Critical Praise for
Books by Paul B. Farrell

"An indispensable roadmap for the financial information highway."
—William J. O'Neil, Publisher
Investor's Business Daily

"Encyclopedic in scope . . . a must read for any Internet investor's library."
—David Brown, Chairman & CEO, Telescan
Author, *Cyber-Investing*

"The TV Guide of Financial Cyberspace, with a vision of how financial markets will operate in the future."
—Ivy Schmerken, Editor-in-Chief
Wall Street & Technology

"Teaches you how to become a profitable twenty-first century-investor before the twentieth century ends."
—Bill Griffeth, Anchor, CNBC-TV
Author, *10 Steps to Financial Prosperity*

"The definitive work on the important and timely subject of investing on the Net."
—Jay Kemp Smith, Chairman
Leading Market Technologies, Inc.

"*Expert Investing on the Net* shows how to best use the top online resources to enhance investment returns."
—Joseph Tigue, Managing Editor
Standard & Poor's *The Outlook*

"Success in online investing starts with this book. Buy it, read it, and laugh all the way from cyberspace to the bank."
—Michael Strangelove, Publisher
The Internet Business Journal

"A provocative and comprehensive guide to the bountiful opportunities scattered all across cyberspace."
—Gordon Anderson, Editor
Individual Investor

"*The Investor's Guide to the Net* tells individual investors how to make use of the wonderful world of cyberspace without getting lost."
—Willard C. Rappleye, Vice Chairman
Financial World

"The investor's megatrends, this book is a must for any investor, beginning to expert."
—Stephen Wendel, President
StockPro Technologies

OTHER BOOKS BY PAUL B. FARRELL

Investor's Guide to the Net: Making Money Online
Expert Investing on the Net: Profit from the Top-25 Online Money Makers

Mutual Funds on the Net

Making Money Online

Paul B. Farrell, J.D., Ph.D.

John Wiley & Sons, Inc.

NEW YORK • CHICHESTER • WEINHEIM • BRISBANE • SINGAPORE • TORONTO

Copyright © 1997 by Paul B. Farrell
Published by John Wiley & Sons, Inc.

Library of Congress Cataloging in Publication Data:
Farrell, Paul B.
    Mutual funds on the net : making money online / Paul B. Farrell.
      p.   cm.
    Includes index.
    ISBN 0-471-17486-6 (cloth : alk. paper)
    1. Mutual funds—Computer network resources.   2. Mutual funds—
Databases.   3. Mutual funds—Computer programs.   I. Title.
HG4530.F364   1997
025.06'3326327—dc21   96-48416

Printed in the United States of America

10 9 8 7 6 5 4 3 2

Welcome to the
Do-It-Yourself Cyberspace Revolution

"Revolution? The word is not too strong. And it's not the same as change. . . . Forget change! The word is too feeble. Keep saying revolution."

—Tom Peters

"It's time . . . to realize the power you have."

—Fidelity Investments

"By 2000, we can expect a billion users on the Net. As recently as a year ago, this number seemed outrageously high. Today it is considered a conservative estimate."

—Nicholas Negroponte, MIT Media Lab

"No one knows more than you do about the future."

—Eric Schurenberg, *Take Charge of Your Future*

"Throw out any preconceived notions that you may have about how you'll retire: A radical new paradigm is emerging."

—Betsy Morris, *Fortune* magazine

"When you become your own portfolio manager, you're in control."

—Gregory Spears, *Kiplinger's* magazine

"Get the same information as the pros."

—Morningstar Mutual Funds

"All the tools of a professional manager . . . you invest like a pro."

—Charles R. Schwab on StreetSmart

"You've got an edge already."

—Peter Lynch, *One Up On Wall Street*

"Do your own thinking. . . . Never listen to the opinions of others."

—Jack Schwager, *New Market Wizards*

"Rule the market. Now the power is yours."

—American Express Financial Direct

Dedication

While at Morgan Stanley some years ago, I had the good fortune of studying with Joseph Campbell, author of *The Hero of a Thousand Faces*, *The Power of Myth, Creative Mythology,* and other classics. Though not your typical Wall Street seminar, it was a major turning point in my life. Campbell challenged us to "follow your bliss," opening my eyes to "the other side" of life, the journey out beyond the money game.

My explorations resulted in a decision to balance a left-brain education in law, city planning, and architecture with a doctorate in psychology. Today, in a strange way, Campbell has had more influence on this book than anything in the "real world" of investment, technology, and broadcasting, and for that I am forever grateful.

The independent "do-it-yourself" investor is also on a similar path, "following your bliss." In a very practical, down-to-earth way, you have awakened an inner spirit that thrives on freedom and independence, especially when it comes to your investments and your future. You are guided by an inner force that goes beyond the cycles (and the chaos) of the financial markets. You know that when the chips are down, you alone are responsible for the results. You are the master of your destiny.

And so this book is dedicated to both Joseph Campbell, for teaching me some of the most important lessons of my life, and to the new do-it-yourself investor, for sharing this exciting adventure with me. Follow your bliss into cyberspace and you will achieve financial independence.

Contents

Acknowledgments

A special thanks to my friends, Steve Wendel, president of StockPro Technologies, and Michael Blodgett, screenwriter, for being there so many times for so many years on so many books.

To all my friends at the Wiley publishing firm for making this book a reality, and more important, making the daily process of writing such a joy: Myles Thompson, Jacque Urinyi, Michael Detweiler, Andrea Abbott, Laurie Thompson, Jeff DeMarrais, Jennifer Pincott, and our publisher, Jeffrey Brown. This team is one of those rare gifts every writer dreams of.

I also want to thank the many teachers whose works have touched me at defining moments through the years: John Naisbitt, Wayne Dyer, Jack Schwager, Adam Smith, Alvin Toffler, Marilyn Ferguson, Anthony Robbins, Jim Bellows, Andrew Grove, Bill Griffeth, Deepak Chopra, Julia Cameron, Robert Schuller, Al Chungliang Huang, Arnold Mindell, John Bradshaw, George Leonard, Chuck Norris, Gail Sheehy, Bowen H. McCoy, George Lucas, Stephen Spielberg, Bill Wilson, Alan Watts, Thomas Merton, Gene Roddenberry, Chuck Chamberlain, Buckminster Fuller, Napoleon Hill, Carl G. Jung, H. G. Wells, Anne Simkin, Calvin Holt, Francis McQuade, and my son, Ian H. Farrell.

And most important, a special thanks to all my dear friends who have been working The Program with me for the past twenty-four years, and to the Higher Power we all share on this exciting journey. Finally, to my wife and best friend, Dorothy, for being there with me every step of the way. What a memorable and thrilling adventure.

Ten Steps to Successfully Building Your Own Portfolio of Winning Funds

This book is a basic, keep-it-simple, how-to course for do-it-yourself investors, people who are ready to build and manage their own mutual fund portfolios online. Today anyone can do it online, on the Internet, and in cyberspace.

If you're reading this, you are a take-charge, do-it-yourself investor. You're already building a portfolio of mutual funds. If you are online already, or *even thinking* about going online and on the Net sometime soon, this how-to course was designed specifically for you. It is the mutual fund investor's electronic-oriented companion to Jack Schwager's *Market Wizards* books and Charles Schwab's classic, *How to Be Your Own Stockbroker*.

The Wall Street cyberspace revolution is indeed transforming the financial world on a global level . . . and leveling the playing field between the Wall Street institutions and the individual Main Street investor. Today the new independent investor not only has the power tools to compete with the top guns from Wall Street, the tools are relatively inexpensive, easy-to-use, and able to get you up to speed fast.

Our goal is to help you get ahead of the technological curve (or at least even with it) and ahead of the game—the new cyberspace investment game. Follow the 10 easy steps in this book and you'll be on the way to building a successful portfolio of mutual fund investments online and on the Internet.

NEW MARKET WIZARDS AND THE INNER GAME OF INVESTING

"Whether you win or lose, you are responsible for your own results. Even if you lost on your broker's tip, an advisory service recommendation, or a bad signal from the system you bought, you are responsible because you made the decision to listen and act. I have never met a successful trader who blamed others for his losses."

SOURCE: Jack Schwager, *The New Market Wizards* (HarperBusiness, 1992). For two of the most enlightening books on the inner game of investing and trading the financial markets, read Schwager's two *Market Wizards* books.

Even more important: If you're not already a cyberspace investor, *you will be soon.* No one will be able to avoid being one. Revolutionary trends are transforming the global investment world so rapidly that by the year 2000, all 42 million mutual fund shareholders along with all 53 million corporate stockholders will be cyberspace investors—all of them, including you! So why wait?

FOUR REVOLUTIONS TRANSFORMING THE MUTUAL FUND WORLD

Words like *revolution* and *transformation* are being tossed around so much these days that we've become immune to them and may miss the message. In fact, a recent IBM ad pictured an exasperated executive with the caption, "Oh great, another *paradigm shift.*" It could easily have been in a *Dilbert* cartoon.

Unfortunately, you'll have to get used to it: The revolution's here to stay! Or rather, *revolutions.* Plural because there are four revolutions going on . . . and every single investor in America and around the globe is being impacted by all four. You can turn your head away and deny seeing them, but not for long. Within a couple years it will be virtually impossible to avoid their impact, no matter how hard you try. *It's time to get in the flow and enjoy the adventure.*

Wall Street, Main Street, and the global investment community race toward the millennium at dizzy warp speed, growing numb to the future shock of daily information overload. Along the way we are all confronted with at least four parallel and unavoidable revolutions *in progress.* That's right, in progress, *not in the future.* The four revolutions hitting all of us individual investors at the same time are as follows:

This revolution is a favorite topic for the press and media. You see it all over the major business and financial periodicals—*BusinessWeek, Forbes, Fortune, Money, Mutual Funds, Kiplinger's, Wall Street & Technology, Information Week,* and many others. Magazines and newspapers are loaded with variations on headlines that announce:

Wall Street Revolution	Cyberspace Revolution
Software Revolution	Digital Revolution
Online Banking Revolution	Technology Revolution
Information Revolution	Internet Revolution
Telecom Revolution	Transaction Revolution

You've probably read every one of these stories and more. As a former newspaper editor and television executive, I know that "revolutions" sell newspapers and hype ratings in our quick-fix, real-time, high-anxiety culture. Yet, even with all the hype, the fact is that these are revolutionary times, and like it or not, you're one of the revolutionaries. Make the most of it.

One: The Do-It-Yourself Revolution

In his *Megatrends* classic, John Naisbitt called this the Age of the Individual, a trend toward self-direction, personal responsibility, and independent decision making. Naisbitt also identified this trend as an Age of the Entrepreneur. And the discount brokers, most notably Charles Schwab, have been helping individual investors become do-it-yourselfers who take charge of their own financial destinies. In brief, the dominant cultural trend is toward independence and individuality.

Quite in contrast, brokers of the Wall Street Establishment remain trapped in the old paradigm, struggling to keep investors *dependent* on Wall Street's brand of advice and decision making. Meanwhile, the new independent investors don't need someone else to do their thinking, so they avoid full-service brokers with all their so-called independent advisors working within the big Wall Street firms.

Two: The Mutual Funds Revolution

Mutual fund assets have exploded by more than five times since the stock market crash of 1987, and the number of funds is now greater than the number of stocks. Retiring boomers are expected to push the DJIA near 10,000 by the year 2000, as fund assets continue climbing, doubling to $6 trillion. Stories about mutual funds saturate the financial media and press on a daily basis.

Until fairly recently, information was not readily available to the individual investor at a reasonable cost. Today the competition among database publishers is so intense, and the costs of electronic data delivery so low, that any investor can now build and maintain their own portfolio as a do-it-yourselfer. And the action is rapidly moving into cyberspace.

Three: The Information Technology Revolution

Cyberspace forecasters predict that by the year 2000 the Internet alone will expand to more that 100 million connections. Other gurus, like Nicholas Negroponte of the MIT Media Lab, say the estimates are too conservative, predicting that at least 1 billion (*that's right, a billion—20 percent of the population of the planet*) will be on the Net by 2000.

Today there's more than $3 trillion invested, and it is expected to explode above $6 trillion by 2000, fueled by retiring boomers and successful Generation Xers, both aware that employer pension plans and the government's Social Security system will fall short. As a result, people are flooding mutual funds with money.

Here, too, the forecasts are far too conservative. This trend will be responsible for moving all 42 million mutual fund shareholders online, on the Net, and "out there" in cyberspace . . . armed with high-powered computers, state-of-the art analytic and portfolio-management technology, and instant access to hot market-turning news and the best financial databases.

Four: The Wall Street Cyberspace Revolution

The major Wall Street institutional investors totally controlled financial cyberspace until four years ago. It was their private club. Moreover, they owned all the electronic power tools for analyzing, managing, and trading securities. The Internet's Web and the PC has changed all that forever.

Today, the small investor has the weapons, too. The playing field is leveling, and individual Main Street investors can compete effectively and independently against the big Wall Street institutions (and without the advice of their brokers).

Wall Street has become a state of mind rather than a physical location. Most likely, you're already aware firsthand that you're being swept up by these revolutionary events (which we'll often call the cyberspace "do-it-yourself revolution" because that fits all the elements of each of the four revolutions). *BusinessWeek* has reported on the increased economic anxiety paralleling this revolution.

However, if you're like most other investors, you'd rather read about revolutions in the press, hear about them on the 11 o'clock news, or watch one in an air-conditioned theater. Revolutions are not *participatory* sports for an investor whose goal is planning for a secure future. The last thing you want is a revolution impacting *your* bank account or *your* investment portfolio. Why? You could *lose* that battle as well as win it! Revolutions are loaded with uncertainty and high risks. We prefer to minimize and control risks.

Nevertheless, you *are* caught by the impact of this Wall Street cyberspace revolution. How do you make the best of it? How can you use this revolution to your advantage? How can you ride the revolution to achieve your goal of economic freedom and financial independence?

THE 10 BASIC STEPS TO SUCCESSFUL MUTUAL FUND INVESTING IN CYBERSPACE

This book is structured around 10 basic steps. These steps are designed to help you successfully build and manage a portfolio of mutual funds in cyberspace—using the most powerful tools online, on the Internet, and on your computer.

This is *not* a get-rich-quick scheme. Rather it is intended to be a disciplined framework for a solid long-term investment strategy using the best of the emerging new information technologies. These 10 steps are as follows.

Step 1. Understanding Mutual Funds: The Perfect Investment
How Mutual Funds Work for the New Do-It-Yourself Investor

The first step focuses on the benefits of owning mutual funds. In this chapter you'll discover why funds are called the perfect investment and what some of the pitfalls are in today's dynamic investment world.

Step 2. The Secrets to Successful Financial Planning
How to Achieve Economic Independence in Cyberspace

In the second step we'll outline the basics of sound financial planning as an essential prerequisite to investing and financial independence, with special attention on the importance of a regular savings program. In addition to the planning process, we'll show how the basics work with other key resources available to cyberspace investors.

Step 3. The Formula for Building a Winning Fund Portfolio
How to Build a Successful Portfolio Using the Right Asset Allocations

In step 3 the emphasis is on asset-allocation strategies, specifically focusing on the key variables—such as lifestyle, goals, age, and risk tolerance—influencing asset strategies. Tax-deferred employee and individual retirement plans are also factored into a sensible, long-term strategy for building a solid portfolio of mutual funds.

Step 4. Learning How to Navigate the Major Types of Funds
Matching Your Asset Allocations to the Fund Categories

Today there are almost 8,000 funds on the market, more funds than public companies. In step 4, this massive database is broken down into the three basic types of funds, and then further categorized into the primary fund categories and types; for example, growth, international, technology, utilities, precious metals. Then we'll review the process of matching the asset allocations from your financial plan with these fund categories.

Step 5. How and Where to Find All the Financial Data You'll Ever Need
Discovering the Best Online Mutual Fund Databases

Here in step 5 we identify the major online and Internet databases covering mutual funds. Fortunately, these databases have been developed and maintained by established, reliable print publishers. Today most of them are also publishing electronically, including large, historic databases on CD-ROMs. We'll show you how to reach them online and on the Internet, directly and through other major vendors such as Dow Jones and America Online.

Step 6. Using the Best Power Tools: Software, Online, and Internet
How to Pick the Right Cyberspace Technologies and Build a Portfolio of Funds

After the key databases have been identified, step 6 will focus on the key analytical tools to help you sift through the 7,000 mutual funds and find the ones that best fit the asset-allocation strategy developed for your personal financial plan. These computerized power tools include commercial online dial-up services, Internet Websites, intranet navigators, and the best offline software.

Step 7. The Best Investment Strategies to Help You Beat the Pros
The Secret to Thinking Like a Mutual Fund Manager

In step 7 you will focus on the key performance criteria used by professional money managers to pick winning mutual funds. In addition, we'll examine 20 specific criteria that are commonly used by both individual investors and fund managers alike in selecting specific funds for inclusion in winning investment portfolios.

Step 8. Picking Superstar Funds and Top-Gun Managers
Screen Top Performers Using Second Opinions of Experts on the Net

In step 8 we'll outline a strategy designed to target the top-gun mutual fund managers, as well as the superstar funds with consistent, long-term track records. These are the jockeys and horses that regularly win the investment race. You'll discover cyberspace resources available to help you get invaluable second opinions from the world's leading experts on mutual funds.

Step 9. Choosing from the Top-20 Mutual Fund Families
The Powerhouses Controlling the Majority of Cyberspace Mutual Funds

Here in step 9 you will be able to quickly home in on the 20 largest families of funds. This is important, because together these 20 fund families control about half of all the mutual fund assets under management and over 2,000 of the major funds in existence. Moreover, these families will grow much bigger in the next few years. We will direct you to their cyberspace and electronic power tools, while reviewing important factors about their management styles and track records.

Step 10. New Mutual Fund Supermarkets: One-Stop Shopping on the Net
How Cyberspace Works as the New Marketplace for Mutual Fund Investors

Networks of funds are spotlighted in step 10. These networks frequently give investors one-stop access to as many as 5,000 funds. Their popularity is rapidly increasing with investors who enjoy centralizing all their trading, managing, and accounting, in contrast to dealing separately with several funds and their managers. Discount brokers have taken the lead here, and the trend will definitely expand. We'll also cover other vehicles for diversification, including fund minimarts and funds of funds (funds that invest only in other funds).

10 BASIC STEPS ON HOW YOU CAN BUILD A SUCCESSFUL PORTFOLIO OF MUTUAL FUNDS IN CYBERSPACE

This book is designed as a working operating manual for the independent investor who wants to build and manage a portfolio of mutual funds using the best possible computer-based power tools. Our goal is to show you how to quickly discover the vast cyberspace resources that are already available to help you do it yourself.

There really is no secret magic to this 10-step process. As millions of other individual investors have already discovered, thanks to the new information technologies in cyberspace, you can now do all your own investment planning and decision making *without ever again sitting down with a broker, financial advisor, or money manager.* All the necessary power tools are waiting for you: computerized, automated, digital, and electronic.

Moreover, the new generation of power tools has become so user-friendly that grade-school kids are now using them with ease; these computerized power tools are natural extensions of their brainpower.

This trend toward cyberspace investing is accelerating so fast that in a few short years mastery of these 10 steps will be essential for all investors. Investors will be unable to survive otherwise. So now is a perfect time to assert your financial independence by becoming a do-it-yourself mutual fund investor in cyberspace.

Just do it: Be an adventurer, join the financial revolution, and become one of the new breed of independent-thinking investors on the Net. You'll improve your bottom line, and more important, you'll have more time to enjoy living.

STEP ONE

Understanding Mutual Funds
The Perfect Investment

How Funds Work for the
New Do-It-Yourself Investors

The first step focuses on the benefits of owning mutual funds for today's do-it-yourself investors. In this chapter you'll discover why funds are the perfect investment, what some of the pitfalls are in today's dynamic investment world, and how you can increase substantially your financial IQ by becoming an online mutual fund investor.

MUTUAL FUNDS ARE THE PERFECT INVESTMENT

When noted CNBC-TV anchor, author, and investment guru Bill Griffeth says that "mutual funds are the perfect investment, period," Griffeth is echoing the sentiments of millions of individual investors as well as investment professionals. Mutual funds are the perfect investment because they fit the special needs of today's investors.

MUTUAL FUNDS . . . THE PERFECT CYBERSPACE INVESTMENT

"A mutual fund is the perfect investment. I don't just mean that mutual funds are the perfect investment for the '90s, or for people saving for retirement or college. I mean: A mutual fund is the perfect investment. Period."

SOURCE: Bill Griffeth, "Let Mutual Funds Be Your Vehicle to Prosperity," *Ten Steps to Financial Prosperity* (Probius, 1994).

Basically, every investor wants to maximize the return on their investment while minimizing the risk of loss. Keep those two underlying objectives in mind as we review the key benefits of mutual funds.

ONE. PROFESSIONAL MANAGEMENT AND RESEARCH TEAM

Certainly the number one reason most investors conclude that mutual funds are the "perfect" investment vehicle for them is the fact that the funds are professionally managed. While diversification will *minimize risks* on the downside, with most funds the primary objective of the fund's professional managers is to *maximize the return* on your investments.

Successful, seasoned fund managers are often responsible for lots of money, anywhere from a couple hundred million dollars in assets to a few billion dollars. The biggest single fund, Fidelity's Magellan, manages over $50 billion, and that is a lot of responsibility.

My experience is that most fund managers take their fiduciary responsibilities *very* seriously, partly because regulatory agencies like the U.S. Securities and Exchange Commission monitor their behavior. But, more important, statistics show that the top performers end up with satisfied investors, favorable press, an inflow of new funds, ego boosts, and of course, increased compensation to the star managers.

Most individual investors are lucky if they find enough time to spend an hour a day on their portfolios (although that's what Charles Schwab recommends in *How to Be Your Own Stockbroker*), what with a full-time job, family responsibilities, and the need to relax.

On the other hand, fund managers are financial experts. Twenty-four hours a day they live and breath money, returns and profits, markets and economic reports, companies and their executives, industry trends and sectors, prospectuses and research analysts, seminars, and daily scanning of tons of newspapers, magazines, books, newsletters, and television coverage.

One of the single biggest objectives of the successful mutual fund investor is to identify some top-gun managers—the right team with the

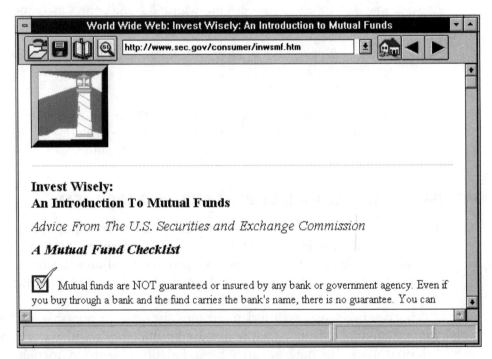

Figure 1.1   SEC Website: An Introduction to Mutual Funds.

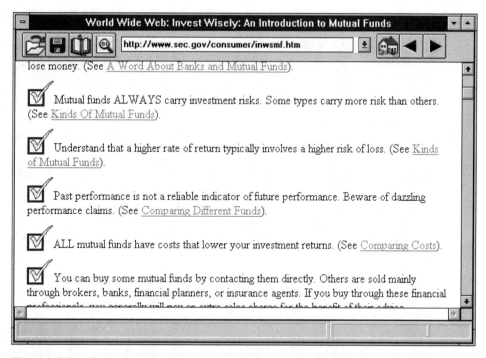

Figure 1.2   SEC educational materials: a mutual funds checklist.

right stuff. Your goal must be to pick the winners and ride them; they will earn their keep while helping you meet your investment objectives.

TWO. DIVERSIFICATION OF YOUR PORTFOLIO RISKS

Risk diversification is also one of the major reasons for investing in a mutual fund. Unless you have a sizable amount to invest—at least $100,000—and both the skill and the time to select a diversified stock portfolio that includes a dozen or more companies in widely varying industrial groups, it would be difficult to diversify adequately.

Instead, you may find yourself with considerable exposure to the risks of the marketplace and the economy or to the specific fortunes of the various companies and their sectors. On the other hand, when you buy into a mutual fund you're actually buying small shares in perhaps 20 to 100 companies.

Mutual funds and fund managers automatically diversify your investment, and that is one of their chief benefits. Diversification, therefore, protects

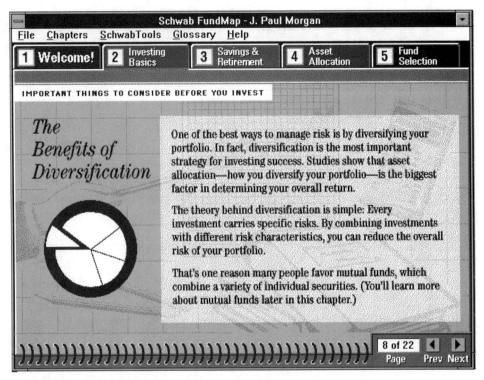

Figure 1.3   Diversification: one of the best ways to manage risk.

the investor on the downside, minimizing the risk of loss within the stated objectives of the fund. Notwithstanding this general rule, some funds (emerging-market funds) are riskier than other funds (asset-allocation funds).

However, when you compare investing in the stock of specific companies to investing the same monies in a single mutual fund made up of similar companies, the mutual fund is clearly ahead as a tool for diversifying your investments. Moreover, a quick check of the fund's prospectus or one of the key, independent, mutual fund databases will identify the major investments in its portfolio: the companies, the securities, and the percentage share of the total.

THREE. THE FINANCIAL INDEPENDENCE TO ENJOY YOUR LIFE

At the risk of sounding a bit too optimistic, here's a plug for being happy, taking walks, and smelling the roses. In fact, this should probably be the number one reason anyone should be developing a financial plan and an investment portfolio—whether mutual funds, stocks and bonds, or any other portfolio of assets. Life shouldn't be just a daily grind based on a rigid plan targeting some distant future.

However, in deference to the conventional wisdom about structuring a book on mutual fund investing, this reason is tucked in here as a reminder about what's really important: Underlying all the money you're accumulating are some more fundamental reasons for investing—principally, the opportunity to enjoy your special lifestyle and live your dream.

You are planning and saving for the future—a comfortable retirement, a new home, college for the children. You are balancing those needs against daily demands for your time and funds. Mutual funds are a perfect investment because they offer diversification of your risk as well as professional management for (hopefully) better returns than you could achieve on your own.

We are definitely living in a revolutionary time, full of exciting opportunities and also considerable uncertainties. Recently we've seen a grow-

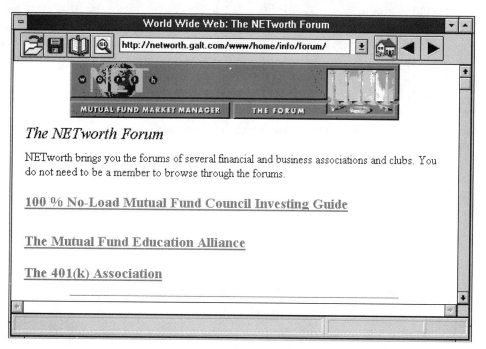

Figure 1.4 The NETworth Forum: mutual fund educational materials.

ing number of stories in major financial publications, such as *BusinessWeek* and *Fortune*, about the increased stress and anxiety created by economic insecurity. Conversely, investors want peace of mind, and mutual funds are, in a way, designed to minimize portfolio-related concerns.

The bottom line is that mutual funds can help you achieve not merely economic freedom and financial independence, but the ability to truly *enjoy* your lifestyle, not just at some future time, but today, while you're moving toward your long-term goals.

MORE SOLID REASONS FOR INVESTING IN MUTUAL FUNDS

The major no-load fund families created the Mutual Fund Education Alliance. Their information is available at the NETworth Website, as well as in printed publications. Members of the Alliance include many of the larger, respected names in the industry, such as Fidelity, Schwab, and Vanguard.

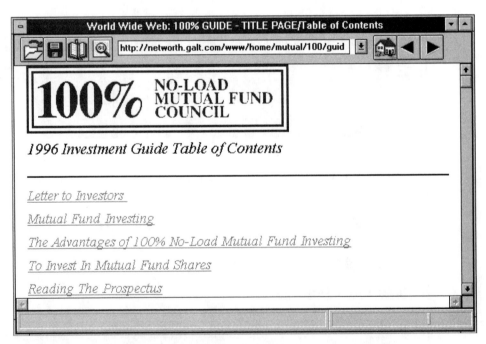

Figure 1.5   The 100% No-Load Mutual Fund Council Investment Guide.

And yes, they obviously recommend no-load funds purchased directly from a fund over load funds where the investor must pay a selling broker's commission (many of which actually do perform better than no-loads). However, that caveat stated, we believe that the Alliance's materials offer the investor an excellent list of many other benefits of mutual funds.

We encourage you to review the Alliance, SEC, and other independent mutual fund educational materials online and on the Web. The following section summarizes some of the other advantages detailed by the Mutual Fund Education Alliance.

FOUR. TOTAL LIQUIDITY: EASE OF INVESTING AND WITHDRAWALS

After opening your account, you can handle all your transactions by phone, mail, and bank transfers. And today, with the growing use of the Internet and online services, everything can be done right from your computer. There is no need to ever go to a branch office again. Moreover, no-load funds offer total liquidity. You can easily redeem them anytime you need cash by contacting the fund.

FIVE. A VARIETY OF FUNDS FOR EVERY POSSIBLE GOAL

With a total of 7,000 funds available, you are guaranteed to find many alternatives designed to fit your unique lifestyle and personal needs. Everything from guaranteed safety of capital to high-risk, high-return funds.

SIX. ACCOUNTING AND RECORD-KEEPING CONVENIENCE

One of the jobs of fund managers is to act as an agent in your behalf with the companies they've invested in. Let's face it, the paperwork involved in administering a large portfolio can be daunting—a big headache. Let the fund take care of clipping coupons, collecting interest and dividends, and holding the companies accountable. Moreover, they'll consolidate all the records into simple statements for your tax purposes and for monitoring your portfolio.

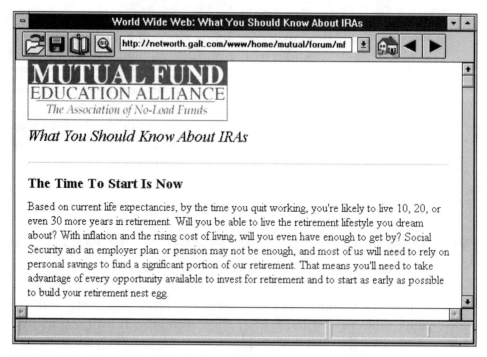

Figure 1.6   Mutual Fund Education Alliance: IRAs and no-loads.

SEVEN. AUTOMATIC INVESTMENT AND DEPOSIT PLANS

Virtually all personal financial planning systems encourage *regular* investing. In fact, it's the key to long-term success as an investor. Mutual funds will help you stick to your plan by setting up a regular, automatic transfer of funds from your bank account into your mutual fund account. That way you can avoid facing the savings decision every single month, while your portfolio grows. You can also arrange automatic deposit of other payments, such as pension and Social Security payments.

EIGHT. PERSONAL SERVICE WITHOUT BROKER'S HUSTLE

You can contact a no-load fund toll-free and get a trained investment specialist for the help you need without getting a sales pitch from a broker. Yes, it's true that the large retail brokerage firms that sell load funds on commission now claim that you'll be talking to a trained "financial advisor," although that's just a new name for a broker.

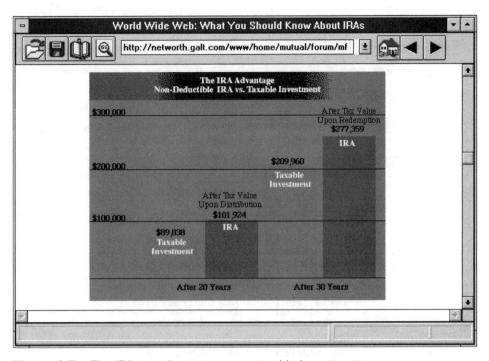

Figure 1.7 The IRA tax advantage versus taxable investments.

NINE. DIVIDEND REINVESTMENTS, COMPOUNDING AND PAYOUTS

Another common recommendation made by most investment experts is that you leave your earnings *on the table* (that is, have them automatically reinvested). And through compounding your returns, your portfolio will grow much faster. Returns not reinvested can be automatically swept into your money market account.

TEN. ONLINE ACCOUNT AND MARKET INFORMATION

In addition to printed reports and telephone information from the funds, NAV quotes and market news are now readily available through many online dial-up services maintained by the funds themselves.

More important, some funds and a number of independent publishers are now providing substantial information on the Internet—covering the financial markets, general business news, economic statistics, and specific research data on companies and mutual funds.

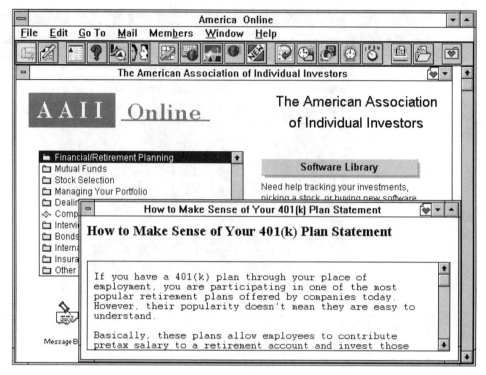

Figure 1.8   AAII: How to Make Sense of Your 401(k) Plan Statement.

Today, through online and Internet connections, you have direct, secure access so you can monitor your accounts and conduct transactions using new encryption technology.

ELEVEN. RETIREMENT PLANS: IRA, KEOGH, AND 401(k)

No-load funds can also be used for government-sanctioned, tax-deferred retirement programs. These include IRAs (individual retirement accounts), Keoghs for the self-employed, and employer-sponsored 401(k) plans. The funds will help investors administer these accounts separately, while structuring how they fit into your overall personal financial planning.

TWELVE. LIFE-CYCLE AND MARKET-CYCLE PLANNING

The Mutual Fund Education Alliance also emphasizes the ability of investors to use mutual funds as a flexible tool in planning over a lifetime

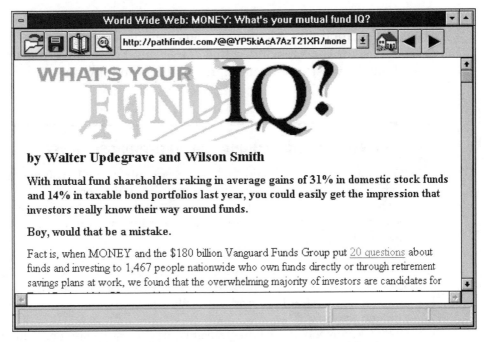

Figure 1.9   Money on the Web: cyberspace quiz on mutual funds.

of changing needs. These include both long-term life-cycle changes as well as short-term market swings.

Fortunately, although the Alliance does mention the possibility of using mutual funds to take advantage of swings in the market, they wisely add a "word of caution: since it is impossible to predict what the market will do at any point in time, a long-term investment view is recommended for most investors." In other words, most investors are well advised to let the fund managers cope with short-term market swings.

The bottom line is that mutual funds are indeed the perfect investment for most investors. And while experts like Griffeth are quick to advise that "people rarely get rich in mutual funds," investors can count on a "slow, steady increase in the value of their money," with downside protection through diversification.

THE BIG TEST . . .
HOW TO BECOME A TOP-GUN CYBERSPACE INVESTOR

Recently, the $200 billion Vanguard Funds Group teamed up with *Money* magazine and gave a 20-question quiz to mutual fund owners. They questioned 1,467 people nationwide about mutual funds and fund investing. The average fund investor answered just half the questions correctly—not a healthy sign. They concluded that "large numbers of investors are clueless about the most rudimentary principles of fund investing."

SCHWAB'S BASIC TRAINING FOR DO-IT-YOURSELF INVESTORS

"You won't find it in a catalog of business schools. Nor will you find it in the training courses of any brokerage house. No, the very best place for you to begin a practical education that will make you piles of money in the market is right where you're sitting now—and that's probably in your own home.

"You don't need an MBA, not even a bachelor's in economics or business, to become a reasonably successful independent investor. But you do need the modest weekly application of your own time, perhaps an hour or two a day, at least at first. And you will need to exercise a great deal of common sense.

"I recommend the following eight steps for anyone who wants to graduate from rank amateur to market-savvy investor:

"Step 1: Read the financial pages of your local newspaper daily . . .
"Step 2: Put your money on the line . . .
"Step 3: Do even more financial reading of a national newspaper . . .
"Step 4: Do still more reading of select magazines . . .
"Step 5: Yes, more reading of key books on the market . . .
"Step 6: Now you're ready to take a formal course somewhere . . .
"Step 7: Consider subscribing to an investment advisory service . . .
"Step 8: Take all advice with a grain of salt . . .

"The eight steps presented in this chapter are not a one-shot route to a 'degree' that certifies you as a know-it-all. You're not supposed to do some reading, get some advice, and then quit. No, the kind of 'course' I'm talking about is an on-going affair. Your education in investments should be a continuing, evolving process."

SOURCE: Charles Schwab, *How to Be Your Own Stockbroker* (Dell, 1984). Schwab's book is designed to help you take charge of your future and become a "reasonably successful independent investor." The updated version is in effect now on the Net! Test drive it with Schwab's software—FundMap, StreetSmart and e.Schwab. Any do-it-yourself investor can quickly become a cyberspace investor, too. Check out their Website . . . http://www.schwab.com.

The results of the survey were published in *Money*'s February 1996 issue. However, you can still take this quiz and have the results calculated for you on the Internet at the Money section of Time Warner's Pathfinder Website. In addition, the editors of *Money* magazine recommend that investors taking the quiz also check to see where they stand in comparison to their peers in the mutual fund world. You may be in for a surprise.

After evaluating the results of this nationwide survey, *Money*'s editors strongly recommend investors thoroughly brush up on these four essential tools necessary to achieving financial success in mutual fund investing:

1. How to evaluate a fund's total return.
2. Know the trade-off between risk and return.
3. Learn more about fundamental investment strategies.
4. Focus on the ongoing costs and fees of mutual funds.

Investors must become much more knowledgeable in these four areas.

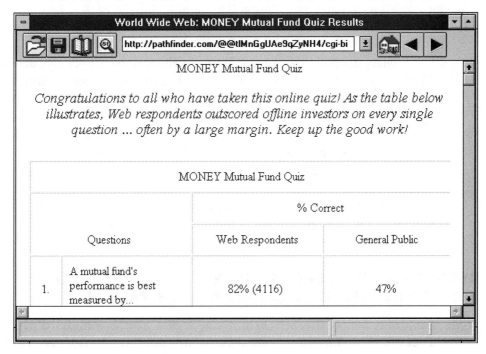

Figure 1.10 *Money* quiz winners: Web users by wide margin!

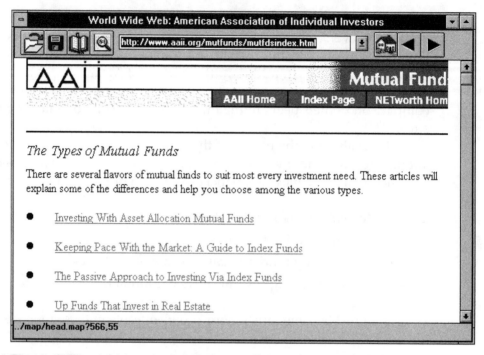

Figure 1.11   American Association of Individual Investors: mutual funds.

Money magazine's bottom-line conclusion is especially disturbing. "With an overall score of 49 out of 100, fund investors' performance on our test of fund and investing knowledge can be summed up in one letter: *F*."

In short, "fund investors need to go back to school," which is the title of this insightful article. And the director of the SEC's Office of Investor Education and Assistance agreed, "This poll brings home in dramatic fashion how much we need to educate investors about the basics of making financial decisions."

Fortunately, the quiz was also given separately to Web users, with substantially different results, which deserve close inspection.

CYBERSPACE INVESTORS ARE SHARPER, MUCH SMARTER OUTSCORING OFFLINE INVESTORS BY WIDE MARGIN!

Yes, there is an extremely bright side to the *Money*/Vanguard poll. However, the most important conclusion of this quiz and *Money*'s editorial analysis was somewhat obscured, hidden in *Money*'s Website where only the

Web elite could see it. On the results page of the *Money*/Vanguard survey, *Money* compares the percentage of correct answers from the following two groups.

❐ Web-based investors who took the quiz
❐ Offline investors among the general public: the 1,467 respondents mentioned in the article; those who as a group got a failing grade

We encourage you to take this short quiz, even if you do it simply to confirm what you already know about your expertise with funds, that you're well informed about funds and investing basics. And while you're out there on the Pathfinder Website, we also encourage you to look closely at the results of the individual questions.

Especially note *Money*'s powerful bottom-line conclusion:

> *Congratulations to all who took this online quiz! As the table below illustrates, Web respondents outscored off-line investors on every single question . . . often by a large margin. Keep up the good work.*

This simple statement is extremely significant and bears emphasis: Web-based investors *outscored* offline investors on *all 20 questions,* and they often outscored the public by big margins. In fact, this summary deserves much more attention and exposure than it got in the general public, as well as the financial press and media.

If we project the importance of this survey, there are a number of parallel conclusions that any sharp observer would have to draw from the totally lopsided results of this test:

1. **More Knowledgeable**
   Based on their superior knowledge, cyberspace investors have a distinct competitive advantage over the general public in the financial markets.

2. **Technologically Proficient**
   The cyberspace investor is computer-savvy and better equipped with a working knowledge of the new electronic and information technologies.

3. **Better Decision Makers**
   Armed with superior knowledge and electronic power tools, the cyberspace investor is more likely to make better investment decisions, resulting in higher returns and lower risk exposure.

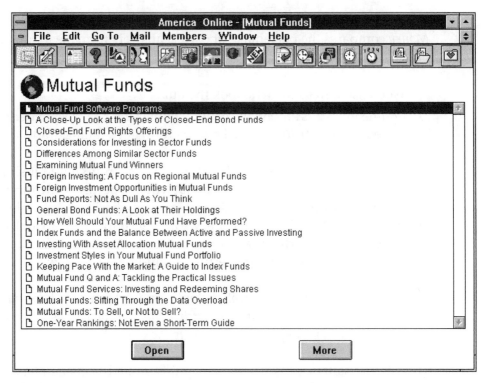

Figure 1.12   AAII at AOL and Web: educational materials on mutual funds.

4. Confident Do-It-Yourselfer

The cyberspace investor tends to have the higher degree of self-confidence necessary to operate independently as a do-it-yourself investor online and on the Internet's World Wide Web.

Arguably, Web respondents were already endowed with all these success characteristics well in advance of taking the quiz, and probably even before going online and on the Internet.

On the other hand, the reason behind superior test scores among the Web users may also be a direct function of the respondents' discipline and use of all the cyberspace resources *after* going online and on the Web. Of course, there's really no way of telling for sure: This is a variation of the old "which comes first, the chicken or the egg" dilemma to which there is no answer.

Still, the cyberspace investor is clearly a significantly smarter investor—more knowledgeable than investors in the general public operating offline. And quite frankly, that fact is critical in forecasting all trends for the Wall Street and global financial communities.

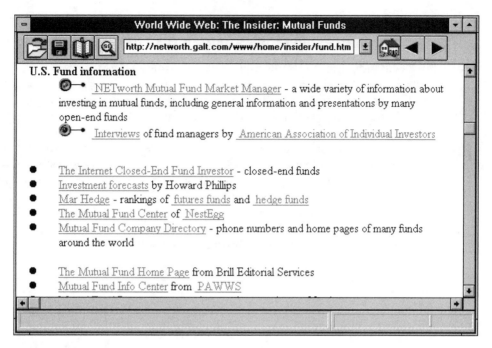

Figure 1.13   NETworth Internet Investor Network: hot links to mutual funds.

TODAY'S CYBERSPACE INVESTORS . . . THE NEW MARKET WIZARDS

Based on the Vanguard/*Money* survey, here's my recommendation: The SEC and the investment community should forget about educating the general public with a flood of *printed* pamphlets . . . instead, the powers that be should encourage and cajole offline investors to buy computers and get online and on the Net.

Then nature will take its course and individual investors will self-educate themselves, drawn in by a fascination with all the new information technologies, tools, and gadgets. Our experience is that many investors have a subtle yet unwarranted fear of computers and the new information technologies. It's temporary. Overcome that and we'll get every investor in the world hooked on the enormous benefits of the new global financial marketplace emerging in cyberspace.

Top-gun pilots, championship ballplayers, and recording stars all have one thing in common. The successful ones endlessly practice their craft, learning new secrets from their mentors. They'll do anything necessary to stay on top of their game, constantly stretching themselves to the limit. Successful investors are no different; get them into cyberspace and you can bet their scores will improve *dramatically* . . . just as we saw happen in the

CYBERSPACE INVESTORS SMARTER THAN OFFLINE COMPETITION

"Galt Industries, an Intuit subsidiary that runs Networth, a popular fund-oriented Web site, recently teamed up with a consulting group called the Center for Strategic Research to survey Networth's users. Among other things, they found that 60% of 'Internet investors' earn at least $60,000 a year.

"In contrast, data from the Investment Company Institute, the mutual-fund trade group, shows that just 40% of all fund investors make that much. Galt also found Net-savvy investors to be younger and better educated than their unwired brethren.

"Feeling an understandable urgency to make a connection with all those mouse-clicking, browser-launching, money-saving Baby Boomers and Gen Xers, the fund biz is furiously Web-spinning."

SOURCE: Eric Savitz, "Haywired," *Barron's* (July 8, 1996).

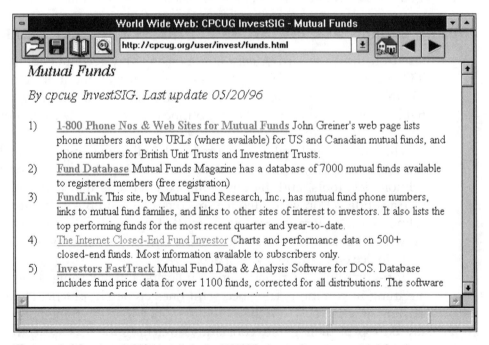

Figure 1.14   InvestSIG: hot links to WWW's best sites on mutual funds.

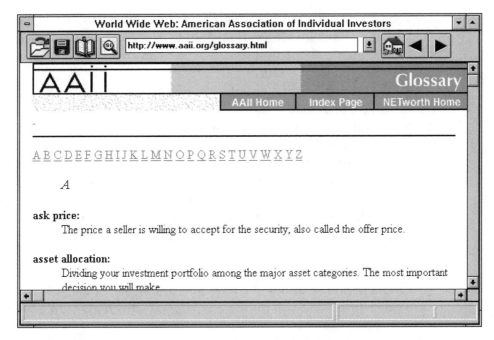

Figure 1.15   AAII Website glossary of terms for individual investors.

comparative results of the *Money*/Vanguard survey, where Web users outscored offline investors by a "World **Wide** Web" margin.

SHORT "OFFLINE" QUIZ FOR INVESTORS WITHOUT COMPUTERS

We purposely did not include the 20-question quiz from the Vanguard/ *Money* survey. We hope you'll go find it on Time Warner's Pathfinder Website and actually take the test, without any advance warning or hints from us. That way you'll go at it fresh. And more important, you will be better able to get an honest comparison of how you stack up against other investors.

Obviously, some of you have yet to get on the World Wide Web, and even those of you who are and who know of the printed Vanguard/*Money* quiz may like the challenge of testing yourself against the competition out there among the investing public. Therefore, we have an alternative, shorter quiz you can take right here on paper.

Shortly after *Money* magazine published the results of its national poll, the Investor Protection Trust, a nonprofit education organization, released a survey with results similar to the Vanguard/*Money* survey.

The Investor Protection Trust focused on investors in general rather than mutual fund investors, quizzing 1,001 people. Nevertheless, it's a solid benchmark about how much American investors know, or rather don't know, about investing.

If you score high, that should encourage you about doing well as an online investor, because the competition is obviously severely handicapped. And if not, well, you learned something.... It's time to take *Money*'s advice and "go back to school." After all, it's your money and your future that's really at stake, not just some scores on a short quiz. Stick with us and read through this book: You will learn the secrets of successful investing right here in these 10 simple steps.

Meanwhile, test yourself right now. Here are the eight questions the Trust gave to investors. After you take the test, see how you stack up (answers are on page 23).

1. Over a period spanning the past 30 years, which of the following types of investments do you think generally gave the highest rate of return?
    a. Stocks
    b. Bonds

NEW SURVEY BY INVESTOR PROTECTION TRUST ENCOURAGES AMERICANS TO STUDY THE BASICS OF INVESTING

"At a time when Americans are increasingly required to make their own investment decisions, the vast majority of them are 'reckless, financially illiterate and sitting ducks for investment fraud and abuse.'

"The survey, believed to be the first look at Americans' investment illiteracy, raises troubling questions about their retirement prospects, given that Social Security is financially ailing and employers are increasingly abandoning professionally managed pension programs in favor of retirement plans that place all the burden of decision making on employees . . .

"Only 18% of those surveyed got the bulk of the questions right, while 32% got fewer than half of them right. . . . Nine out of 10 investors who have received professional financial advice never bothered to check the disciplinary history of their broker or financial planner . . . Two-thirds of investors have never prepared a specific financial plan, even though having one is considered the cornerstone of wise investing."

SOURCE: Kathy Kristof, "Trouble in the Offing—Survey Shows Few Americans Know Basics of Investing," *Los Angeles Times* (April 1996).

    c. Savings accounts

    d. Certificates of deposit

2. When an investor diversifies their investments, does the risk of losing money increase or decrease?

    a. Increase   b. Decrease

3. Is the following statement true or false? "A no-load mutual fund involves no sales charges or other fees."

    a. True   b. False

4. If you lose money in a mutual fund that you invested at a bank, will the Federal Deposit Insurance Corporation cover your losses?

    a. True   b. False

5. Is the following statement true or false? "The Securities Investor Protection Corporation, known as the SIPC, protects you from loss on investments of up to $500,000 if the stock market goes down."

    a. True   b. False

6. When interest rates go up, what usually happens to the price of bonds?

    a. Bond prices go up

    b. Bond prices go down

    c. Bond prices stay about the same

7. How do you think most full-service brokers and financial planners are paid? Are they mainly paid:

    a. Based on the quality of advice they offer and how much their clients earn

    b. Based on the amount and type of investments they sell to their clients

8. What is a "blue-chip" stock?

    a. A stock offered by a high-tech company

    b. The stock of an established company with a history of paying dividends

    c. A low-priced security usually traded for less than a dollar a share

In scoring the Vanguard/*Money* quiz, the Trust ranked investors as "very knowledgeable" if they got seven or more correct. Investors answering five or six of the questions right are classified as "somewhat knowledgeable."

Answers: 1. a 2. b 3. b 4. b 5. b 6. b 7. b 8. b

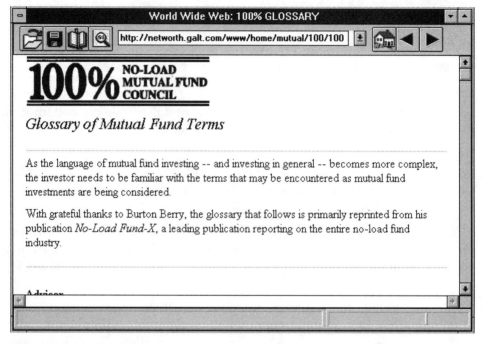

Figure 1.16   100% No-load Mutual Fund Council Website glossary.

Thirty-two percent of the survey group were "not too knowledgeable," with less than half their answers correct.

In evaluating the results, Barbara Roper, investor protection director at the Consumer Federation of America, concluded, "The appalling lack of basic financial knowledge revealed by this survey calls into serious question the ability of most Americans to make sound, informed financial decisions that would allow them to achieve [their] goals." Now that's scary.

One interesting side note: The Investor Protection Trust was created and financed as part of a multistate settlement resolving misconduct charges against the Wall Street investment banking firm of Salomon Brothers in 1993. The Trust, however, is an independent agency with directors from various state regulatory commissions.

INVESTOR'S CHOICE: EITHER DO IT YOURSELF IN CYBERSPACE . . . OR LET SOMEONE ELSE DO YOUR THINKING!

So far we've learned that Internet Web users are better prepared and more knowledgeable mutual fund investors than offline investors surveyed in

Figure 1.17 Carnegie Mellon University: directory of funds.

SOME KEY BOOKS IN PRINT ON MUTUAL FUNDS

Bogle on Mutual Funds, John Bogle (Dell, 1994)

BusinessWeek Guide to Mutual Funds, Jeffrey Laderman (McGraw-Hill, 1995)

Guide to Planning Your Financial Future, Kenneth Morris et al. (Lightbulb Press and Dow Jones, 1995)

Investor's Guide to Low-Cost Mutual Funds (Mutual Funds Education Alliance, 1996)

Keys to Investing in Mutual Funds, Warren Boroson (Barron's, 1992)

Morningstar Mutual Funds (Morningstar, 1996)

Mutual Fund Buyer's Guide (Institute for Economic Research, 1996)

Mutual Funds for Dummies, Eric Tyson (IDG Books, 1995)

Mutual Funds Made Easy, Gerald Perritt (Dearborn, 1995)

Mutual Fund Profiles (Standard & Poor's/Lipper, 1996)

Yes You Can . . . Achieve Financial Independence, James Stowers (Andrews and McMeel, 1994)

10 Steps to Financial Prosperity, Bill Griffeth (Probius, 1994)

100 Best Mutual Funds, Gordon Williamson (Adams, 1995)

401(K) Take Charge of Your Future, Eric Schurenberg (Warner Books, 1996)

the general public. In addition, we discovered that the average offline investor on Main Street is a "sitting duck for investment fraud and abuse," because he or she is basically "investment illiterate," according to the Investor Protection Trust survey.

The recommendations of the Trust are sound—some strong measures are necessary in order to educate the investing public. You could also argue that an equally valid solution would be to assume that a substantial majority of investors may continue in the "not too knowledgeable" category.

As a result, the Trust, the SEC, exchanges, and others should seriously consider encouraging investors to employ professional advisors to help them and make their investment decisions for them. Just as we have our accountants, doctors, and ministers, in this day and age perhaps *all* investors should also have their own financial planners. Well, that's exactly what the brokerage industry is betting on.

With those two potential alternative strategies in mind, let's consider the conclusions of several other studies to see what kind of outside advice and third-party advisors today's investors can rely on . . . if not themselves:

Money Managers: The Majority Can't Beat the Indexes

Burton Malkiel, a former member of the Council of Economic Advisers, Princeton professor, and author of a *Random Walk Down Wall Street,* concludes that 65 to 70 percent of all pension and mutual fund managers fail to beat the market indexes over the long run.

Financial Advisory Newsletters: Even Weaker Track Records

The National Bureau of Economic Research released a 1995 survey of 237 investment newsletters published between 1980 and 1992. They concluded that less that 25 percent achieved returns higher than would a buy-and-hold investor with a passive portfolio.

Similarly, Mark Hulbert's highly respected *Hulbert Financial Digest* publishes a quarterly performance review of the major financial newsletters. Hulbert cautions that almost 90 percent of financial newsletters fail to beat the indexes.

Brokers as Financial Consultants: Conflicts of Interest

The big Wall Street full-commission brokerage firms are now retraining their brokers, giving them professional-sounding titles like "financial consultants." Aside from the fact that this may be no more than handing out new name tags, their objectivity and independence must be questioned if their employers are brokerage firms that charge commissions and fees.

Independent Financial Planners: Professionalism Questioned

Money magazine recently surveyed professional financial planners. Their investigation revealed that nearly one-third were taking commissions, even though they claimed to be on a fee-only basis. In addition, 13 percent had brushes with the law, and 43 percent had no professional accreditation that would suggest appropriate training.

Mutual Fund Rating Agencies: Even Facts Can Be Misleading

In his book, *The 100 Best Mutual Funds,* Gordon Williamson quotes a Lipper Analytic Services report on the star-rating system of Morningstar, revealing that five-star equity funds typically underperformed the average

Figure 1.18   Investment Company Institute: members trade association.

return of their peers in the subsequent year. Williamson also cites several other surveys, in *BusinessWeek* and *Personal Financial Planning* magazine, that reached similar conclusions.

So the ball's in your court. . . . It's your money, your lifestyle, and your future. And if you're one of the "highly knowledgeable" investors—within the definitions set by Vanguard/*Money* and Investor Protection Trust surveys—you're probably on the way to finding the *minority* of high-performing money managers, truly independent consultants, trust-worthy brokers, and reliable rating systems. They are out there (if you need one).

However, there are so many obstacles to successful investing today that if you do rely on advice from someone else, you *still* have to know enough about what your advisors are doing to determine whether they're really doing their job right. In the final analysis, given today's dynamic, rapidly changing financial world, you must be prepared to take over the process and do it yourself as necessary. At minimum, you need the skill to double-check your advisor and to select one in the first place.

BOTTOM LINE: THE FUND INVESTOR'S BEST STRATEGY . . . DO IT YOURSELF IN CYBERSPACE

Now we have come full circle. Mutual funds are the perfect investment for today's do-it-yourself independent investors for many reasons, the most important ones being that with a mutual fund you get the following:

INTERNET WEBSITES FOR MUTUAL FUND EDUCATION

American Association of Individual Investors http://www.aaii.org
Fidelity Investments http://www.fid-inv.com
Mutual Fund Education Alliance http://www.mfea.com
Mutual Funds Online http://www.mfmag.com
NETworth: Internet Investors Network http://networth.galt.com
      100% No-Load Mutual Fund Council
      Mutual Fund Education Alliance
PAWWS Financial Network http://pawws.com
U.S. Securities and Exchange Commission http://www.sec.gov
Vanguard Group of Funds http://www.vanguard.com

Figure 1.19   Mutual Fund Info Center: at the PAWWS Website.

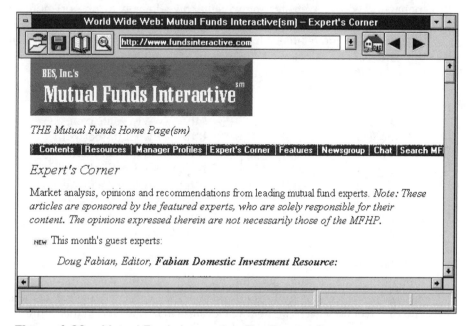

Figure 1.20   Mutual Funds Interactive: The Experts' Corner.

❏ A professional management and research team

❏ Diversification of your investment portfolio

❏ The freedom to enjoy your unique lifestyle

❏ Many other perks, such as centralized record keeping, automatic deposit and reinvestment plans, checking, retirement plan management, personal financial planning, market information, portfolio management, and more

Mutual funds are the perfect investment for today's do-it-yourself investor because of all the dozens of benefits of owning funds. Moreover, cyberspace fund investors have a decided edge in the investment game.

Fortunately, in cyberspace you can and will discover all the databases and analytical power tools necessary to make your job as an investor easy.

CAN'T FIND IT IN CYBERSPACE? SEARCH THE WEB!
START WITH ONE OF THESE TOP-NINE SEARCH ENGINES

If you're ever having trouble finding something on the Internet—funds, managers, books, Websites, news, *anything*—log on to one or more of these Websites and do some exploratory word searches. Think of it as getting help from the reference librarian at the main library, or checking out the card catalog. Explore! With practice, you will discover what you need . . . if it's out there anywhere on the World Wide Web.

Altavista	http://www.altavista.com
Excite	http://www.excite.com
InfoSeek	http://www.infoseek.com
Lycos	http://www.lycos.com
Magellan	http://www.mckinley.com
Metacrawler	http://www.metacrawler.com
Netscape	http://www.netscape.com
Webcrawler	http://www.webcrawler.com
Yahoo!	http://www.yahoo.com

These are the top-nine Internet search engines: bookmark them. Although they are all cataloging the *exact same* gigantic Web database, each has a different technology, format, and style. So experiment with all of them and discover how each can help you do research, now and in the future.

For example, with a little effort today's investors can identify consistently high performing funds and fund managers, independent financial consultants, and first-class rating systems that will help you build a successful portfolio of mutual funds.

They do exist, and you'll learn all about them before you finish this book. However, when the chips are down, you are your own best broker, your own best financial planner, your own best research analyst . . . and your own best decision maker. You never again have to turn your life and your financial independence over to anyone else.

The Key to Successful Financial Planning

How to Achieve Economic Independence in Cyberspace

In this second step we will outline the basics of sound financial planning, showing how planning is essential to building a winning mutual funds portfolio online, and the importance of a regular savings program. In addition to the planning process, we'll also identify other key resources available to investors in cyberspace.

HOW AMERICA'S SAVINGS
SHORTFALL IS IMPACTING YOU AS AN INVESTOR

Merrill Lynch's "Baby Boom Retirement Index," which they began publishing in 1993, is an extremely valuable service. While it focuses primarily
on the baby boomers—the 76 million Americans born between 1946 and
1962—the Boomer Index is one of many loud alarm bells in a rising chorus
encouraging not only boomers, but Americans in general, as well as other
investors worldwide, to start planning for the future, to shift their thinking
from current consumption and debt accumulation to savings and investing
for the future.

As recently as 1980, Americans were in the habit of saving about 8 percent of their disposable income. However, in a relatively short 15 years, the
personal savings rate had dropped to about half the 1980 level.

FORTUNE: A RADICAL NEW PARADIGM FOR AMERICA'S FUTURE

"Throw out any preconceived notions that you may have about how
you'll retire: A radical new paradigm is emerging that will change how
you invest, dream, and plan for the future. . . . Savings? . . . The numbers
alone are grim enough to make you want to run and hide . . .

"We may end up with a new model of retirement that future generations might aspire to. We might finally do the downscaling we've
always talked about. Our next career might just possibly turn out to be a
labor of love."

SOURCE: Betsy Morris, "The Future of Retirement: It's Not What You Think," *Fortune*
cover story (August 19, 1996).

Today, we are saving only about 4.5 percent of our disposable income.
Moreover, that's only about one-third the savings rate of our major competition among industrialized nations. Eventually this emphasis on consumption will impact not only individuals but the nation as a whole. Here
are the most significant conclusions in Merrill Lynch's latest report:

1. **Saving and Investing Are Too Little to Achieve Goals.**

   A typical baby boomer is saving only 35.9 percent of the amount necessary to maintain his or her standard of living in retirement. This assumes no systematic tax increases or reduction of retirement benefits by the government, a questionable assumption.

2. **You Will Change Lifestyle Now . . . or Later.**

   If the current behavior of the baby boomers is not adjusted considerably, they will be forced to either substantially reduce their lifestyle expectations for retirement or delay retiring.

3. **Solution: You Must Triple Your Savings!**

   Therefore, baby boomers would have to triple their saving's rate in order to invest, build their nest egg, and retire securely.

Fortunately, the popular media and financial press have been recently accelerating their coverage of this shortfall. In fact, hardly a week goes by without an article somewhere about the dire consequences—individually and nationally—of this enormous savings shortfall. When common sense isn't enough encouragement, fear tactics are always a powerful motivator.

TRIPLE YOUR SAVINGS . . . AND YOU'LL RETIRE IN STYLE!

"Do you really need that big-screen TV or new suit? Today's workers who want a secure retirement have to start saying 'No.'

"In 1994, Americans on the average saved an abysmal, decades-low 3.8% of their income after taxes. The amount ticked up—barely—to 4.5% in 1995.

"To provide just a modest $35,000 of annual income from age 65 to 90, in 1996 dollars, today's 40-year-old will need $1.7 million—that's no typo—by age 65. Today's 25-year-old will need $3 million. Even with $50,000 already saved, the 40 year-old would have to start putting away an additional $12,000 . . .

"Merrill Lynch's just released 'Baby Boom Retirement Index,' a kind of yearly ding on the head for boomers, shows that most would need to triple their savings rate to retire at 65 without a severe decline in living standards. Financial journalist Philip Longman, in his recent book, The Return of thrift, calls the behavior of most of today's consumers 'slow-motion bankruptcy.' "

SOURCE: "Save Now, Live Later," cover story in *U.S. News & World Report* (June 10, 1996).

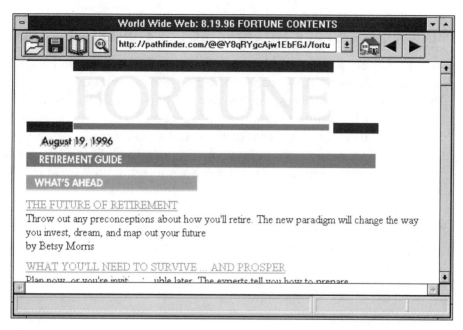

Figure 2.1 *Fortune:* new paradigm for future retiring and investing.

Figure 2.2 Planning *is* the difference. . . . Increase your savings *today!*

THE SECRET FORMULA TO
BECOMING A CYBERSPACE MILLIONAIRE . . . AND RETIRE EARLY!

What is happening to the baby boomers is also turning out to be a massive wake-up call to all Americans, including the Generation Xers, who are turning out to be more responsible than early pundits predicted. This new generation is becoming very aware of the need for early savings and, as a result, is focusing on long-term savings and investments.

The message is loud and clear: Wake up. As incredible as it may seem, we have to become millionaires if we want to retire with an even modest lifestyle!

Fortunately, the investment community is also rising to the occasion, especially the mutual funds and brokerage industries who will be handling the increased investments and who stand to profit as the savings pendulum swings up and new capital flows in. After all, mutual funds have about quadrupled in the 1990s to more than $3 trillion, and they are forecast to exceed $6 trillion by 2000.

ECONOMIST'S ADVICE: YOU'LL NEED TO BE A MILLIONAIRE

According to Robert Goodman, senior economic adviser, "Social Security cannot continue to exist in its present form. Neither can Medicare, Medicaid, or welfare. These and other entitlements, heretofore politically sacrosanct, will be dramatically altered, reduced, or eliminated. To live a financially secure life in this changing economic environment, you will need a much larger nest egg than in any prior generation . . . you can earn $1 million . . . and you'll need it."

SOURCE: Robert Goodman, *Independently Wealthy—How to Build Financial Security in the New Economic Era* (John Wiley, 1996).

Small wonder, then, that we are seeing many excellent new books on personal financial planning. Perhaps more important, we are also seeing a flood of new computerized planning tools, designed to operate online and on the Internet, as well as many new *offline* software products, which operate without tying up network connect time, while at the same time the better products are being developed as fully integrated one-stop, total-service navigational systems for investors.

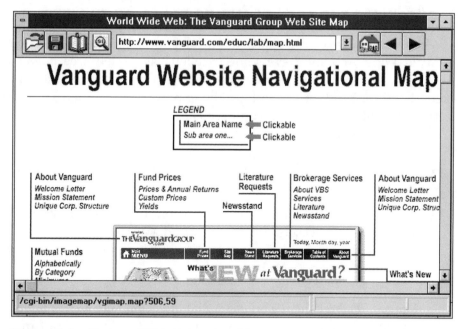

Figure 2.3 Vanguard Web University: #1 do-it-yourself funds education.

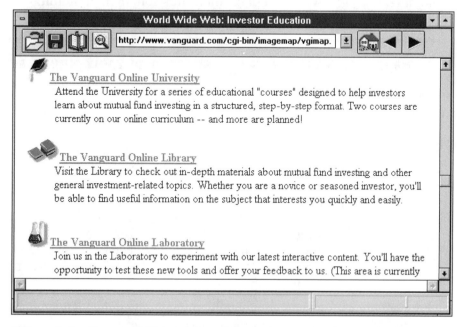

Figure 2.4 Vanguard Website: best free graduate school in cyberspace.

FIRST: CHECK OUT THE FREE PLANNING TOOLS ON THE WEB

When it comes to cyberspace financial planning, the Internet and the World Wide Web still have some excellent, absolutely free power tools, thanks to mutual fund giants like Vanguard and Fidelity. Moreover, as good as these products are today as beginning tools for financial planning, it appears likely that as the communication technologies improve on the Internet, these products will:

❒ Not only improve on par with the generally higher quality offline software systems, but

❒ It's also likely that many of them will continue as free services (that is, loss leaders or teasers) on mutual fund Websites, in much the same way that stock and fund quotes and news headlines have developed on many other financial Websites today.

Vanguard's Website deserves special attention because it has so much information available for the cyberspace investor. In fact, staff members take so much pride in what they have done, they even call it *The Vanguard Online University*, which defines their mission in maintaining a high-

---

THREE SECRETS TO PLANNING A SUCCESSFUL EARLY RETIREMENT

"Financial planner Jonathan Pond, host of the December PBS TV special, 'Finding Financial Freedom,' says successful early retirees invariably share these characteristics:

1. **They plan early.** Often beginning in their 20s and 30s, successful early retirees set their goal and take action to achieve it.
2. **They sacrifice during their working years.** Where most of us have trouble saving 10 percent of our income, early retirees may save 20 or 30 percent. 'They are experts at living below their income.' Pond says.
3. **They sacrifice after their working years.** Successful early retirees cut back even further during retirement because they know their savings will have to last them 25, 30, or more years. This could mean locating to a less expensive area of the country."

SOURCE: Jonathan Pond, "Keys to Early Retirement Success," *Your Money* (January 1996). You'll find more of Pond's wisdom online and in his books.

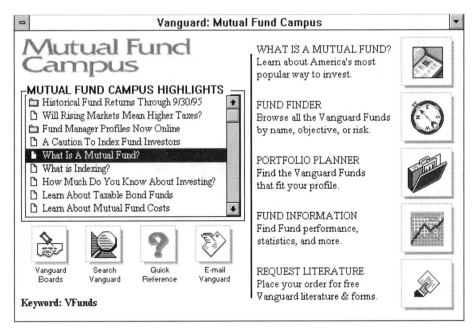

Figure 2.5   Vanguard Campus at AOL: online alternative to Website.

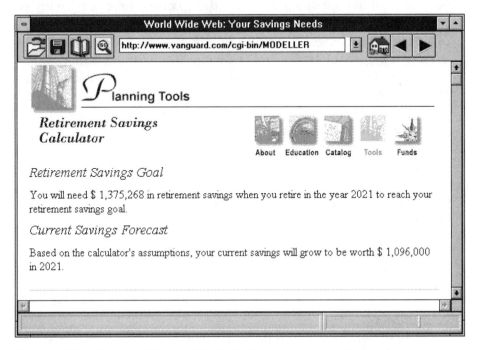

Figure 2.6   Vanguard Planning Tools: Retirement Savings Calculator.

quality Website planner, as well as encouraging their audience to take this personal financial planning process very seriously.

While the Vanguard planner is an excellent starter before you move on to some of the more sophisticated and integrated systems we'll discuss, even the more advanced investors would do well to go back and review Vanguard's Website—even if you are convinced you're a "very knowledgeable" investor.

This Website is packed with files containing courses, lessons, calculators, and quizzes—hey, it's The Vanguard *University*. You're bound to pick up a few helpful pointers, and it may help you refresh the fundamentals. Perhaps even more important, the Vanguard Website is a classic example of the high quality of Internet content and technology that's now available for the new cyberspace investor.

HOW TO CALCULATE YOUR SAVINGS USING THE FREE PLANNING TOOLS ON THE WORLD WIDE WEB

"Two-thirds of investors have never prepared a specific financial plan, even though having one is considered the cornerstone of wise investing," according to the *Los Angeles Times* in covering the Vanguard/*Money* survey of investor knowledge. Planning—or rather, the lack of planning—is one of the single biggest obstacles and challenges facing today's investors.

This fact is central to your success as a cyberspace investor, indeed, *for any investor.* In fact, it is so important that it bears repeating for emphasis: *Having a personal financial plan is generally recognized as the cornerstone of successful investing. And yet almost 70 percent of all investors never prepare a personal financial plan.* The winners do.

The solution is simple:

❏ Make financial planning a **regular habit.**
❏ **Start by preparing** a financial plan.
❏ **Review and update** your financial plan periodically.
❏ **Integrate it** with your other computer systems for investing and banking.

Learn to manage and control your finances *today,* and you'll be in control of your future.

Here's a way to get a jump start. Whether novice or expert, go directly to the Vanguard University on the World Wide Web. Now jump over to

THE SIX BEST WAYS TO FUND YOUR RETIREMENT

"There are two inescapable truths: More is better than less, and the sooner you start saving, the better. You know that. So don't get hung up about being too precise with the calculations, because life isn't all that precise. . . . Whether your calculations tell you you're well on your way to a secure retirement, or serve as a wake-up call to start savings hot and heavy, your goal should be to exploit any of these options available:

❒ **401(k) Plans** . . . squeeze every possible dollar out of your employer's match . . .
❒ **IRAs** . . . an excellent retirement savings vehicle . . .
❒ **Pension** . . . if you're in one, you can count on receiving these benefits.
❒ **Social Security** . . . perhaps not as soon and not as much as is currently provided . . .
❒ **Part-Time Work** . . . the real wild card. . . . Every 40-something person interviewed . . . had some sort of retirement work plan . . .
❒ **Inheritance** . . . estimated $10 trillion will be inherited by baby boomers from their parents—roughly $130,000 for each and every boomer . . .
❒ **The House** . . . the fact that you have to live somewhere . . . leads most financial planners to suggest that home value not be included in a retirement portfolio . . .

"A lot of your retirement income will come from savings. And where is all that money supposed to come from? No mystery here. It comes from you—in whatever way makes the most sense and hurts the least. . . . Saving now is a guaranteed lead-pipe cinch to pay enormous dividends later."

SOURCE: William Giese, "Retirement: How Boomers Can Avoid a Bust," *Kiplinger's Personal Finance Magazine* (October 1995).

Vanguard's Planning Tools section. Start with their Retirement Savings Calculator, and work through the questionnaire.

Here's a preview of one of the relatively simple planning modules available on the Vanguard Website to help the new do-it-yourself cyberspace investor. They're "simple" because you don't even have to buy and install any new computational software. With the Internet now an extension of your computer, you're using programming installed out there in cyberspace on Vanguard's superpowered computers. All you have to do is fill in the blanks with the following eight sets of information from your records, *and do all the work on the Web:*

- ❑ **Marital status.**
- ❑ **Household income.**   Pretax, including spouse's.
- ❑ **Retirement goals.** As a percent of income.
- ❑ **Current savings.** Seven categories include employer-based retirement programs, IRAs, mutual funds, bank accounts, stocks, CDs, and other savings
- ❑ **Investment personality.** Vanguard also has a more detailed risk-profile analysis. Here you select one of three:
    - ❑ *Conservative:* Few or no stocks.
    - ❑ *Moderate:* About half your investments are in stocks.
    - ❑ *Aggressive:* Most of your savings are stocks.
- ❑ **Current age.**
- ❑ **Retirement age.**
- ❑ **Life expectancy.**   Your period in retirement.

Then all you do is hit the **Calculate** button and zip . . . the great computer out there in Vanguard cyberspace will do the rest. Remember, *the Net is now*

FREE GRADUATE PROGRAMS FOR CYBERSPACE INVESTORS

"Vanguard University is one of the most innovative features of the Vanguard Website, and it represents the primary goal of the site: education. Our approach was to come up with something based on service, not advertising. . . . We want investors to understand as much as they can about what they are looking for in an investment vehicle . . .

"Vanguard University contains about 20 'classes' . . . 1,500 pages of information [and] is highly interactive . . . simple and intuitive. In the 'laboratory' section of the 'investor education' is a map that shows all of the site's segments . . .

"Vanguard puts all its prospectuses on the Web, whereas other companies may only offer online prospectuses for their most popular funds."

SOURCE: Arlene Weintraub, "Leaders of the Pack," *Individual Investor* magazine (July 1996). Fidelity Investment's 1,000-page Website was also highly recommended.

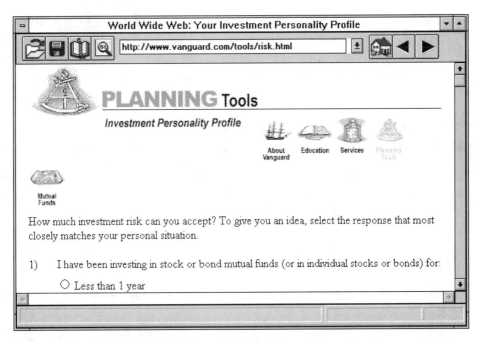

Figure 2.7 Vanguard: Web quiz to determine your risk profile.

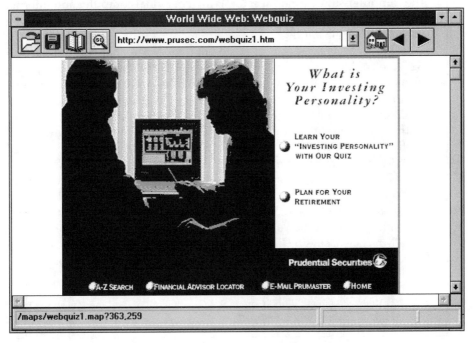

Figure 2.8 Prudential: determining your investing personality.

your computer, and this planning tool proves it one more time. You don't have to do any of the tedious, laborious, longhand number crunching that kept you from doing this kind of personal financial planning in the past, which is a fate worse than a trip to the dentist for most individuals.

WHY YOU MUST (AND CAN) BECOME A MILLIONARE: PLANNING, DISCIPLINE, AND ONE SMALL STEP AT A TIME

With all the new high-powered computer software, online, and Internet tools like the one on the Vanguard Funds Website, the planning process is now becoming fast and painless.

In order to test Vanguard's system to see if it's in line with the Merrill Lynch forecasts of the funds necessary for retirement—*namely, the necessity to become a millionaire*—we used an example of a 40-year-old couple with

---

CYBERSPACE: INSTANT INFORMATION, NO MORE WAITING

"Forget those mail-in coupons for mutual fund prospectuses. Even calling toll-free telephone numbers for information is rapidly becoming passe for the computer-savvy fund investor. With a personal computer and Internet access, mutual fund investors can get much of the information they are seeking almost instantly . . .

"Fidelity says 59% of its customers have personal computers, and 52% are equipped to go on-line. A survey of 11,000 individuals using Galt Technologies [Intuit] NetWorth site (which has information on 56 funds) by the Center for Strategic Research found that investors who use the Internet tend to be younger, single, better educated and more aggressive with investments than those who are cyberspace-shy. They have more cash to invest and hold 52% of their portfolios in mutual funds, compared to 38% for general investors.

"Take Salil Gangal, for example. The 32-year-old computer consultant in Portland, Ore., invests in 22 mutual funds and tracks most of them using the Internet. He recently took a four-week course in mutual fund investing as part of the Vanguard Group Inc.'s on-line university.

"Mr. Gangal says he likes reading Fidelity prospectuses while he is on-line, without having to save them to his computer's hard drive, or provide his home address. 'And I don't have to wait for the mail to arrive,' he says."

SOURCE: Kathryn Haines, "Fund Companies Offer Plenty of On-Line Investing Data," *The Wall Street Journal* (July 3, 1996).

household income of $75,000, a current nest egg of about $150,000, an annual savings rate of about $10,000, and other facts. Here's the bottom line for this family:

Retirement savings goal	$1,375,000
Current savings forecast	$1,095,000
Shortfall (goal minus forecast)	$280,000

Yes, there is a sizable shortfall here. In fact, it's a very big one: almost $300,000. Actually, it's "easy" to correct—*if you start early enough, plan ahead for a solution, get into action . . . and have the tenacity and discipline to stay in action, no matter what.*

We can also look at the positive side: Even under the current scenario, this 40-year-old couple is on its way to $1 million! In other words, there are a number of important observations we can make from this brief, initial effort:

1. You now know that you really do have to become a millionaire in order to retire in your current lifestyle.

2. Now you actually know your current financial status; no denial, no wishful thinking.

3. You have the tools to go the next step and work out a solution to correct the shortfall.

Moreover, this initial process—logging on to the Website, answering the questions, and getting the results—took less than 15 minutes. In that short a period, any investor can develop an initial financial plan. And in

---

BOOMERS AND GEN XERS:
IT'S *NEVER* TOO LATE (OR TOO EARLY) TO START SAVING!

"Consider this: The life expectancy of the typical 55-year-old woman today is more than 82 years—meaning that a portion of her cash must last at least 27 years. By any measure, 27 years is long-term investing."

SOURCE: Mark Bautz, "Five Steps to Earning Great Returns on Your 401(k)," *Money* (June 1996).

the case of an investor already doing regular planning who just wants to double-check those plans, it may take even less time.

Take this test. It could be more important than your annual physical this year.

To Vanguard's credit, you're not left hanging without a diagnosis of the problem. They also offer six recommended ways to deal with shortfalls, with some detailed explanations:

1. **Reduce the retirement period.** Retire later.

2. **Reevaluate your investment strategies and asset allocations, become more aggressive** (recognizing that will require more risk in your portfolio).

3. **Reduce your retirement income goals.** Live on less.

4. **Plan on part-time work** during retirement.

5. **Trade down your home** to reduce expenses and increase cash.

6. **Cash out life insurance.** Borrow, cancel, roll over into annuity.

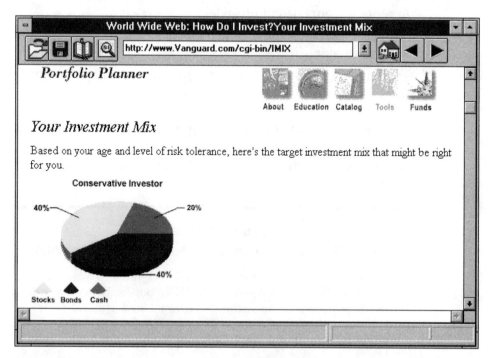

Figure 2.9   Vanguard: your investment mix based on risk profile.

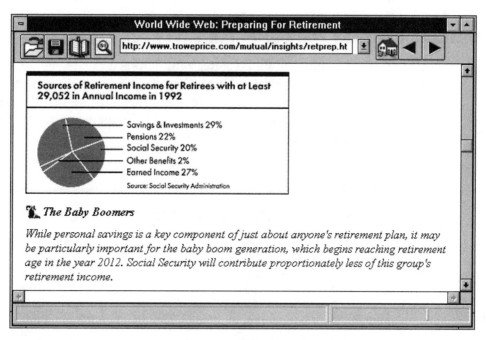

Figure 2.10   T. Rowe Price: actual sources for income in retirement.

Vanguard also has a more detailed investor's risk-tolerance quiz with its own calculator and, in addition, a subroutine program to help you develop a portfolio mix based on an asset allocation that fits your particular risk profile.

START EARLY AND BECOME A MILLIONAIRE ON $2.78 A WEEK!

"If you invest just $2.78 per week in an index fund or a diversified portfolio of common stocks and earn an average of 10.5% per year, which is the long-term average return generated by the market as a whole since 1926, your nest egg will exceed $1 million in 65 years . . .

"Of course there are a lot of caveats . . . but don't let that discourage you. Focusing on the future value of your portfolio in today's dollars instead of in nominal dollars simply means that you need to save and invest more—much more—to afford a comfortable retirement for yourself."

SOURCE: Joel Whittenberg, "How to Become a Multi-Millionaire," *Your Money* magazine (June/July 1996).

VANGUARD UNIVERSITY'S FREE GLOBAL
RESEARCH LIBRARY FOR COMPUTER-SAVVY FUND INVESTORS

With over 1,500 pages on its Website, Vanguard is a must-see first stop for the cyberspace mutual fund investor. You'll discover a wealth of educational materials—organized training lessons and courses—on all aspects of mutual fund investing. Here are just a few of the many resources filed in their extensive learning modules:

FIDELITY'S FINANCIAL PLANNING CALCULATOR ON THE WEB

Questionnaire also allows inputting data separately for spouse.

1. Marital Status
2. Birth Date
3. Planned Retirement Age
4. Life expectancy
5. Pretax Salaries
6. Other Incomes
7. Retirement Income Goals
8. Social Security Benefits
9. Pension Benefits
10. Cost of Living Index with Pension
11. Part-Time Job Income in Retirement
12. Years Working Part-Time
13. Income from One-Time Sales of Assets
14. Total Investments in Tax-Deferred Accounts
15. Total Investments in Taxable Accounts
16. Current Annual Savings Amount: Tax-Deferred
17. Annual Taxable Savings Amount
18. Assumed Inflation Rate
19. Pre-Retirement Investment Return Rates
20. Post-Retirement Return Rates

Once you input your information, the Fidelity computers become your computer. They handle all the calculations, and the processing is done for you in a flash. You get your financial bottom line within seconds: retirement nest egg, retirement goals and needs, and the gap, shortfall, or cushion. All right there with your computer while logged on to the World Wide Web.

❐ Primer on funds: stocks, bonds, money markets

❐ Risk/return trade-off: market, credit, investing, inflation

❐ Management styles

❐ Rating fund performance

❐ Deciphering newspaper listings

❐ Fund costs and expenses

❐ Understanding fund documents: prospectuses, annual reports, accounting reports

❐ Market indexing

❐ Special funds: global, sector, balanced

❐ Taxation and tax deferral

❐ Market timing

❐ Dollar cost averaging

❐ Cost basis and accounting

❐ Sources of information

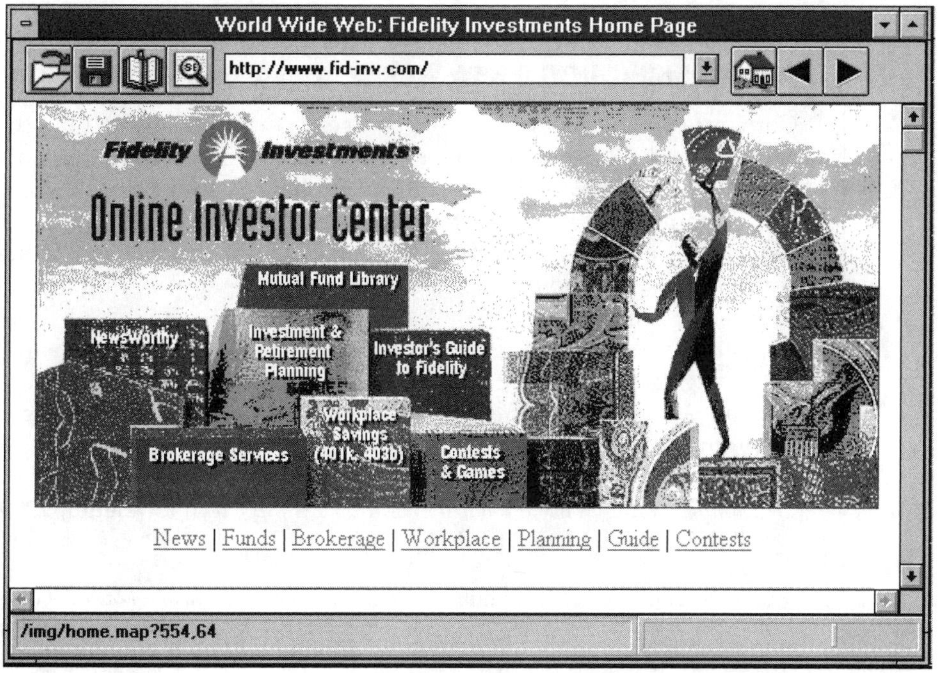

Figure 2.11 Fidelity Website: cyber-university for fund investors.

Vanguard is the ultimate cyberspace university. Its catalog of course materials at Vanguard University Website goes on and on. So whether you're a skilled investor who needs to look up something about mutual funds in this cyber–public library or a novice who's ready to get serious about planning for your future, enroll now.

Sign up now and start working on a "graduate" degree in do-it-yourself mutual fund investing. There are no tuition fees! It's free. Vanguard is clearly committed to higher education at this cyber-university.

Not only is it free, but cyberspace investors are definitely better prepared to make all the right decisions in the financial markets, so this free "investment" will help you hone a winning edge. Remember, that was the conclusion of the Vanguard/*Money* "Investor Literacy" quiz results.

FIDELITY'S FREE CYBERSPACE UNIVERSITY FOR FUND INVESTORS

Fidelity and Vanguard are intense competitors for cyberspace investors on the Web. Fortunately, both families of funds got a head start in cyberspace

---

**HOW YOU CAN REDUCE THE STRESS OF FUTURE SHOCK:
"DOWNSHIFT" INTO A NEW WORLD OF "VOLUNTARY SIMPLICITY"**

Corporate downsizings, increased stresses in the work world, the savings shortfall, and a long list of other cultural factors are *forcing* many individual investors to downshift into a life of "voluntary simplicity."

"Resources for DownShifters: The trend toward simple living, which has an especially strong foothold in the Pacific Northwest, has spawned a cottage industry of books and other resources for people trying to live life at a slower pace.

❑ *Living the Simple Life*, Elaine St. James (Hyperion Press)
❑ *Your Money or Your Life*, Joe Dominguez and Vicki Robin (Viking Penguin)
❑ *Voluntary Simplicity*, Duane Elgin (Quill Publishers)
❑ *Simple Living: The Journal of Voluntary Simplicity* Newsletter, 2319 N. 45th St., Box 149, Seattle, WA 98103"

SOURCE: Kirstin Davis, "DownShifters," *Kiplinger's Personal Finance Magazine* (August 1996). Also see Bradford Swift, "Living Simple in a Complex World," *Yoga Journal* (August 1996), *The Utne Report* and other alternative lifestyle periodicals that regularly advise individuals on how to downsize and enjoy life.

by creating their initial cyberspace programs on America Online. And they have both taken a "higher education" approach, including help in your financial planning.

Fidelity may be bigger in terms of the number of funds and money under management. However, the Websites and AOL menus for both companies run neck and neck in terms of quality and benefits to investors.

Fidelity has a 1,000-page site complete with features that rival the Vanguard site. In fact, you could even call this the Fidelity Web university, except Vanguard beat them to the punch. Besides, as a matter of pride, they probably don't want to come across as second best.

What the Fidelity Web university does have is a series of subdirectories covering everything from screening fund information to brokerage services, as well as personal financial planning. We already suggested that you take the quiz and work the Retirement Calculator at the Vanguard University site.

Well, you're in luck. Fidelity has similar educational services available, so you can double-check the results. In particular, Fidelity also has some neat interactive calculators to help you do your initial financial planning on the Web:

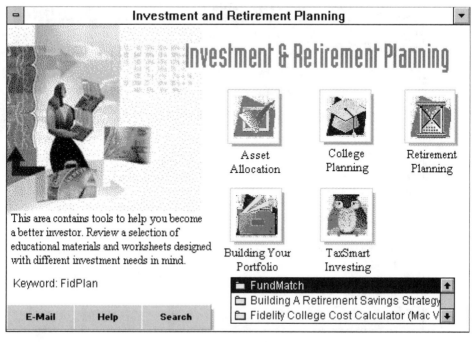

Figure 2.12 Fidelity: Investment and Retirement Planning courses.

❏ Retirement needs and goals analysis

❏ Risk-tolerance questionnaire

❏ Financial planning calculator

❏ Portfolio-building asset strategies

In short, you can start your financial planning in both universities, Vanguard's and Fidelity's. Call it a dual-enrollment with double major! And see how fast you can get up to speed as a "highly knowledgeable" cyberspace mutual funds investor. It's faster than you might imagine.

In fact, here's a suggestion. Take the Vanguard/*Money* 20-question quiz before spending much more time on the Vanguard and Fidelity Websites—or for that matter, any of the other key ones for mutual funds (NETworth, Mutual Funds Online magazine, etc.). Then, in a month or so, after taking the time to "study" the "courses," go back and take the 20-question quiz again. See the improvement.

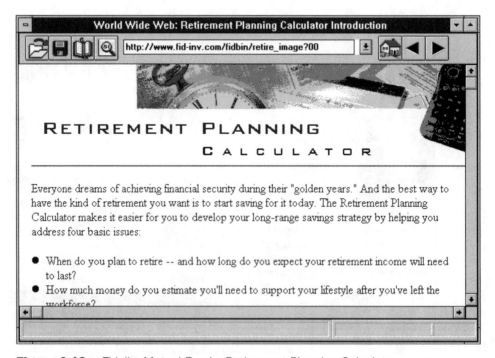

Figure 2.13   Fidelity Mutual Funds: Retirement Planning Calculator.

BOTTOM LINE:
START THINKING LIKE A MILLIONAIRE . . . AND YOU WILL BECOME ONE

Most investors are getting the message loud and clear: You must plan to become a millionaire if you want to retire. Period. That means the average investor must develop a mind-set that includes a new way of thinking:

❑ **Start thinking like a millionaire (because you have no choice).**
Since you *must* become a millionaire if you want to retire comfortably and securely, and since you *can* become a millionaire with regular, disciplined savings and wise investing, *believe and know that you can!*

PLANNING EARLY RETIREMENT? EXPECT THE UNEXPECTED!

"We visited some early retirees a few years after they took the plunge. They're doing just fine, thanks, but not always in the way they anticipated. . . . The realities of their experiences may help you shape your own plans for an early retirement:

Reality #1: **You'll still be working.** Over half are still working because they have to or want to.

Reality #2: **Life expands to fill available time.** Many retirees are still on 50 hour weeks, consulting, volunteering, travel, sports . . . doing what they really want.

Reality #3: **Your best-laid plans may fail.** A second career may not pan out, health problems, market reversals, etc.

Reality #4: **Your money has to keep working, too.** It is essential you stay on top of your portfolio to maximize returns while minimizing risks for your changing needs.

Reality #5: **You don't both have to retire.** In fact, one of you may be more likely to want to continue working.

Reality #6: **You can retire more than once.** That's right, plan to retire early, and plan ahead and do it again after succeeding in a new venture in doing something you always wanted to do. And maybe even a third career!"

SOURCE: Adapted from Gregory Spears, "Retiring Early: A Reality Check," *Kiplinger's Personal Finance Magazine* (July 1996).
Also review *Fortune's* Website for "The Future of Retirement: It's Not What You Think," by Betsy Morris, and other excellent articles in *Fortune's Midyear Retirement Guide* (August 19, 1996).

Figure 2.14 Fidelity Investment's Workplace Savings course.

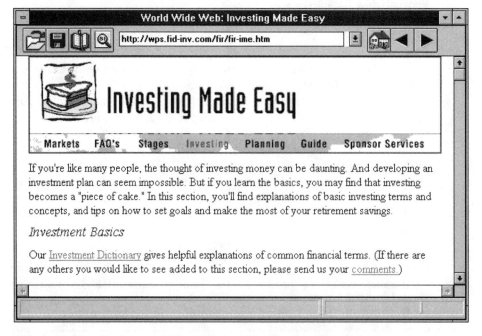

Figure 2.15 Do-it-yourself "Investing Made Easy" on the Web.

❏ **Develop a personal financial plan, today.**
Studies show that most investors neglect this most fundamental and essential tool in preparing for the future. Get online and on the Net; buy and install some financial planning software; plan your future now.

❏ **Increase your savings, and enjoy life.**
Substantially increase your savings, probably by as much as three times over the current rate, and start doing it regularly.

WHEN TO DO IT YOURSELF (AND WHEN TO HIRE AN "ADVISOR")

The trend toward do-it-yourself investing is growing rapidly throughout the world. Establishment brokerage firms are counterattacking, even renaming themselves "financial consultants," implying that their advice is *independent and objective.* Are you independent enough to do it yourself? Or do you need someone to make your decisions for you? Here's what one expert has to say:

"You may decide that it's too much trouble to research mutual funds and plan the rest of your finances. So you'll be tempted to find a financial advisor to relieve the burden.

"Don't do it!

"If you're like many people, you may hire an advisor for the wrong reasons. . . . Don't hire an advisor because of what I call the crystal ball phenomenon. . . . No one that you're going to hire has a crystal ball. . . . Lots of smart folks are following the markets, so it's highly unlikely that you or an advisor, myself included, could outfox them . . .

"Besides, investing intelligently in mutual funds isn't that complicated.

"The right reasons to hire an advisor. Consider hiring an advisor if you're:

Too busy to do the investing yourself . . .
Always putting it off because you don't enjoy doing it . . .
Uncomfortable making investment decisions on your own . . .
Wanting a second opinion . . .
Needing help with establishing and prioritizing financial goals."

SOURCE: Eric Tyson, *Mutual Funds for Dummies* (IDG Books, 1995).

Mediation is perhaps the single biggest reason for hiring an advisor when spouses or partners have conflicting goals.

For specific recommendations contact The Institute of Certified Financial Planners for a copy of their guide to selecting a financial planner, along with a list of three planners in your area (800) 282-7526.

❐ **Study and improve your IQ as an investor.**
Increase your "investor intelligence" by educating yourself and becoming more knowledgeable about the market and investing skills.

❐ **Start using all the new investor cyberspace power tools.**
Become skilled in using the vast arsenal of new cyberspace technologies designed for do-it-yourself mutual fund investors.

❐ **Patiently build a successful investment portfolio.**
Yes, you can do it. And your chances of success increase with do-it-yourself cyberspace power tools and action. Just do it!

As with so many things, the chief hurdle and challenge facing individuals is the need to overcome their denial of the need for change. In the past two decades our economy has been driven by consumption and debt. As a result, as a nation and individually we had dramatically reduced savings.

Fortunately, the times are changing. In the past couple years more individuals are changing to this whole new way of thinking with a stronger sense of responsibility. Indeed, this wake-up call is creating a whole new generation of do-it-yourself independent investors who are taking charge of their futures. And cyberspace is where the future is for this new generation.

HOW TO GET INTO ACTION TODAY: IT'S EASIER THAN YOU THINK

So what are the next action steps for you? Well, there are many powerful tools reviewed here in this chapter. Imagine yourself as Tom Cruise, the hero in *Mission Impossible*. If you're ready to get into action, here is your mission . . . if you choose to accept it. And here's a summary of the actions that will ramp you up into full-fledged cyberspace financial planning:

Action step 1:
Take the 20-Question Mutual Fund Quiz on the Web

The Vanguard/*Money* questionnaire is one of the quickest ways to discover your current level of investor intelligence and probably a resounding wake-up call to action. You can't afford to be ignorant about investing—it's your future folks. If you're not on the Web, you *must* get on the Web now. Very soon *all* mutual fund investors will be cyberspace investors, just as all investors have a telephone. So get on board and enjoy the benefits.

Action step 2:
Start Planning, Buy Some Financial Planning Software

And do it today. That's right, pick up the phone and call Vanguard, Fidelity, or one of the others reviewed here to order their basic planning software. For about $25 you can move to the next level in your education and get a more detailed financial plan for your future.

HOW TO FIND VANGUARD AND FIDELITY EDUCATIONAL MATERIALS

America Online	Free (part of AOL fee)	(800) 827-6364
Vanguard Website	Free	www.vanguard.com
Fidelity Website	Free	www.fid-inv.com
Retirement Planner	Vanguard software ($15)	(800) 876-1840
Thinkware Planner	Fidelity software ($15)	(800) 457-1768

Action step 3:
Commit Time and Energy Studying about Investing

You'll probably find all you need to know in cyberspace, online, on the Net, and offline with your new software. In his book, *How to Be Your Own Stockbroker,* Charles Schwab recommends an hour a day at the start.

Okay, sounds like a lot, but you're probably already reading periodicals and even some books on investing. It's your future we're talking about here, and you're worth every minute of the time you invest in it. So get on the Net where the action is, and you'll experience a rapid learning curve.

Action step 4:
Quickly Move into a Graduate Course in Financial Planning

The "graduate course" is the ongoing, disciplined practice of planning, saving, investing, and long-term portfolio management. And it takes a commitment, time, and eternal vigilance to manage your money.

To make your job easier, you'll need at least one of the integrated planning and investing power tools reviewed here. So your next step is to buy and install an integrated system that works for you. It might be the Intuit/Quicken system, WealthBuilder from Reuters Money Network, or another. Test-drive one, and if it's not right for you, be brave and get another. Keep your eye focused on your goals.

You'll also find several other top navigational systems listed in the appendix. They are covered in much more detail in our companion book, *Expert Investing on the Net: Profit from the Top-25 Online Money Makers*. And while most of these systems lack personal financial planners comparable to the ones here, many of them may be just right for you when you enter the ongoing path to becoming a millionaire in cyberspace.

THE FOUR RISKS IMPACTING ALL MUTUAL FUND INVESTMENTS

These computer power tools for mutual fund investing will help minimize many risks, but they'll never eliminate them. All investment decisions are subject to four inherent risks or uncertainties that impact your portfolio:

❏ **Inflation risks**

The purchasing power of future goods and services will erode so that future dollars won't be worth as much as today's money. Your portfolio should be designed so that your return will be much higher than the rate of inflation.

❏ **Interest rate risks**

Fluctuating economic conditions, productivity, Fed policies, government fiscal policies, and many other variables create volatility in interest rates, inversely affecting bond prices and indirectly impacting stock prices.

❏ **Market risks**

The up-and-down cycles of industry sectors, inherent uncertainties of individual companies, public perceptions of the future, and external factors, such as a war, can all influence stock prices and market indices.

❏ **Credit risks**

There is always the possibility of a default and bankruptcy, as remote as it may appear. Individual companies, junk bonds, even governments, are not immune, as we saw with the Orange County municipal bond fiasco.

The reality is that for the vast majority of investors, professional and individual alike, and especially the mutual funds investor, you have very little or no control over most of these risks, in spite of all your efforts. And that is why mutual funds—providing you with professional management and diversification—are the perfect investment. You are "partners" with experts, plus you're spreading your risks over many companies.

STEP THREE

The Formula for Building a Winning Fund Portfolio

How to Build a Successful Portfolio Using the Right Asset Allocations

Here's the simple formula for building a winning mutual funds portfolio. Master it and you'll be in control of 90 percent of your portfolio's return. Step 3 emphasizes asset-allocation strategies—such as lifestyle, goals, age, and risk tolerance—that influence long-term asset strategies, plus the major software programs that can simplify your personal financial planning.

THE SECRET OF A WINNING PORTFOLIO: IT'S 90 PERCENT IN YOUR ASSET ALLOCATIONS, ONLY 10 PERCENT IN THE FUNDS YOU PICK

Here's the keep-it-simple rule, the key to building a winning mutual funds portfolio. Here's how the professionals do it. The key to success is not in picking the right fund, not in screening and selecting another five-star fund, not in picking one of those top-gun portfolio managers.

It's very important that you understand this crucial distinction, because the financial press will relentlessly numb you with titillating articles about this week's or this quarter's hottest funds, top-performing managers, and fund sectors.

THE WINNING FORMULA: 90 PERCENT ON ASSET ALLOCATIONS AND ONLY 10 PERCENT ON PICKING SPECIFIC FUNDS

"In a celebrated 1991 study, researchers Gary Brinson, Brian Singer and Gilbert Beebower statistically proved what 90% of investing is. It is asset allocation . . . the way you divide your money among the investment options.

"The researchers found that the investment mix accounted for 91.5% of the variation in total return among the investors they surveyed. Security selection (whether the investor chose stocks or bonds that did better or worse than the pack) and market timing (when an investor decided to buy and sell) together explained a measly 6.4% of the difference in returns.

"This may not make much sense at first. After all, had you bought Intel stock in the spring of 1994, you'd have more than doubled your money by the end of last year. Had you bought the retailer Bradlees instead, you'd have lost 90%. How, you may wonder, could securities selection not be more important than asset allocation?

"The real question is: Can anyone consistently make those brilliant calls in advance? Obviously not: The average equity fund manager has earned just over 12% for his shareholders since 1980, while the market overall rose more than 14%. Clearly the pros have a hard time keeping their portfolios brimming with Intels."

SOURCE: Eric Schurenberg, "Get This Strategy Right, and Your 401(k) Investing Will Be 90% Sewn Up," *Money* magazine (February 1996).

As a result of the constant drumbeat in the financial press, you may have come to believe that chasing and picking one of the currently hot five-star funds or the latest top-gun manager with the most news coverage is the key to a winning portfolio. This is especially true today, with all the emphasis on improving your retirement savings shortfall and the pressure to go for the highest possible returns.

However, the answer lies not with the stars. For the vast majority of individual investors, the key to a successful mutual fund portfolio is in making the right asset allocations . . . *not in picking star funds and top-gun managers.*

In fact, research studies have proven that over 90 percent—that's right, 90 percent—of the success of your mutual fund portfolio will be *directly* related to your asset categories and *not* the specific funds you'll pick!

Now you can see why we consistently put so much emphasis on your personal financial plan. Yes, picking the right funds will always be important . . . but only *after* you develop your portfolio's asset allocations using your personal financial plan. And then you need to exercise the necessary discipline to stick to those allocations rather than chasing hot news items.

WARNING: LAST YEAR'S WINNERS WILL NOT REPEAT THIS YEAR

"Don't just compare your fund to the market, says Roger Ibbotson; rank it against funds with the same style . . . The unfortunate truth is that a list of last year's winning funds isn't going to tell you much about who's going to be a winner this year . . .

"Ibbotson, a Yale School of Management professor . . . began analyzing year-by-year rankings of funds over the period 1976 through 1995. His conclusion, not at all surprisingly, is that there is *next to no consistency* of raw returns from one year to the next. Only 52% of the time did a fund that landed in the top half one year repeat its performance the next. Using longer periods (two or three years) didn't improve the picture."

SOURCE: Thomas Easton, "The Funds: Compared to What?," *Forbes* (October 21, 1996).

Think of investing as a sport: Financial planning is analogous to all the preseason training, the game plans, and pregame warm-ups. It's absolutely essential to prepare *before* you step onto the field and play the game. Planning leads to winning.

Figure 3.1 Ninety-four percent of mutual fund returns are based on asset allocations.

Figure 3.2 Vanguard Investment Planner: A Guide to Asset Allocation.

STAY FOCUSED ON YOUR ASSET ALLOCATIONS . . .
AVOID CHASING AFTER THE HOTTEST FUND OF THE MONTH!

Today's financial and popular media are loaded with examples of asset allocations for model portfolios. In fact, if you subscribe to several publications, you're probably well aware of the new trend toward the "fund-of-the-month" club (or "manager," or "portfolio"). None are immune. Even the best financial periodicals are guilty of luring in readers with titillating lists of the hottest, latest, and best superstars.

Some of the better magazines for the serious fund investor include *Kiplinger's, Money,* and *Mutual Funds.* Several others regularly include fund coverage, although with somewhat lesser editorial content focused on mutual funds. These include *Your Fortune, Forbes, Barron's,* and *The Wall Street Journal.* And occasionally you'll run across some interesting articles on mutual funds in magazines such as *Working Woman, Playboy,* and other large-circulation, popular magazines.

And of course, with major trends such as the predicted massive inflow into mutual funds, you can expect the coverage of mutual funds to increase even more . . . with new funds, new model portfolios, and new asset allocations.

JUST WHEN YOU THINK YOU'VE GOT IT ALL FIGURED OUT,
THEY MOVE THE TARGET AGAIN!

Kiplinger's Mutual Funds annual is one of the best printed guides for mutual fund investors who are computer-savvy and always looking to improve "the edge," as well as the computer phobic or computer illiterate.

A recent issue quotes a teacher, Judy Johnson, "Every time I think I've got it, I hear something new. So I go back and start over. It's very confusing—I feel like I've been going in circles."

Kiplinger's says, "Millions of people feel just as lost as Johnson. It's hard for them to put together a good investment plan to prepare for retirement, their children's college education or other goals. Many do nothing—the worst possible solution. Others limp along with portfolios that they really don't understand or that may not be right for them."

Sound familiar? You bet. Most investors share the feeling. With the rate of new money pouring into funds, and the number of funds on the increase, the level of confusion is also guaranteed to increase. Stay alert.

SOURCE: Steven Goldberg, "Your Investments, Are They in Harmony?," *Kiplinger's Mutual Funds '96.*

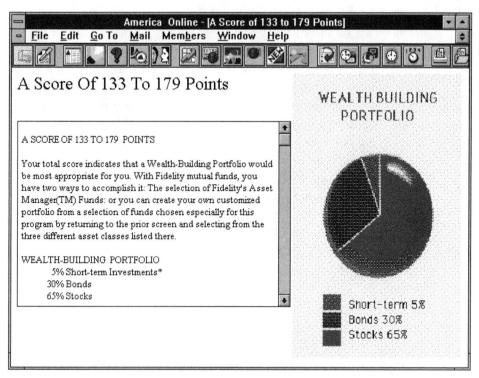

Figure 3.3   Aggressive three-part asset allocation: stocks, bonds, and cash.

Our recommendation is quite simple: Keep all your subscriptions; occasionally you will get some solid advice. Besides, it'll keep you sharply focused on your portfolio. However, notwithstanding the occasional tidbits of information about funds and their managers, you must *first* get yourself anchored in your own financial plan, with an asset allocation that works for you, staying focused on *your* plan. And that's where the new personal financial software programs become important. First, let's review the process of developing your asset allocations.

THE CLASSIC EXAMPLE:
BASIC PORTFOLIO STRATEGIES
WITH THREE SIMPLE ASSET ALLOCATIONS

In the simplest form, asset allocations of individual investors require balancing these elements: the time horizon (when they want to make withdrawals) with risk tolerance (personal anxiety about price volatility, especially the possibility of loss) and the ability to diversify or spread the risk.

One of the simplest and best explanations available of this balancing act is in an excellent book, *The Wall Street Journal Guide to Planning Your Financial Future,* written by Kenneth Morris, Alan Siegel, and Virginia Morris. In their section on asset allocation, the trio keeps it very simple: "You don't have to reinvent the wheel to plan your asset allocation. It's already been done. Fortunately, there are a limited number of ways to split up your assets. If you're a cautious investor, you'll stress bonds and cash. And the more aggressive you are—the more you'll put into stocks."

The second major factor is the number of years you have before retirement, and in "an asset allocation model, stocks represent growth," so "financial experts may recommend that you have as much as 80% of your total portfolio in stocks (or stock mutual funds) while you're in your 30s and 40s . . . as you get older, say in your 50s and 60s, the percent of stocks in your portfolio is usually scaled back to 60% or sometimes less." The result is a general asset-allocation model that looks like this:

Years Until Money Needed	Stocks	Bonds	Cash
30 years	80%	15%	5%
12 years	60%	30%	10%
5 years	40%	40%	20%

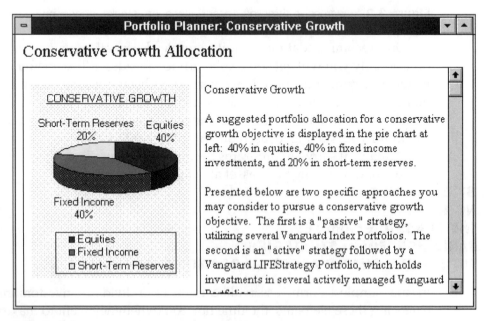

Figure 3.4   Conservative risk taker's portfolio: three-part allocation.

The closer you get to the time you need the money, the more is shifted out of the stock's slice of the asset-allocation pie and into the bonds and money market slices. Actually there's no special magic here, just the discipline of staying focused on your own asset allocations, without chasing after the most recently touted portfolio-of-the-month, five-star fund, or top-gun manager in the financial press. It's that simple.

TIME IS THE INVESTOR'S BEST ALLY. . . . PATIENCE *IS* A VIRTUE (AND THE LATEST HOT NEWS TIP IS YOUR ENEMY)

"Time, the risk killer. Some investors can't get past the fear of losing money. They seem to think that the longer you stick with the stock market, the greater your chance of experiencing a big loss. But investing is not like Russian roulette. In fact the opposite is true: The easiest way to reduce the risk of stocks is to increase the time you hang onto your portfolio . . .

The lesson is simple: The stock market will bite you only if you cash out too early. And now you know why only seven U.S. equity funds have lost money over the past 10 years. Even the badly managed funds have time and the market working for them . . . Time is on your side."

SOURCE: Jersey Gilbert, "Ride Out the Risk—The Long-Term Favors a Steady Hand," *Smart Money* (November 1995).

Keep in mind that this basic model must be adjusted for your personal tolerance for risk. Fortunately, all the best Website and software planners include risk-tolerance questionnaires that compute and factor into the plan's recommended asset allocations your unique personality and risk tolerance.

STICK WITHIN YOUR ASSET ALLOCATION RANGE NO MATTER WHAT. . . . STOP CHASING HIGHER RETURNS

After reviewing many, many of these recommended model portfolios in the financial press, in the software programs, on Website calculators, in pamphlets from the fund managers, and in proposals from various expert financial advisors, you soon understand that, while there are some variations, most of these asset-allocation models follow this general pattern, give or take a few percentage points.

True, some of the more sophisticated ones break up the *stock* slice into large companies, small companies, and internationals, as we'll see more closely in the next chapter, but the principle is the same.

THE THREE LEVELS OF ASSET ALLOCATION USED BY THE PROS

"The way professional money managers go about it, asset allocation usually takes place at three levels. There isn't any reason you can't or shouldn't do it the same way.

"The first level . . . strategic asset allocation . . . the process by which you determine your willingness to take risks. . . . Your conclusions about yourself and your goals will help you construct a portfolio that is aimed at reaching your goals without giving you high blood pressure . . .

"The second level . . . dynamic rebalancing . . . nothing more than the occasional adjustment of the portfolio to keep its relative risk at a predetermined level . . . a buy-and-hold strategy that gets out of kilter over the years, becoming more risky than you might like . . .

"The third level . . . tactical asset allocation . . . moving funds from what they believe are high-priced assets to what they hope are low-priced assets . . . the dream of every investor: buy low and sell high. They tend to use computer models to make those decisions."

SOURCE: Douglas Sease and John Prestbo, *Barron's Guide to Making Investment Decisions*, (Prentice Hall, 1994).

In addition, the major families of funds all have asset-allocation funds that actually do the asset allocation for you in a single fund. For example, Twentieth Century's three Strategic Asset Allocation funds ("a new way to diversify") follow *The Wall Street Journal* model quite closely:

Twentieth Century's Three Asset-Allocation Funds	Stocks	Bonds	Cash
Aggressive	75%	20%	5%
Moderate	60%	30%	10%
Conservative	40%	45%	15%

You will note that there are only minor differences between *The Wall Street Journal*'s model and Twentieth Century's three asset-allocation funds. If you're choosing among Twentieth Century's three Strategic Asset Allocation funds, all you have to do is connect the dots, that is, understand the basic principle that investors can and should be more aggressive the more years they have before retiring. Conversely, they should be more conservative the closer they are to retirement.

These basic options are common throughout the mutual fund industry. The danger today (if there is one) is that as more investors become conscious of their savings shortfall and increase savings, they are also likely to look for quicker fixes, and therefore lean more toward investment alternatives that will potentially generate higher returns, but that also have higher risks.

And that tendency could be a big problem. The pressure to employ a more aggressive asset allocation than justified (based on the number of years until your retirement, or your risk tolerance, or your personal financial plan) can lead to paradoxical results and actually lower your returns because of higher risks.

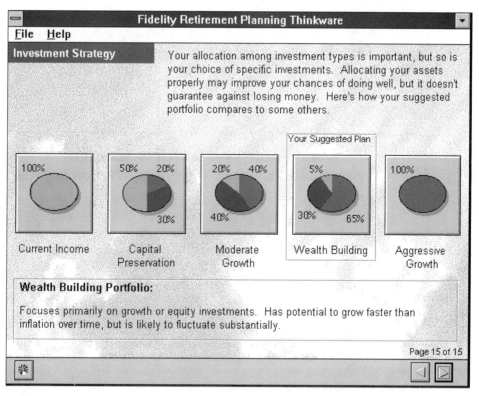

Figure 3.5 Fidelity Thinkware: five portfolios with three-part allocations.

In order to protect yourself against this, we strongly recommend regular use of some financial planning software to test and confirm your risk tolerance, your asset allocations, and the performance of your funds, so you can successfully build and manage your portfolio over the long term.

THE BEST PERSONAL FINANCIAL PLANNERS ARE THE OFFLINE SOFTWARE PROGRAMS

In the last chapter we urged you to start and continue an ongoing study program as an investor. We have already had a chance to review the best of the Web-based financial planners. One thing becomes obvious very quickly. The best planning tools are not yet on the Web.

Yes, the Web is a great place to start. However, if you want the real cyberspace power tools and, more important, the ability to integrate online resources with offline power tools, you'll need to look beyond the Web . . . at least for the near future.

For example, the extensive financial planning information on the Vanguard's Website is quite rare, and their Web-based planning program, great as it is, lacks many features of the offline systems. True, in the very near future some of the best of today's mutual fund resources (perhaps, for

---

THE WALL STREET JOURNAL DISCOVERS
TOP FINANCIAL PLANNERS ARE OFFLINE, NOT ON THE WEB

"All the hype about the Internet, and the whole concept of going on-line, make it easy to forget that what most people do with their computers most of the time has nothing to do with using a modem to connect with the outside world. Most computer owners are still concerned with running useful or entertaining software programs that live in a single machine.

"Nearly every software maker is trying to build some Internet-oriented feature into its software, because that's what attracts the attention of reviewers and dealers these days. But the real meat of most software remains on the hard disk or CD-ROM of a single PC."

SOURCE: Walter S. Mossberg, "Personal Technology Column," *The Wall Street Journal* (July 20, 1996).

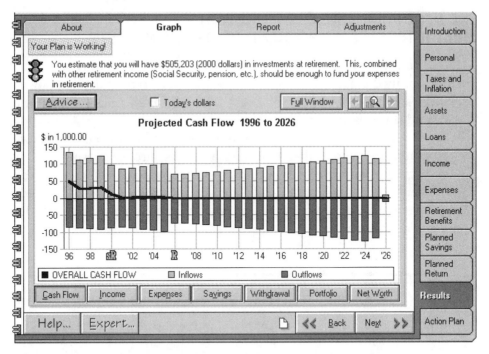

Figure 3.6   Quicken Financial Planner: long-term cash-flow projections.

example, Morningstar or NETworth) will try to outdo the Vanguard and Fidelity Websites, and put a supersophisticated version on their Website for free.

However, right now virtually all of the more sophisticated cyberspace financial planners are *offline* software systems that you have to purchase and install on your hard drive. Fortunately, although these systems are neither free nor easily accessible on the Web, they are:

❏ usually designed to interface with Web-based programs, and

❏ more important, they operate as ongoing portfolio-management programs, so you're not just getting a one-shot plan in a vacuum.

Moreover, they are typically quite inexpensive, and worth every penny in terms of saving you headaches and money. So let's review the arsenal of available offline planning products.

THE BEST FINANCIAL PLANNING TOOLS
MUST INTERFACE WITH YOUR INVESTING SOFTWARE

The cyberspace revolution is disrupting the status quo on Wall Street so rapidly that it's becoming nearly impossible to predict what new technologies will still be important a year ahead, let alone guess what new products and services are coming in the next generation.

One thing is certain: There is a clear trend toward creating totally integrated systems, rather than just a single-purpose planner executed in a vacuum. Valuable as they are as starter kits and for cross-checking, the planners on the Fidelity and Vanguard Websites are not designed to interface with and readily exchange data with the other critical functions in the investing process:

THE ONGOING BATTLE: WEB TOOLS VERSUS OFFLINE SOFTWARE

❑ **The Case *against* mutual fund website power tools.** In "Haywired," a recent cover story on Web resources on funds, *Barron's* writer Eric Savitz concluded: "It should come as no surprise to see the frantic efforts of fund companies and computer geeks to set up mutual-fund sites on the World Wide Web. . . . So far, the choices are underwhelming. There's simply not a lot out there, at least not yet.

"For the most part, the fund-company sites consist of 'brochureware,' digitized sales literature. . . . Not many, however, offer compelling reasons for anyone to make a return visit. That's one of the conclusions of a recent study by Coopers & Lybrand and the Cyber Solutions Group . . ."

❑ **The case *for* online/software systems off the web.** The same issue of *Barron's* had a separate article, "The Race Goes to the Quick," by columnist Howard Gold ("The Electronic Investor"), comparing Quicken's Investor Insight and Reuters Money Network, and concluded they were the two major competitors for the cyberspace investor's online/software business. In particular, "Investor Insight combines just about everything needed in one program."

Note the marked contrast between Gold's praise of the online/software systems and Savitz' skepticism of World Wide Web resources. This reinforces our belief that, generally, today's combination online/software systems are superior to Web-based systems.

SOURCE: *Barron's* (July 8, 1996).

1. Developing your personal financial plan
2. Picking the right database for your searches
3. Database screening based on selection criteria
4. Selecting specific securities for your portfolio
5. Executing trades with electronic discount brokers
6. Managing an ongoing investment portfolio
7. Timing and disposition of assets

As a result, a committed do-it-yourself cyber-investor will soon move past the Fidelity and Vanguard systems because the Website planners are not designed to integrate your plan from the Website into an integrated system that allows the all-important ongoing portfolio-management function. Nevertheless, the Websites are important tools for providing investors with a jump start, a cross-check on other planning efforts, or a refresher course.

Let's look at some of the software systems that more closely fit an ideal financial planner designed to work as part of a totally integrated navigational system for investors.

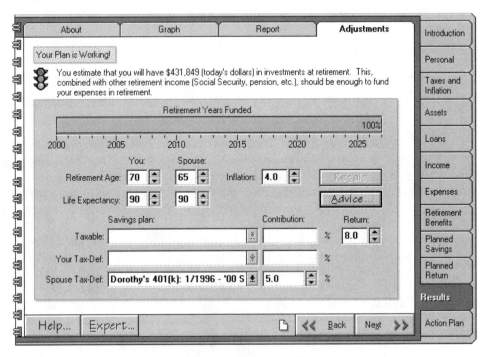

Figure 3.7   Quicken planning: easy testing what-if scenarios.

INTUIT'S QUICKEN:
THE ULTIMATE PLANNER FOR CYBERSPACE INVESTING

Quicken's parent company, Intuit, has had software for financial planning almost as long as Microsoft, starting back in the early 1980s. Intuit's software is important for cyberspace mutual fund investors because its financial planning systems are being developed as part of larger integrated systems:

❐ The software is interactive *within* the Intuit family of financial software modules.

❐ It also interfaces with *external* computerized systems for cyberspace investors, such as Schwab's StreetSmart software for trading and Reuters Money Network for portfolio management.

Moreover, with the flood of banks now moving onto the Web and into online banking, Intuit's alliance with the over 40 commercial banks gives them an even further entrée to investors. Quicken is in a perfect position to offer its total package of services and even further expand an already huge 70 percent market share in the personal finance software field.

QUICKEN FINANCIAL PLANNER: TOPS WITH THE JOURNAL

"There are a number of similar products, but the Quicken Financial Planner, now in version 2.0, stands out from the pack for offering the best balance of depth and ease of use. Unlike many of the others, it also has a somewhat broader focus than merely planning for retirement . . .

"While retirement is the main focus . . . paying for college and buying life insurance . . . a good database of mutual funds, and primers on inflation and rates of return . . .

"The program is organized clearly, and takes a hand-holding, step-by-step approach. It appears usually like a notebook, with tabs across the top and sides. . . . But Quicken Financial Planner seems to be blind about two big realities of modern financial life: excessive debt and emergency medical costs."

SOURCE: Walter S. Mossberg, "Personal Technology Column—Intuit Helps You with Future Finances, but Overlooks Debt," *The Wall Street Journal* (July 20, 1996).

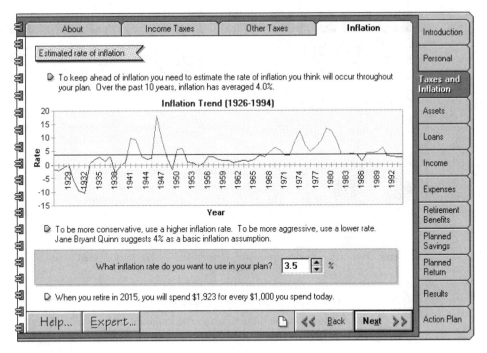

Figure 3.8   Quicken financial planning: taxes and inflation.

We're putting the Quicken/Intuit system in the spotlight at this point to illustrate the current trend toward totally integrated systems for cyberspace investment. These one-stop systems allow do-it-yourself fund investors to integrate all their investment needs into one single cyberspace system. Here's Intuit's rather extensive package of integrated products:

1. **Personal Financial Planner**
2. **Quicken Deluxe:** Personal finances
3. **Investor Insight:** Stock and fund analytics
4. **Mutual Funds Finder:** In Investor Insight
5. **NETworth Internet Investor Network: Website with Morningstar and Disclosure**
6. **Reuters Money Network:** Portfolio management
7. **Exporter:** Interface with StreetSmart trading
8. **TurboTax:** Software and online tax planner

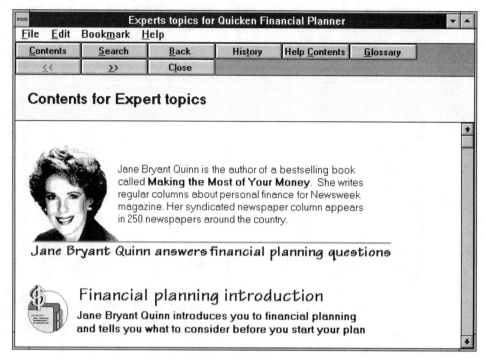

Figure 3.9   Quicken's inhouse expert answers your questions.

 9. **QuickBooks Pro:** Small-business accounting
10. **PocketQuicken:** Mobile financial management
11. **Expendable:** A personal expense tracker
12. **Family Lawyer:** Software program
13. **Parent's Guide to Money:** Software
14. **Intuit's Online Banking Consortium**
15. **Quicken Financial Network:** Website

Moreover, whether a cyberspace investor is operating solely with Intuit/Quicken software (which is rapidly becoming a feasible alternative) or linking into other necessary tools (e.Schwab, StreetSmart, and Reuters Money Network), it's clear that in this arena the wave of the future is integration of information systems and products for investors. The Intuit team is pushing the envelope of this unique wave of technology.

QUICKEN'S MAJOR SOFTWARE COMPETITORS FOR FINANCIAL PLANNING, BUDGETING, AND ONLINE BANKING

Other personal financial planning software on the market includes the three main runners-up to Quicken. These are MECA Software's Managing Your Money, Microsoft's Money software, and Kiplinger's Simply Money (sold by Computer Associates). Together, these three software products have about 25 percent of the market dominated by Quicken. MECA has about 15 percent, while Microsoft and Kiplinger's offerings share about 5 percent each.

Managing Your Money: MECA Software

Like Quicken's Personal Financial Planner and Quicken Deluxe, Managing Your Money includes programming modules for banking and investment tracking, as well as planning for retirement and other goals such as buying a home. This MECA Software is obviously designed as an integrated banking and investing platform, but it lacks the sophistication a serious investor might expect.

Kiplinger's Simply Money: Computer Associates

Simply Money is a product of Computer Associates, one of the largest software developers in the world. The program is one of many marketed by Computer Associates under the trademark title of "Simply." Simply Money has many of the same features as Quicken for banking and investment management, although it is not yet integrated with one of the major portfolio-management systems like Schwab and Reuters.

Although *Kiplinger's Personal Finance Magazine* frequently reviews mutual funds and also offers Steele System's Mutual Fund Expert Analyzer, Simply Money would need further development and upgrades to compete effectively with Quicken's Personal Financial Planner.

Microsoft's Money

In spite of Microsoft's unsuccessful takeover attempt of Intuit, Microsoft seems to have become much more aggressive about promoting the Money software through the commercial banking system. On a regular basis, the press makes note of other banks offering Microsoft's Money along with the

HOW AN EXTRA 2 PERCENT RETURN CAN BE WORTH $1.7 MILLION

"People are beginning to realize the decisions they make regarding these plans really do matter. Working to get an 8% return rather than settling for 6% will mean a difference of as much as $1.7 million over the course of a forty-year career."

SOURCE: Eric Schurenberg, "How Do You Spell Relief? For Retirement, the Answer is 4-0-1-k," *Money* magazine (June 1996).

Ask yourself, however, is the extra two percent worth it? Is the added risk tolerable? What if it doesn't work as planned?

Quicken program to their customers. They are clearly not surrendering to Quicken, but Microsoft has a long way to go.

It should again be emphasized that, as a group, these three systems have only about 30 percent of the personal financial planning software market, compared to 70 percent for Quicken Deluxe. Moreover, their focus is on personal finance—family budgeting, bill paying, online banking, and the like—rather than as a power tool for online and Net investing.

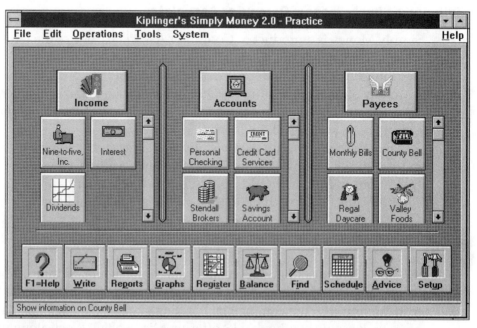

Figure 3.10 Kiplinger's Simply Money from Computer Associates.

Figure 3.11 MECA Software: basic tools for Managing Your Money.

Quicken, however, is in a league by itself with its Mutual Fund Finder, the Investor Insight package, its interface with StreetSmart and Reuters Money Network, and other features specifically for investors. Moreover, there are several other financial planning software packages designed specifically for investors rather than primarily for online banking. Let's take a look at some of them.

WEALTHBUILDER: AN INVESTOR'S FINANCIAL PLANNER INTEGRATED WITH REUTERS MONEY NETWORK

The WealthBuilder personal financial planning software was originally developed by Reuters Money Network in conjunction with *Money* magazine. WealthBuilder is primarily their *offline* software package for planning, analytics, and management, whereas the Reuters Money Network software is part of Reuters online link to current news updates, market quotes, and fundamental research. Reuters also offers the Money Network to Quicken users as an alternative to WealthBuilder. The WealthBuilder performs a set of eight functions:

1. **Personal Profile:** Risk tolerance and investment philosophy
2. **Retirement Planning:** Goals, savings, investments, shortfall
3. **Investment Strategies:** Test alternative portfolio strategies
4. **Timeline Graphics:** Forecast of long-term portfolio growth
5. **Goals Analysis & Budgeting:** Income, expenses, controls
6. **Financial Statements:** Assets, liabilities, and networth
7. **Portfolio Management:** Monitor-accounts and transactions
8. **Reuters Money Network:** Portfolio updating and integration

The WealthBuilder/Reuters Money Network system is also designed to interface and work with Schwab's StreetSmart system, and they jointly pro-

Figure 3.12   Reuters Money Network Website: WealthBuilder plus.

FINANCIAL PLANNING SYSTEMS: OFFLINE SOFTWARE DIRECTORY

Financial Planner	World Wide Web	Telephone
Fidelity Retirement Planner	www.fid-inv.com	(800) 544-0246
FundMap	www.schwab.com	(800) 435-4000
Kiplinger's Simply Money	www.cai.com	(800) 225-5224
Managing Your Money	www.mymnet.com	(800) 537-9993
MS-Money	www.microsoft.com	(800) 426-9400
Plan Ahead	www.dowjones.com	(800) 815-5100
Portfolio Manager	www.telescan.com	(800) 824-8246
Prosper	www.ey.com	(800) 277-6773
Quant IX & Pulse	www.compuserve.com	(800) 848-8990
Quicken Financial Planner	www.intuit.com	(800) 964-1040
Retirement Planner	www.vanguard.com	(800) 662-7447
Retirement Planning Kit	www.troweprice.com	(800) 541-4041
WealthBuilder	www.moneynet.com	(800) 346-2024

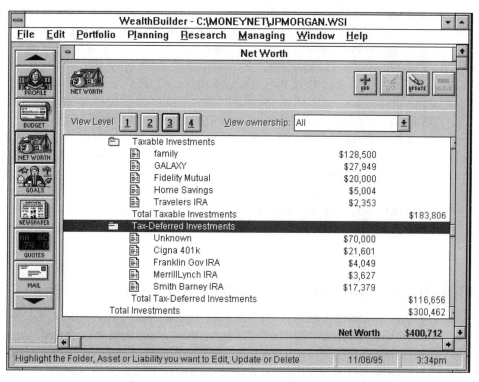

Figure 3.13   Reuters WealthBuilder: portfolio planning and management.

mote their systems. There is some overlap between the two systems. The StreetSmart software, however, is a one-shot expense and works with a trading account at Schwab.

Reuters, on the other hand, is primarily a financial planner, fund and securities analyzer, and portfolio manager—an excellent complement. In addition, the WealthBuilder/Reuters Money Network system has now been designed to work with other discount brokers, such as PCFN, Quick & Reilly, and AccuTrade.

Bottom line: Perhaps the most important point to understand with this example of the WealthBuilder software is that an investor will have considerably more long-term overall power using *offline* financial planning software than relying on the Web-based systems. Moreover, several of the offline systems, such as WealthBuilder and Quicken, are designed to manage all your assets, rather than just your securities portfolio.

Of course, investors can now find, if they choose, Web-based systems for portfolio management, primarily in conjunction with an account at one of the discount brokers. Aufhauser, Jack White, and Lombard are some examples of Web-based discount brokerage systems designed for portfolio management as well as for news and analysis. Each has received top ratings on recent comparisons of brokerage firms in key financial publications like *Barron's* and *SmartMoney.*

Does the fact that the offline software planners like WealthBuilder are preferred, and actually essential for serious investing, mean that investors should skip the miniplanners on the Fidelity and Vanguard Websites? Absolutely not. As we've said a few times, it's a great way for novices to get up to speed quickly, and for experienced investors to get a second opinion.

If you're really serious about moving forward with the financial planning process, we strongly suggest that you head for CompUSA or any of the other discount computer software superstores and test-drive some of the other software packages we're reviewing here.

FIDELITY AND VANGUARD: RETIREMENT PLANNING SOFTWARE

The Vanguard University Website has a host of excellent resources for planning, such as the Portfolio Savings Calculator, Investment Personality Profile quiz, and a Portfolio Investment Mix or asset allocator. They are valuable yet limited products, at least until the Web-based technologies develop further.

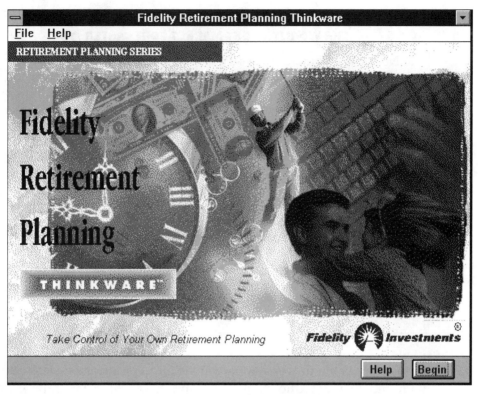

Figure 3.14   Fidelity Thinkware: Take Control of Your Own Planning.

If you want a more powerful planner, try Vanguard's Retirement Planning software, a user-friendly, sophisticated system that costs only $15. In fact, the cost of most of these financial planners is usually less than $50, even the more powerful ones like WealthBuilder and Quicken's Personal Financial Planner, and they are often in the $25 range. Fidelity also offers it's Thinkware, a system comparable to Vanguard's Retirement Planner.

If there is any limitation with this system for the astute cyberspace investor, it'll likely be corrected in one of the future upgrades. Keep in mind that these are planners designed by and for a particular mutual fund family. They are likely to be biased and unlikely to include the entire universe of available funds.

You may want other software for a more objective and thorough comparison. On the other hand, since together Fidelity and Vanguard manage about 500 funds and 20 percent of *all* mutual fund assets between them,

---

THE WORLD'S BEST MARKET FORECASTER: YOU!

"No one knows more than you do about the future.

"Every time the stock and bond market makes a major move, the air waves are filled with well-dressed experts confidently predicting the level of the market in six months or a year. Learned as these experts may seem, you should regard what you hear mainly as entertainment . . .

"In fact, savvy investors tend to get nervous when a majority of experts agree about the market's direction—because they are so often wrong.

"According to Investor's Intelligence, a research service that tracks optimism or pessimism among investment newsletters, the expert consensus is often misguided just when it matters most—right before a major turn in the market.

"For example, only 20% of the newsletter editors foresaw the crash of 1987, when the market fell 36%. Equally discouraging, only 31% of these supposed savants were calling for a rally in late 1990, just before stocks went on a three-year 68% tear."

SOURCE: Eric Schurenberg, *401(k) Take Charge of Your Future* (Warner Books, 1996).

---

this is a pretty big universe for any investor to pick from. Besides, you'll do your independent due diligence through Morningstar, Lipper, Mutual Funds Online, or some other cyberspace databases, anyway.

Charles Schwab's Fundmap: First-Class Financial Planner from a Discount Broker

Charles Schwab has developed a host of software products in the past 10 years, and his firm has been the leading pioneer of the financial cyberspace revolution. Schwab's StreetSmart system is frequently sold in conjunction with Reuters WealthBuilder or Quicken as a financial planner and portfolio manager.

One of Schwab's excellent products for the independent investor is its FundMap software. Although the name suggests that it is merely a guide to selecting funds, it's actually a very helpful personal financial planner and educational tool for investors. The software is structured in four modules:

1. **Investing Basics.**   Review course on key concepts and terms.
2. **Savings & Retirement.**   Calculation of your savings goals and retirement, with flexibility to test alternative scenarios.

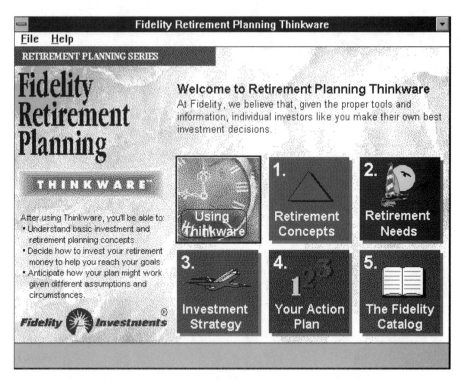

Figure 3.15 Fidelity Thinkware: You make your own best decisions.

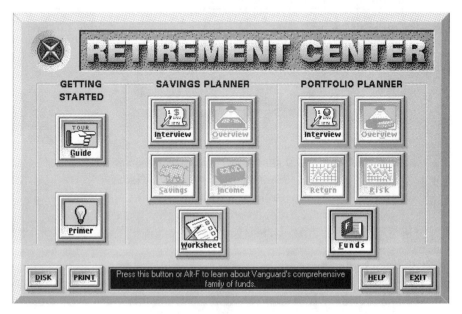

Figure 3.16 Vanguard Planner: portfolio building, savings, and investing.

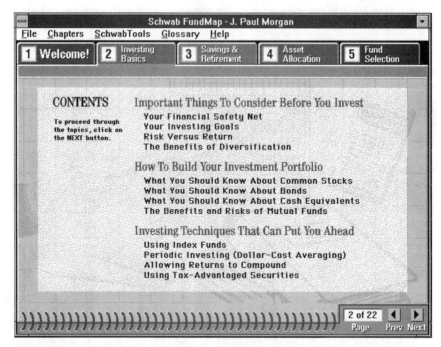

Figure 3.17   FundMap: solid planning tool for investment portfolio.

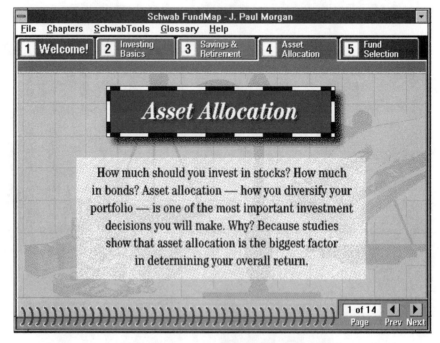

Figure 3.18   Asset Allocation: the biggest factor in your returns.

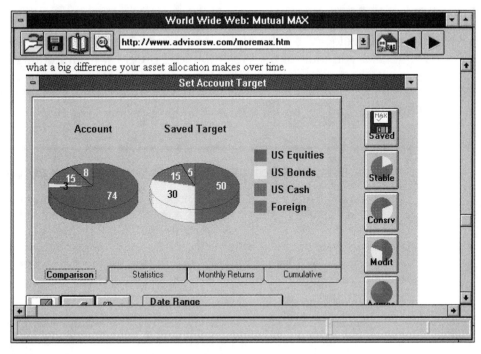

Figure 3.19 Mutual MAX: asset allocations make a big difference.

3. **Asset Allocation.** Risk-tolerance and portfolio strategies.
4. **Fund Selection.** Includes almost 1,000 funds in addition to funds offered by the Schwab family.

Schwab's FundMap is a sophisticated program that you might consider an intermediate-level program. It is an excellent, and quite objective, personal financial planner, even though it was developed by a discount broker. Therefore, FundMap should be considered by every investor before moving on to a more sophisticated operating system using Quicken's Investor Insight or Reuters' WealthBuilder.

OTHER POPULAR FINANCIAL PLANNERS: SOFTWARE SYSTEMS DEVELOPED SPECIFICALLY FOR INVESTORS

Several other financial planners are also available from a variety of providers, each of which deserves consideration. In considering these options, be aware of the following conditions of use that may limit your interest, depending on your existing needs:

Ernst & Young's *Prosper*

Prosper, developed by the highly respected accounting firm of Ernst & Young, is a variation of the WealthBuilder program from Reuters. One of Prosper's major advantages is that it is an excellent companion to E&Y's *Personal Financial Planning Guide,* a book that investors should add to their library regardless of which *software* planning system you choose.

TAXES AND FUND INVESTORS: IT'S WHAT YOU KEEP THAT COUNTS

"There are some lucky investors earning 30% returns who will owe virtually no taxes at all. No, they don't live in tax havens like the Bahamas or Guernsey. They simply own tax-efficient index funds at Vanguard and Charles Schwab.

   "What's a tax-efficient fund? One that focuses on after-tax, not pretax, returns. That means holding onto winners, avoiding high-yielding stocks and selling losers to get tax losses."

SOURCE: Suzanne Oliver, "What Counts Is What You Keep," *Forbes* (November 20, 1995).

"Investors have long believed they could earn more money by choosing funds that minimize shareholder's taxes. That turns out to be a myth, according to a new study by Ken Gregory, editor of the *No-Load Fund Analyst* newsletter. . . . The lesson for investors: Buy funds based on how well they perform, not how tax efficient they are."

SOURCE: Penelope Wang, "Why Winning Funds Often Aren't Tax Efficient," *Money* magazine (Forecast 1996).

There are two major advantages to Ernst & Young's Prosper: First of all, it is designed as an integrated package with Reuters Money Network. And second, Ernst & Young publishes one of the best annual tax-planning guides available. However, for trading and brokerage accounts, investors must switch to programs like StreetSmart.

Dow Jones' *Plan Ahead*

Dow Jones has released a financial planning software. However, it is currently available only on CD-ROM and is too basic for the serious investor. Perhaps in the near future the Digital Dow team will add a disk version, or better yet, upgrade and create an interactive planning system on the Web.

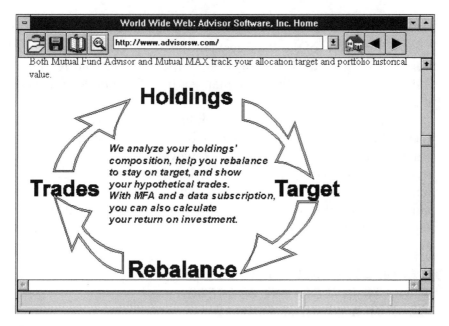

Figure 3.20 Mutual MAX Software: Rebalance to stay on target.

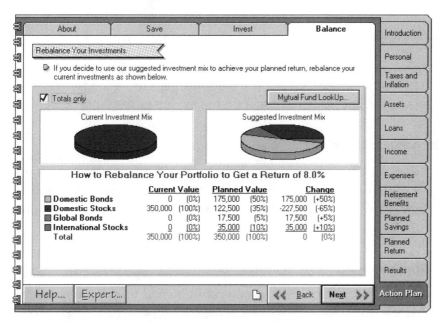

Figure 3.21 Quicken's Planner: built-in portfolio rebalancing.

T. Rowe Price's *Retirement Planning Kit*

T. Rowe Price, one of the 20 largest families of funds, has offered its Retirement Planning Kit to clients for some years. While its features are the basic ones you'd expect in a financial planner, this Planning Kit will soon come in a Windows version.

Generally speaking, investors should be aware of each of these alternatives, which all offer some clear benefits, within limited parameters, and deserve examination by investors. However, in terms of graduating to an investor system that's totally integrated and capable of handling all the primary steps in the investing process—plus other functions, such as online banking—it would be wise to compare each one of them with the ones reviewed earlier in the chapter.

BOTTOM LINE: ASSET ALLOCATIONS ARE THE KEY TO INVESTMENT SUCCESS . . . 90 PERCENT OF A WINNING PORTFOLIO

If rule number one in building a winning portfolio is "prepare a plan," then rule number two is "start saving on a regular basis." And number three is "stick with your asset allocations," *no matter what.* Let's review the key recommendations that have already been discussed:

Prepare a Financial Plan

Since most investors never do any planning, they never start saving, and therefore are unable to build for the future. Professional investment advisors unanimously agree that a financial plan is absolutely essential.

Save on a Regular Basis

Recent studies indicate quite clearly that most investors are saving only one-third of what's necessary for retirement. Obviously, the trick now is to substantially increase savings in accord with the recommendations of your financial plan.

Stick with Your Asset Allocations

Assuming you're one of the new, enlightened breed of responsible, do-it-yourself investors who are rapidly becoming active in cyberspace, you will have a financial plan and will be regularly investing your savings. On a regular basis, *review* your asset allocations, and *rebalance* your portfolio as necessary.

Resist Chasing the "Portfolio of the Month"

Avoid the temptation to chase after the latest, hot, five-star fund or top-gun manager being hyped by the financial press. If you do, it will mean higher risks, and will most surely be at the expense of your asset allocation developed using your financial planner.

The Best Financial Planners Are Offline

Finally, although today's cyberspace investors will find many, many useful electronic tools on the Internet's Web, the technology still favors the offline software products that are available. And most of these offline software planners are also (1) integrated with other investor tools for real-time market news, securities quotes, screening, analytics, portfolio management, and trading and (2) interfaced with the World Wide Web and/or a particular online service for investors, because it's designed as a superpowered offline component of a single operating system.

ALL PORTFOLIOS GET OUT OF WHACK AND NEED REBALANCING

"If you started off last year with a carefully constructed asset-allocation plan for your mutual funds, you now may notice something is out of whack . . . the huge run-up in stock prices likely increased the equity component dramatically, thus raising your risk. . . . It's portfolio rebalancing time . . .

"Make sure your rebalancing benefits aren't lost to transaction costs from broker fees. It's best to do the process through no-load funds or load fund families that allow no-cost shifts within the family.

"Even better are the automatic rebalancing services offered by some mutual fund companies, such as Stein Roe, Fidelity and T. Rowe Price. . . . The fund company will do a monthly review of the account."

SOURCE: Amy Dunkin, "A Rebalancing Act to Protect Your Portfolio," *BusinessWeek* (June 17, 1996).

If you want to create a winning mutual fund portfolio in cyberspace, start by test-driving a few of the best software planning products reviewed here, *even if you already have one.* This technology is changing rapidly, and the newer models may be better suited to your personality and easier to use.

Then, once you know what your options are, get adventurous and leap into cyberspace with the other winners. Install your first-choice planning software and start using it right away. Start planning a successful future as a do-it-yourself investor.

HOW TYPICAL AN INVESTOR ARE YOU?

Using sources from the Investment Company Institute and Access Research, Inc., the *Los Angeles Times* offered investors a "look at mutual fund ownership by the numbers." Keep in mind that there are over $3 trillion in mutual funds. Some of the more important facts are:

How many funds owned: 28 percent own four to six funds, which is almost enough for a diversified portfolio; 57 percent own three or less funds; and only 15 percent had seven or more funds.

Most popular stock funds: Of $1.53 trillion in stock fund assets, 40 percent were in growth-and-income/equity-income funds and another 27 percent in growth funds; and there were 16 percent each in aggressive growth and foreign/global funds.

Most popular bond funds: 57 percent were in tax-exempt municipal funds and flexible or balanced funds; 16 percent in govt/GNMAs; 8 percent in high-yields; only 4 percent each in corporate and global bonds.

What's in 401(k) plans: Employees put 23 percent in their company's stock; 22 percent in guaranteed investment contracts; 21 percent in stock funds; 14 percent in balanced funds; 8 percent in bond funds and 6 percent each in money market funds and "other" investments.

SOURCE: Tom Petruno and Kathy Kristof, "Is It Time to Clean House?" *Los Angeles Times* (October 6, 1996).

Learning How to Navigate the Major Types of Funds

Matching Your Asset Allocations to the Fund Categories

Here's how you can navigate through the basic categories of funds. Today there are about 8,000 funds on the market, and a new fund is added each day. In step 4, we'll review the primary types of funds, their objectives and risk levels, and show you how to fit this massive database into the simple asset allocations of your financial plan.

THE BIG CHALLENGE: HOW TO SCREEN THROUGH 8,000 FUNDS AND FIND THE PERFECT ASSET ALLOCATION FOR YOU

Today, the number of mutual funds exceeds the number of publicly held companies, and is growing fast, with more than one new fund added every day. Investors have almost 8,000 mutual funds to choose from. Talk about information overload. That's enough to make most people throw up their hands and avoid the investing process. Fortunately, do-it-yourself investors now have everything they need at their fingertips—all the power necessary to build a successful portfolio is just a mouse click away, thanks to the following:

❏ The major mutual fund *databases* now available in cyberspace

❏ New online and offline *computer tools* for analysis and management

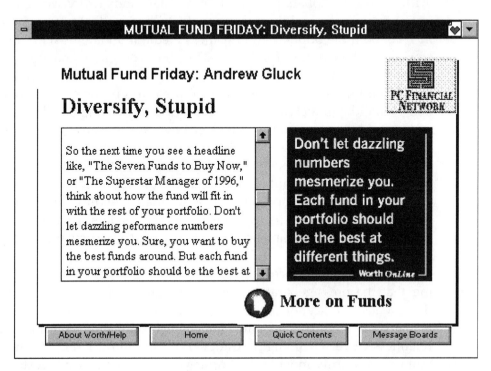

Figure 4.1 Worth on asset allocation: Diversify your portfolio!

**PORTFOLIO SUCCESS:
DISCIPLINE, INDEPENDENCE, AND SELF-CONFIDENCE**

"Discipline is probably the most frequent word used by the exceptional traders that I interviewed. . . . There are two reasons why discipline is critical. First, it is a prerequisite for maintaining effective risk control. Second, you need discipline to apply your method without second-guessing . . .

"You need to do your own thinking. Don't get caught up in mass hysteria . . . by the time a story is making the cover of the national periodicals, the trend is probably near an end. . . . Never listen to the opinions of others."

SOURCE: Jack Schwager, *The New Market Wizards* (HarperBusiness, 1992).

STICK TO THE ALLOCATIONS IN YOUR PLAN AND IGNORE THE SENSATIONALISM IN TODAY'S FINANCIAL MEDIA

With billions of dollars pouring into mutual funds every week, the total invested has risen rapidly from about $1 trillion in 1990 to over $3 trillion in 1996. Both the popular and business media inundate us with hot news stories about the hottest funds, top-25 sectors, top-gun managers, best and worst performers, secrets of wealth building with little-known funds, and many more hot tips. Today's financial press has become sensationalistic, using tabloid gimmicks like MTV graphics and shocking headlines, teasers we've come to expect on the 11 o'clock news. Browse any good newsstand and you'll have an anxiety attack.

In order to sell newspapers and magazines in this highly competitive market targeting the mutual fund buyer—all 42 million of them—there seems to be an intense pressure driving financial editors, reporters, and publishers to create a sense of urgency in their readers. That may be a reasonable goal . . . getting a reader to actually read a particular article or buy a particular magazine.

However, in the process, investors are being led into the trap of believing that the press-generated urgency is real. As a result, this obsessive drive to sell publications and information may have the indirect effect of actually creating the investor anxiety—a self-fulfilling prophecy—by relentlessly overwhelming investors with fund information. What should you do? Be a truly independent do-it-yourself cyberspace investor. Make your own decisions.

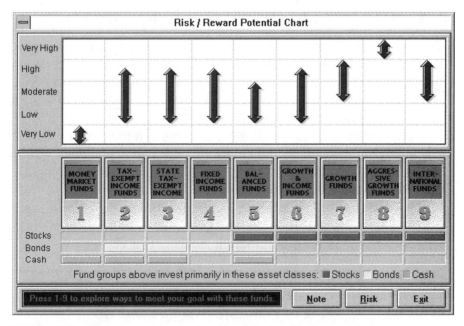

Figure 4.2   Relative risk-reward ranges for nine fund categories.

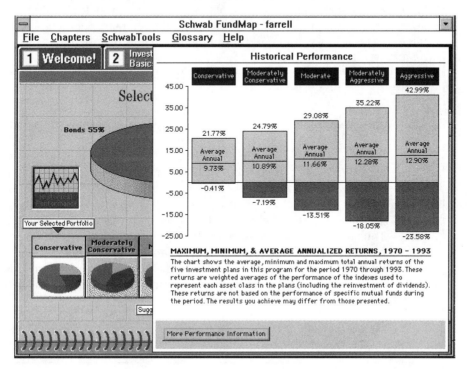

Figure 4.3   Historical performance ranges: five asset allocations.

THE THREE MAIN TYPES OF MUTUAL FUNDS IN CYBERSPACE

For the average fund investor with a portfolio of perhaps 6 to probably no more than 12 funds, it's easy to feel the urgency as a need to get into action and do something—often prematurely, such as buying a fund because it's the featured five-star performer this month—or to throw up your hands, tune out, and turn on TV reruns.

Rather than responding to the urge, filter out the media/press chatter, while staying focused on the emerging new world of cyberspace mutual funds. What you'll see is a fascinating collection of new technologies online and offline, Websites, and intranets.

Stay focused on these technologies. Because, paradoxically, very soon all mutual funds will be in cyberspace, and mastering the technologies may well be more important than the funds themselves.

HOW MANY FUNDS DO YOU NEED?
SIX TO EIGHT STOCK FUNDS WILL DO

"Everyone agrees, there's no magic number. Most financial planners and money managers believe a portfolio should contain at least three but probably no more than a dozen funds, and money managers who invest in funds generally recommend a number in the middle range."

SOURCE: Ken Sheets, "How Many Funds Are Too Many?," *Kiplinger's Personal Finance Magazine* (February 1996).

"How many mutual funds should you own? . . . According to a new study, when it comes to investing in domestic stocks, six funds are really all you need. . . . More surprising was the fact that most of the risk reduction—about 75% of it—occurred with just four funds. . . . After eight funds, there was very little further lessening of risk, and after 15 almost none . . .

"They also believe in choosing funds that target stocks of different sizes. Thus their recommended portfolio would consist of six funds: one growth and one value fund specializing in small, medium-size and large companies. . . . Put the finishing touches on their portfolios by adding two overseas offerings—one international and one emerging markets fund."

SOURCE: Prashanta Misra, "Why Six Stock Funds Are Enough and 15 Are Too Many," *Money* magazine (June 1996).

From the perspective of every new do-it-yourself investor, it is essential that you begin making this transition now, because cyberspace mutual funds are at the center of the new electronic Wall Street. There,

❑ the new *mutual funds networks* are merging with the

❑ new *electronic discount brokerage,*

❑ all your new *online banking transactions,* and

❑ the new world of *commercial shopping.*

This revolution is happening at such an accelerating speed that it is critical for you to move into the cyberspace world in order to build your mutual fund portfolio.

Perhaps the most important secret of success in mutual fund investing is to stick with long-term fundamentals—a basic method and style of investing that fits you—and screen out the relentless short-term noises shouted at you from the press. With that in mind, we'll look at the basic types of mutual funds, breaking them down into manageable size.

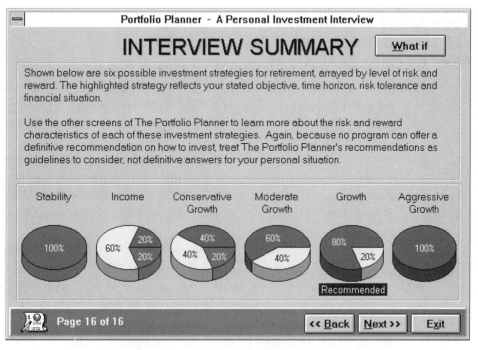

Figure 4.4 Vanguard: a range of six asset allocations based on risk.

MUTUAL FUNDS: WHERE DO INVESTORS PUT THEIR BILLIONS?

Type of Fund	1975 Total	1995 Total Invested
Stocks	$37 (82%)	$1,058 (44%)
Bonds	5 (10%)	683 (28%)
Money Market	4 (8%)	688 (28%)

SOURCE: *Mutual Fund 1995 Fact Book*, Investment Company Institute.

To begin with, from the conventional *personal financial planning* standpoint, there really are only three basic types of mutual funds, in spite of what you see reported in the popular and financial media. There are stock funds, bond funds, and money market funds. However, the real world of more than 8,000 funds quickly complicates the neat, conventional trinity used for planning.

YOUR ASSET ALLOCATIONS:
THE LINK BETWEEN YOUR FINANCIAL PLAN
AND THE MANY FUND TYPES

It becomes quickly apparent, however, that the division of mutual fund investments between stocks and bonds (or stocks, bonds, and money market funds) is perhaps too overly simplistic for a complex world with thousands of mutual funds.

However, thanks to the major cyberspace fund databases, we can categorize this potentially overwhelming collection of investment alternatives into a couple dozen sectors, used by most professionals. More important, however, is their value to you as an investor. The investment professionals can take care of themselves.

The crucial link between your personal financial plan, on one hand, and the vast universe of 8,000 mutual funds, on the other hand, is the general asset allocations developed as a part of your plans, those typically pie-shaped percentages that suggest how much of your investment portfolio you should have in stocks, bonds, and money market funds.

The classifications used by the major databases, including Morningstar and Lipper, each vary from the generally accepted standard of the Invest-

---

KIPLINGER'S "STYLE" TEST: DOES IT QUACK LIKE A DUCK?

"The proliferation of funds has caused rampant confusion about what funds are really seeking to invest in and how they differ from one and other. For example, Fidelity Asset manager is categorized by Micropal (our data supplier) as a growth-and-income fund, by Lipper Analytical Services as a flexible-portfolio fund, and by Morningstar Mutual Funds and Value Line as an asset allocation fund. But none of these applications gives you a clue to what fund manager Bob Beckwitt invests in or what to expect from his fund . . .

"If you see a web-footed bird that quacks, you can be fairly certain you're looking at a duck. And if you can see a fund who's monthly ups and downs match those of indexes in such a way that the fund appears to be invested two-thirds in small-company value stocks, and one-third in midsize-company value stocks, then you can be fairly sure that it is."

SOURCE: Fred Frailey, "Fund Styles: Looking Beyond the Name," *Kiplinger's Mutual Funds* (1996).

---

ment Company Institute, a membership association of mutual fund organizations. Moreover, individual funds often deviate from their stated objective and categories. Figures 4.5 and 4.6 show the main fund types divided into asset-allocations categories by their risk level.

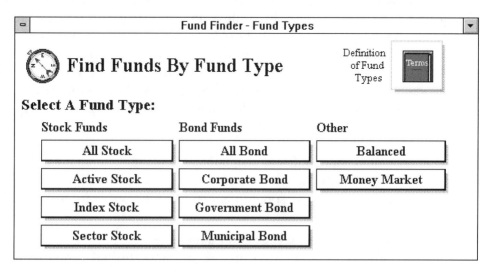

Figure 4.5   Vanguard Campus: three-part division into ten fund types.

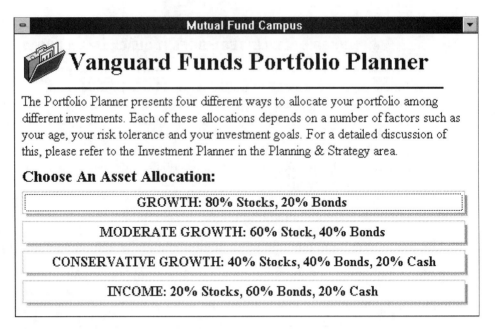

Figure 4.6   Portfolio planning: a range of four basic asset allocations.

MAKING THE BIG CUT:
FROM 8,000 FLAVORS TO THREE NEAT PIE SLICES

First, let's see the particular sectors or categories of individual funds based on risks involved. Keep in mind, however, that while each of these terms is widely accepted within the mutual fund industry, and they identify, or at least imply, something about the objectives and characteristics of the types of funds included, there is still enormous latitude between individual funds.

The objective of this chapter is very specific and very crucial: Help the cyberspace do-it-yourself investor make the all-important transition from personal financial planning allocations to the real world of fund types and databases.

❑ **Personal financial planning allocations**

The simplistic, slice-of-the-pie asset allocations you have developed with your personal financial planning software discussed in the last chapter.

❑ **Real world of fund types and databases**

The more complex universe of 8,000 mutual funds in probably more than 20 general fund types and categories that you will be con-

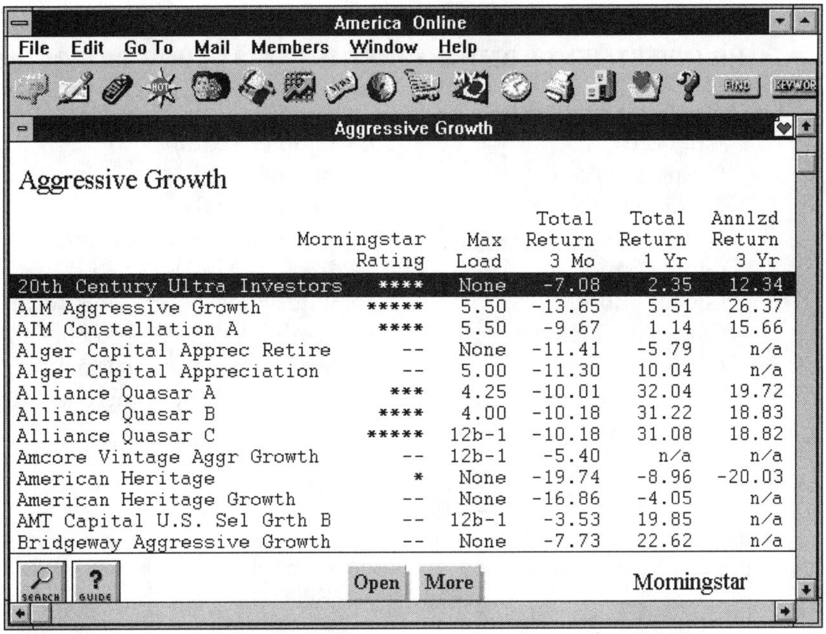

	Morningstar Rating	Max Load	Total Return 3 Mo	Total Return 1 Yr	Annlzd Return 3 Yr
20th Century Ultra Investors	****	None	-7.08	2.35	12.34
AIM Aggressive Growth	*****	5.50	-13.65	5.51	26.37
AIM Constellation A	****	5.50	-9.67	1.14	15.66
Alger Capital Apprec Retire	--	None	-11.41	-5.79	n/a
Alger Capital Appreciation	--	5.00	-11.30	10.04	n/a
Alliance Quasar A	***	4.25	-10.01	32.04	19.72
Alliance Quasar B	****	4.00	-10.18	31.22	18.83
Alliance Quasar C	*****	12b-1	-10.18	31.08	18.82
Amcore Vintage Aggr Growth	--	12b-1	-5.40	n/a	n/a
American Heritage	*	None	-19.74	-8.96	-20.03
American Heritage Growth	--	None	-16.86	-4.05	n/a
AMT Capital U.S. Sel Grth B	--	12b-1	-3.53	19.85	n/a
Bridgeway Aggressive Growth	--	None	-7.73	22.62	n/a

Figure 4.7   Aggressive growth funds: Morningstar database at AOL.

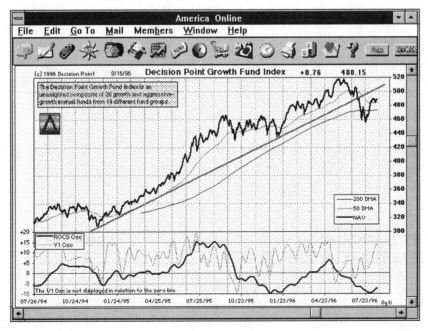

Figure 4.8   Growth Fund Index: Decision Point Mutual Fund Center.

THE INVESTMENT COMPANY INSTITUTE'S 21 FUND CATEGORIES

Aggressive Growth	Income—Bonds
Balanced	Income—Equity
Corporate Bond	Income—Mixed
Flexible Portfolio	International
Ginnie Mae (GNMA)	National Municipal Bond
Global Bond	Precious Metals/Gold
Global Equity	State Muni. Bond Long-Term
Growth & Income	Taxable Money Markets
Growth	Tax-Exempt Money Markets
High-Yield Bonds	U.S. Government Income
Capital Growth	

SOURCE: *1995 Fact Book,* Investment Company Institute.

These are the 21 "official" mutual fund categories agreed upon by ICI, the mutual fund trade association. Note that labels often given to the funds by their managers will frequently vary from these official classifications, and also differ from the category they are placed in by the independent rating organizations, each of which may have its own set of categories. Ultimately, the investor has the responsibility of determining the "fit" of a particular fund to the investor's special needs and unique risk tolerance.

fronted with by the rating agencies, the financial press, and the funds themselves.

This transition from the simple, pie-shaped, bottom-line asset allocations in most financial plans into the complex real world of mutual funds is a critical step in the process of building and managing a successful mutual fund portfolio in cyberspace. And it's not an easy step. Most advisors, funds, and planning systems fail to help investors make this transition, because it really is not as simple as the neat little pie-shaped asset-allocation charts imply.

1. ASSET ALLOCATIONS: THE *STOCKS* SLICE OF YOUR PIE (HIGH-RISK/HIGH-RETURN FUNDS)

Generally speaking, if you're shooting for the higher returns, you're taking higher risks. Conversely, if you want to minimize your risk and sleep better at night, you may tend to shy away from these funds, except in carefully prescribed terms according to the asset allocations in your financial plan.

MORNINGSTAR MUTUAL FUNDS: "TOP-25" REPORTS

Top-Performing Funds at America Online: by Category

❏ Top-25 **Overall**
❏ Top-25 **Aggressive** Funds
❏ Top-25 **Growth** Funds
❏ Top-25 **Growth & Income** Funds
❏ Top-25 **Equity-Income** Funds
❏ Top-25 **Small Company** Funds
❏ Top-25 **World Stock** Funds
❏ Top-25 **Foreign Stock** Funds
❏ Top-25 **Europe Stock** Funds
❏ Top-25 **Pacific Stock** Funds
❏ Top-25 Specialty—**Unaligned**
❏ Top-25 Specialty—**Health**
❏ Top-25 Specialty—**Financial**
❏ Top-25 Specialty—**Natural Resources** Funds
❏ Top-25 Specialty—**Precious Metals**
❏ Top-25 Specialty—**Technology** Funds
❏ Top-25 Specialty—**Utilities** Funds
❏ Top-25 Specialty—**Asset Allocation** Funds
❏ Top-25 Specialty—**Balanced** Funds
❏ Top-25 Specialty—**Income** Funds

In considering how these 20 or more types of funds fit into the three asset allocations from your financial plan, keep in mind that, in spite of all the fancy new technologies, your selection of some general type of funds, or of a specific fund, is actually

❏ as much a *subjective art* as it is a science and
❏ very much tied to *your personal needs.*

Ultimately, you and you alone are best suited to make the decision, functioning as your own professional advisor.

Aggressive Growth Funds

These funds are chasing the highest possible yield, with minimum interest in current income. They are likely to include some wild-card, gun-slinging investments that could include new or struggling companies, less than hot industries, possibly even short sales and options. These funds carry some of the highest potential returns—and risks.

Growth Funds

Much less risk here than with the aggressive growth companies. These funds are looking for the more established, stable, typically blue-chip companies with solid capital appreciation rather than steady income.

PASSIVE BUY 'N' HOLD FUNDS ARE BEATING MOST STOCK FUNDS

"Is 'active' investing—what most fund managers are paid handsomely to do—worth the cost, trouble and risk, versus simply owning a 'passive' portfolio that represents the market as a whole?

"Passive, or index, investing in the S&P gives you a stake in the biggest companies in America. . . . Actively managed stock funds, on the other hand, by definition aren't content to own a static portfolio of big stocks. They promise, often in so many words, to try to beat the market . . .

"In the modern history of investing, reaching back as far as 35 years, the evidence indicates that the majority of stock funds haven't beaten the S&P but rather have continually lagged it:

❏ In the 35 years . . . only 33% of the funds in existence for that era topped the S&P, according to Lipper Analytical.
❏ Over the past 10 years, the figure was a more dismal 21%.
❏ The last five years provided the most favorable comparison for active managers, as 43% beat the S&P. But that meant 57% did not . . .

"For the true long-term, buy-and-hold fund investor, the evidence is compelling: It's tough to beat simply owning the market."

SOURCE: Tom Petruno, "Which Way to Wealth," *Los Angeles Times* (June 30, 1996). Index funds are only 4.5 percent of the total $1 trillion in stock funds.

Small-Company and Mid-Cap Growth Funds

These are investments limited to companies based on size, with strong upside growth potential, more volatility, and higher risk than the established blue-chip companies.

Sector and Specialty Funds

These funds focus specifically on a single industrial or economic sector, including technology, financial services, biotech, health care, real estate, energy, natural resources, and utilities. Because sector funds are concentrated in single sectors, they tend to be more volatile and risky than those that are more diversified, and the returns are potentially higher.

FUND TRACK: *MONEY* MAGAZINE'S 13 FUND CATEGORIES

Money magazine summarizes Morningstar's database into 13 categories:

Stocks	*Bonds*
Aggressive Growth	**U.S. Government**
Capital Growth	**Investment-Grade Corp.**
Growth & Income	**High-Yield Corporate**
Total Return	**Mortgage-Backed**
Overseas	**World Income**
Foreign Regional	**Tax-Exempt**
Specialty [sectors]	

SOURCE: Fund Track, *Money* magazine (1996).

Kiplinger's, Fortune, Mutual Funds, and *Your Money,* to name a few of the prominent print publications, each uses its own set of categories, with many similarities. Some have as few as 13 types (*Money* magazine and *Kiplinger's*); others (Morningstar on AOL) use 26 categories. Lipper has 57 categories in its ProFiles, and 27 in its Associated Press releases.

While the categories used by the periodicals create unique periodical identity and invite reader interest, most periodicals draw from a select few well-known databases, reviewed in the next chapter, such as the 28 categories used by the Morningstar research organization.

Obviously, their performance is directly linked to their sector's performance and volatility, which even for presumably secure sectors such as utilities can be quite volatile. And the precious-metal fund sectors are the highest of all risk categories, and therefore are not recommended for the average portfolio.

International, World, and Global Funds

This is another broad class of funds that invest in stocks and/or bonds worldwide. International funds invest outside the United States. Global and world funds may invest in both foreign and U.S. companies. There is a wide variety of specialty regional funds, for example, Europe, Asia/Pacific, Latin America, and developing regions, as well as single-country funds. Diversity of the fund's assets will influence risks. However, the track record of the fund manager will be a major factor in assessing your risk and return.

Growth and Income Funds, Equity Income Funds

Growth and income funds attempt to blend the best of both worlds, investing in securities that produce both steadily increasing appreciation in the value of the stock and a steady income through regular dividend payments. Equity income funds are similar to growth and income funds, with somewhat more emphasis on the income.

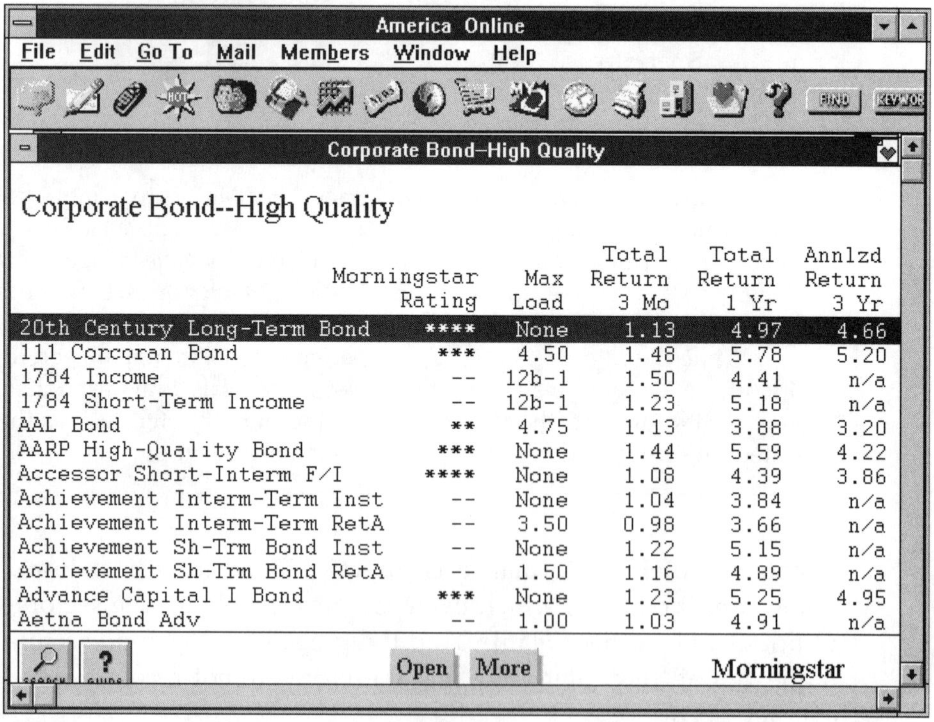

```
─                          America Online                          ▼ ▲
 File  Edit  Go To  Mail  Members  Window  Help

 [toolbar icons]                                          FIND  KEYWORD

─                    Corporate Bond–High Quality                      ♥ ▼ ♦
```

Corporate Bond--High Quality

	Morningstar Rating	Max Load	Total Return 3 Mo	Total Return 1 Yr	Annlzd Return 3 Yr
20th Century Long-Term Bond	****	None	1.13	4.97	4.66
111 Corcoran Bond	***	4.50	1.48	5.78	5.20
1784 Income	--	12b-1	1.50	4.41	n/a
1784 Short-Term Income	--	12b-1	1.23	5.18	n/a
AAL Bond	**	4.75	1.13	3.88	3.20
AARP High-Quality Bond	***	None	1.44	5.59	4.22
Accessor Short-Interm F/I	****	None	1.08	4.39	3.86
Achievement Interm-Term Inst	--	None	1.04	3.84	n/a
Achievement Interm-Term RetA	--	3.50	0.98	3.66	n/a
Achievement Sh-Trm Bond Inst	--	None	1.22	5.15	n/a
Achievement Sh-Trm Bond RetA	--	1.50	1.16	4.89	n/a
Advance Capital I Bond	***	None	1.23	5.25	4.95
Aetna Bond Adv	--	1.00	1.03	4.91	n/a

```
 [🔍]  [?]                  Open   More                    Morningstar
 SEARCH GUIDE
```

Figure 4.9   High-grade corporate bond funds: Morningstar ratings.

New Software Planning Tools

By now, the sophisticated investor will have observed that many of the newer software packages for personal financial planning have more than three slices in their pies. Often, these asset allocations are sliced into five pieces. Why?

Although it'll seem like a comment on the obvious, we're going to make it anyway: Please note that where there are five primary slices, it's usually a division of the *stock* allocations into three separate allocations, some with a clearly higher risk-return profile than others. Charles Schwab's FundMap, for example, slices the pie into five allocations:

1. **Large Company Stocks**
2. **Small Company Stocks**
3. **International Stocks**
4. **Bonds**
5. **Cash**

Keep in mind that the investor is still left with the same basic question, whether you're working with three-part or five-part asset allocations, namely:

❏ How do you take a universe of 8,000 mutual funds,

❏ which are divided into anywhere from 13 to 27 categories

❏ by several different independent rating agencies, and

❏ make them fit into the three (or five) asset allocations from your personal financial planner?

This question isn't easy to answer. However, as with most of the key issues in life, *caution is advised.* Please note a subtle but critical point. These planners with five pie-shaped slices are telling you that a *prudent* investor *should* put some money into riskier small-cap and international stocks.

The Bigger Question: Should All Investors Buy Small-Cap and Global Stocks? What about You?

Investing in small caps and international stock funds is probably a good idea if you're shooting for higher returns and your plan calls for it. Never-

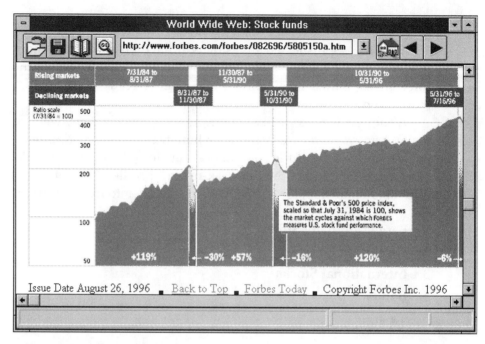

Figure 4.10   U.S. stock fund performance on Forbes great Website.

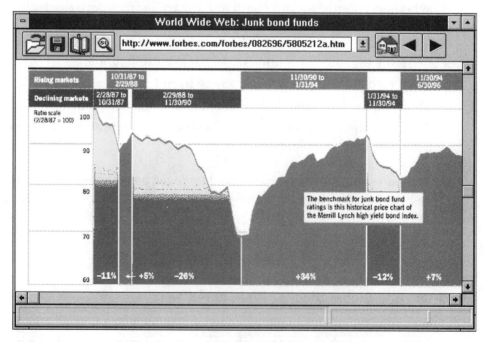

Figure 4.11   Junk bonds index: historical prices and volatility.

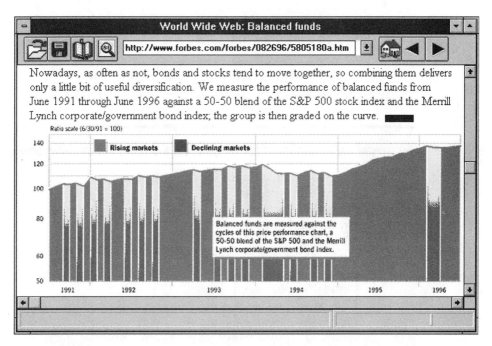

Figure 4.12   Balanced funds and their recent price performance.

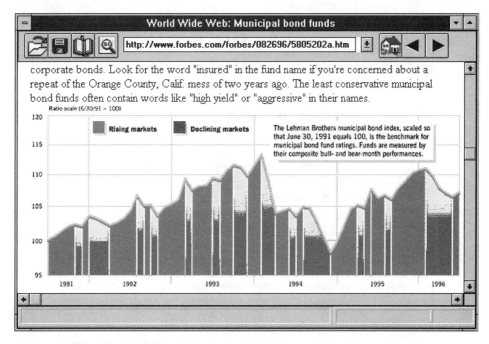

Figure 4.13   Municipal bond funds: volatility versus tax advantages.

theless, stick to your guns. Don't let the pressure for higher returns force you to do either of the following:

❐ Give up your comfort range regarding risk tolerance
❐ Abandon the asset allocation targets in your financial plan

---

LIPPER AND ASSOCIATED PRESS: 28 MUTUAL FUND CATEGORIES

Long-Term, Investment-Grade Corporate Bonds
Capital Appreciation
Equity Income
Growth and Income
Global
General Municipal Bond
Growth
General Taxable Bond
High-Yield Taxable Bond
High-Yield Municipal Bond
Intermediate-Term, Investment-Grade Corporate Bond
Intermediate-Term Treasury/Government Debt
International
Intermediate-Term Municipal Bond
Long-Term Treasury Government Debt
Mid-Cap Companies
Mortgage
Stock and Bond (Mixed Portfolio)
Insured Municipal Bond
Short-Term, Investment-Grade Corporate Bond
Small-Company Growth
Sector Funds
Short-Term Treasury/Government Debt
Short-Term Municipal Debt
Single-State Municipal Debt
Unclassified
World Bonds

SOURCE: Lipper Analytical Services, *Los Angeles Times*. These are the standard 28 categories you see in most national newspapers, with data provided by Lipper and distribution by the Associated Press news services. Compare them with the classifications of Morningstar and ICI or in various magazines such as *Kiplinger's, Mutual Funds*, and *Money*. And also see S&P/Lipper's Mutual Fund ProFiles for their detailed set of 57 categories and profiles of "the 800 largest investment companies."

On the positive side, today's small-cap companies and global markets look increasingly more favorable because of the following factors:

❐ Sixty percent, or $9 trillion, of the world's stock market capitalization is outside the United States.

❐ There are many free-market economies in the international arena with growth rates much higher than that of the domestic economy.

Presumably, the questions you answered for your risk profile led to these allocations. However, the ball is really back in your court, for 8,000 funds is too many, *and three is definitely not enough.* In the final analysis, you and you alone must decide which categories of stock funds to invest in.

Keep in mind, however, that no simple $25 or $49 software program can solve all your investment strategy problems, any more than a mutual fund manager with small-cap and international funds to sell. Ultimately, you must pull the trigger and pick a specific fund that feels right to you based on your financial plan, savings budget, and gut instincts.

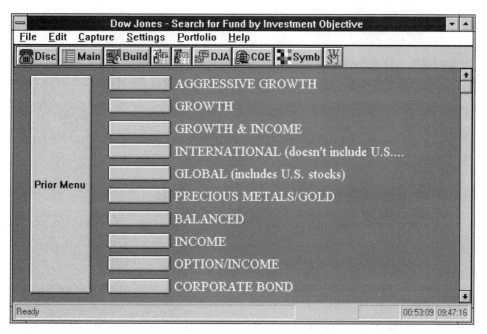

Figure 4.14   Ten categories of funds used by Dow Jones News/Retrieval.

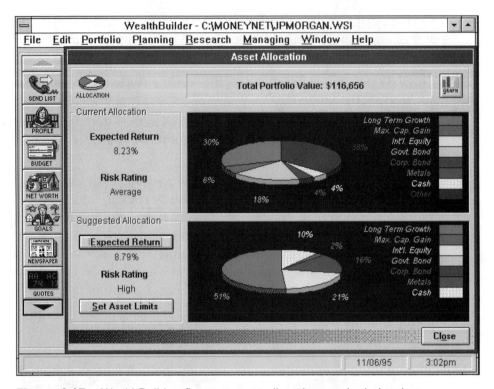

Figure 4.15   WealthBuilder: five-part asset allocations and rebalancing.

2. ASSET ALLOCATIONS: THE *BONDS* SLICE OF YOUR PIE (MODERATE-RISK/MODERATE-RETURN FUNDS)

Fixed-Income, High-Grade Corporate Bond Funds

These bond funds invest for high incomes, generated mainly by well capitalized, established, blue-chip American corporations.

Fixed-Income, High-Yield Corporate Bond Funds

The majority of these portfolios are loaded with non-investment-grade corporate bonds. The income is higher with many of the so-called junk bonds, and so is the risk compared to a blue-chip bond fund.

Convertible Bond Funds

This is a narrow-sector corporate bond fund structured to pay interest, with the added advantage of some capital appreciation from the conversion of the bonds.

THE NEW RULES: HOW MUCH EMERGENCY CASH DO YOU NEED?

"Keep a cash reserve for emergencies to cover three to six months' expenses, goes the age-old rule of thumb. Some financial planners even recommend a six- to 12-month cushion. But do you really need to tie up half a year's wages in a low-yielding certificate of deposit or money-market account before you start saving for long-term goals? Probably not.

"The New Rules. Some rainy-day money is a must. But how much you need depends on your age, health, job outlook—and your borrowing power in an emergency . . .

"You may need a fat reserve when:

❑ Your income fluctuates because your work is seasonal, you own a business, or rely on commissions.
❑ Your job may be at risk.
❑ Facing long-term disability or illness.
❑ Expect to make a large cash outlay, such as payment for a parent's nursing home care.

"You can get by with less when:

❑ You can easily borrow against assets, using a home-equity line of credit, brokerage margin account or policy loan against life insurance cash value . . .
❑ You have multiple sources of income. In a two-income household, for instance . . ."

SOURCE: Tracey Longo, "How Much Emergency Cash Is Enough?," *Kiplinger's Personal Finance Magazine* (November 1995).

Municipal Bond Funds, Tax-Exempt

These are funds invested in tax-free securities issued by local municipalities, multiple- and single-state securities, as well as high-yield government bonds. Selection of munis brings into consideration your unique tax position.

Government Bond Funds

These are guaranteed secure funds invested in U.S. Treasury securities; also mortgage-backed government bonds issued by GNMA and FNMA. As such, many essentially function as money market funds.

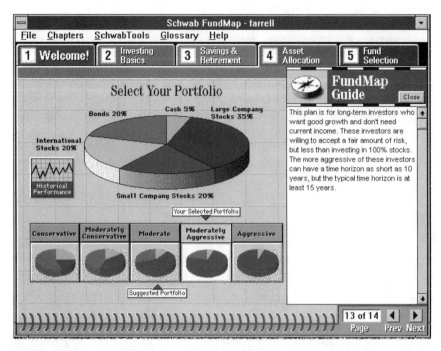

Figure 4.16   FundMap: asset allocations for a five-part portfolio.

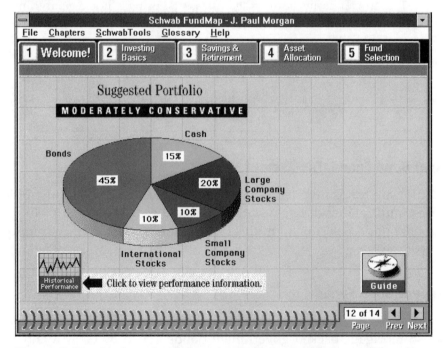

Figure 4.17   Moderately conservative portfolio: five-part asset allocation.

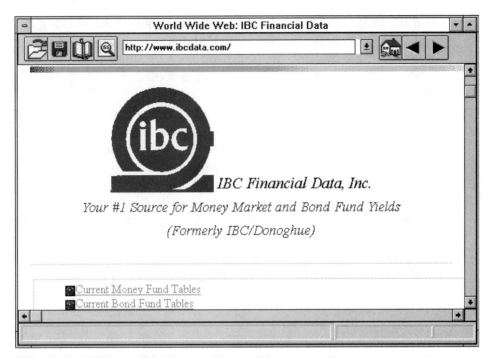

Figure 4.18 Money market and bond yields from IBC Financial Data.

3. ASSET ALLOCATIONS: THE *MONEY MARKET* SLICE OF YOUR PIE (LOW-RISK/LOW-RETURN FUNDS)

Money Market Funds

These are funds invested in a blend of government bonds and high-grade corporate bonds. This also includes separate taxable and tax-exempt money market funds. These fall into the category of *cash* or *cash equivalents*.

4. ASSET ALLOCATIONS: ONE-STOP SHOPPING FOR YOUR PIE (VARIABLE-RISK/VARIABLE-RETURN FUNDS)

Most personal financial planners generate pie-shaped asset allocations that simply categorize funds into three types:

- Equities (stocks)
- Fixed-income investments (bonds)
- Cash equivalents or short-term reserves (money markets) . . .

But the task of the mutual fund investor becomes considerably more complex as soon as you examine the vast statistics available from any one of the major rating organizations (for example, Morningstar, Value Line, or Lipper) and move on to selecting one of the specific 8,000 funds from any one of 650 fund families.

As a result, there are certain types of funds specifically designed as hybrids, mixing and blending stocks, bonds, and even money market securities. In effect, the managers of these funds are saying, "We 'do-it-yourself' for you!" The objective of these funds is to create, at least in theory, a no-brainer for the investor who doesn't have an investment advisor to help select funds to fit the asset allocations in his or her financial plan.

Bingo! Here's the solution to your dilemma. If you don't want to make the conversion from the asset allocations in your plan to picking 8 funds out of 8,000, let some sharp fund managers do it for you as part of their job and get into some *balanced, asset-allocation,* and *index funds.* Many of these funds give their managers specific authority to move funds back and forth between bonds, stocks, and money market instruments to take the best advantage of the market.

INDEX FUNDS: A NEAR-PERFECT ASSET-ALLOCATION TOOL

"Extraordinary short-term performance has propelled indexing into the limelight. . . . Historically, the broad stock market index has outperformed the average general equity fund. Over the past ten years, the 15% return of the S&P 500 Index handily outpaced the 12% return of the average general equity fund. Long-term performance superiority is one of the merits of the indexing approach . . .

"The average equity fund incurs annual expenses (excluding sales charges) of 1.4%, which, combined with portfolio transaction costs of .5% to 1%, brings the total to at least 1%. Vanguard manages its index funds at about one-sixth the cost . . . a built-in advantage of at least 1.6%.

"Consistent Investment Results . . . Relative Performance Predictability . . . Tax-Efficiency . . . Diverse Choice . . . more than 150 index funds available to investors today, so your choice is not limited to portfolios that are solely based on the S&P 5000.

"For these reasons, index funds should be considered for a core portion—say, 50%—of an investor's equity and bond investments."

SOURCE: George Sauter, "The Case for Index Funds," *Mutual Funds* magazine (November 1995).

In effect, the fund's manager becomes your *independent* investment advisor and handles your asset allocations for you—blending, mixing, matching, and actively switching securities within the ebb and flow of the fluid dynamics of the market.

Let's take a quick look at the three main fund types that serve this purpose. You might want to slot one of them into your portfolio as the whole pie . . . and forget all about the picking and choosing. In effect, turn over your asset allocations and your portfolio to your new investment advisor, the manager of one of these special types of funds.

Index Funds

Notwithstanding their name, index funds that actually do match the performance of a market average are anything but "average." Why? Because they usually outperform other funds, too, the majority of which fall short of the market averages. By tracking and matching the market averages, index funds become winners, although less so than some of the more aggressive and riskier funds.

Balanced Funds

The ultimate no-brainer. Managers of balanced funds actually attempt to balance three sets of objectives, maintaining moderate growth and income, with moderate stability of principal. They typically work within a specific mandate to invest half their assets in stocks and half in bonds, with perhaps as much as 10 to 15 percent in other instruments.

Asset-Allocation Funds

Although similar to balanced funds, asset-allocation funds will give their managers more latitude to invest in a broader range of securities in order to take advantage of changing economic and market opportunities.

Keep in mind that these hybrid funds clearly do not fit into one of the basic pie-shaped categories of the financial planners we're working with—they straddle both the bond and stock slices. However, they may well provide the overall diversity you need. Just make certain that before selecting one of them, you examine the following:

❐ The **tax impact** of mixing dividends and interest payments

❐ The **potential of higher expenses** due to more aggressive trading, which may reduce your overall return

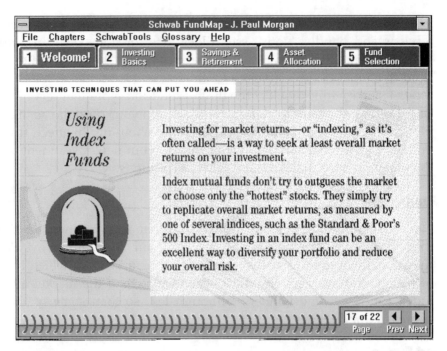

Figure 4.19   Index funds replicate overall market returns.

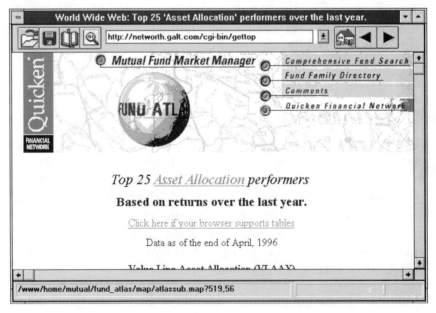

Figure 4.20   Morningstar: top-25 asset-allocation performers.

❏ How well the mix of stocks and bonds matches **your stage of life;** generally, more stocks when younger, and more fixed income later

By way of review, the primary objective of this chapter has been to help do-it-yourself mutual fund investors make the critical transition from the general pie-shaped asset allocations in their personal financial plan to specific funds in a vast universe of 8,000 funds, usually divided into about 25 types of funds depending upon which database and which rating organization you're using; or conversely, to help you avoid the headaches of the process by investing in balanced, index, and asset-allocation funds, letting the fund's managers do the job for you.

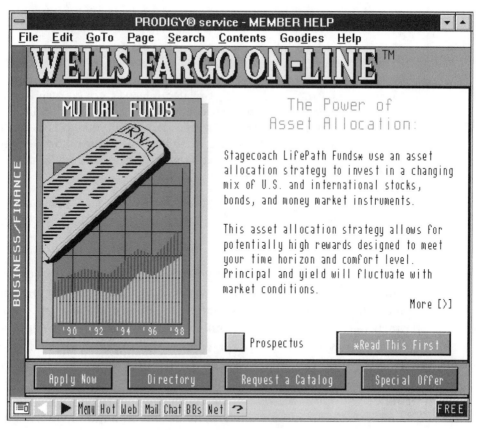

Figure 4.21 Online banking: mutual funds and discount brokerage.

DO-IT-YOURSELF INVESTING IN CYBERSPACE:
THE NEW DIGITAL CHECKBOOKS MAKE IT VERY EASY

Look at it this way: A money market fund is no more than the checking account you keep at your favorite mutual fund family out there in financial cyberspace. It'll pay you interest, which in some cases may even be non-taxable. The rate beats what you'd get at your local bank. You can write checks on your deposits, arrange debit cards, and set up automatic deposits and withdrawals.

Virtually everything you could do if you walked into your local bank and talked to a teller can be handled through your computer, in the privacy of your home.

CYBERSPACE INVESTORS WAVING GOODBYE TO THEIR BANKS

"For many people, old-fashioned checking accounts leave much to be desired. . . . But for investors like Dr. Bamberger, there is an alternative. Asset-management accounts, which combine stock and bond trading with money market funds, pay market-related interest rates on cash balances and can be just as easy to use as checking accounts. Many come with staple checking-account features, such as direct deposit, unlimited check-writing and debit cards that can be used to withdraw cash from automated-teller machines. Some even offer such extras as home banking and bill-payment services."

SOURCE: Vanessa O'Connell, "Tired of Banks? Try Checking Out an Alternative," *The Wall Street Journal* (September 8, 1995).

You can electronically transfer your money right from the convenience of your computer. Plus you can move the money back and forth, in and out of other funds and brokerage accounts, pay bills, and make purchases. For all practical purposes, your computer is your branch bank, except there are no waiting lines, no tellers to deal with, no waiting until tomorrow to make your move. Your money management account is the perfect home base for your banking needs and for storing the cash reserves in your investment portfolio.

Moreover, your money is virtually as safe in a money market account as it is in a bank account. True, there's no FDIC insurance, but the SEC regulations limit money market funds to investing in short-term securities of

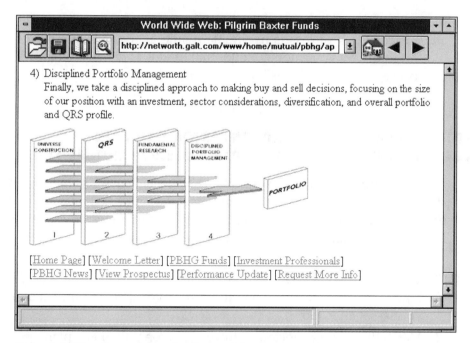

Figure 4.22   Screening a database of funds to match your criteria.

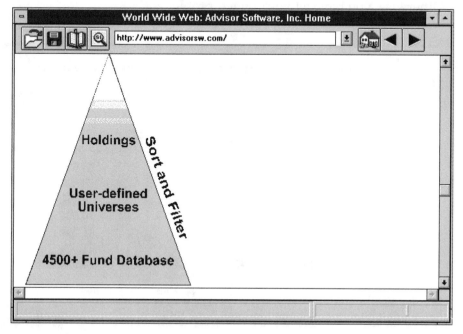

Figure 4.23   Filter through huge databases for your asset allocations.

the highest credit ratings. So for all practical purposes, the funds are guaranteed. Your risk of loss is negligible, while at the same time you get a modest return on your money, better than it would get with a bank deposit or most certificates of deposit. It's a great deal.

BOTTOM LINE: ANY CYBERSPACE INVESTOR CAN PICK AT LEAST 8 WINNERS FROM THE TOTAL OF 8,000 MUTUAL FUNDS

Effective mutual fund investing in cyberspace demands that you move strategically and easily around a universe of about 8,000 mutual funds. In order to do this like the professional do-it-yourself investor you're becoming, you must first understand how to do the following:

❏ Screen through several of the standard 25-category databases and see how they are all related, so you can uncover specific funds that match your asset allocations.

❏ Match those asset allocations to your personal financial plan.

Otherwise, you have a two-pronged problem:

FORTUNE MAGAZINE'S KEEP-IT-SIMPLE "RISK-O-METER"

"Investments that promise high returns over long periods of time carry high risk."

Type of Investment		*Expected Annual Return*
Cash	**Lowest risk**	4.5%
Treasury Bonds		6.0%
Junk Bonds		8.0%
U.S. Stocks		10.0%
U.S. Small Stocks		11.2%
Foreign Stocks		11.5%
Emerging-Market Stocks	**Highest risk**	14.5%

SOURCE: Susan E. Kuhn, "Creating A High-Powered 401(k) Strategy," *Fortune* (August 19, 1996).

❐ Your financial planning may exist in a vacuum and have little value.

❐ Without a plan, your database searches are no more than random accesses chasing the latest news and the hottest tips . . . and *that* investment strategy is guaranteed to create problems down the road.

The solution requires a knowledge of how a set of 25 or so fund *types* fit into the simpler three-part (or five-part allocation—for example, Schwab's FundMap or Quicken Planner) asset allocation in your plan.

As we've shown here, once you are armed with your planned asset allocations designed for your risk profile and economic needs, you can match your allocations with mutual fund types and categories that work for you.

The importance of this planning concept cannot be overstated, and we'll expand on it even more in the next chapter: *Successful mutual fund investing is more dependent on selecting the right types of funds than it is on selecting specific funds.* That principle should be indelibly committed to memory.

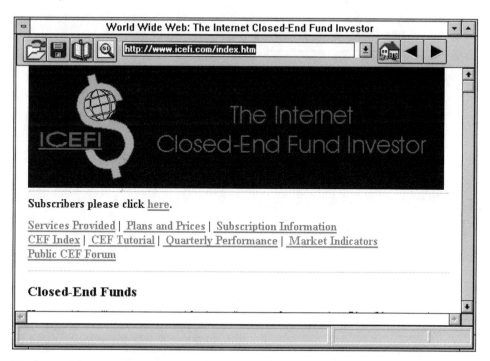

Figure 4.24   The Internet Closed-End Fund Investor (ICEFI).

SMARTMONEY: "IT'S TIME TO BURY CLOSED-END FUNDS"

How about a closed-end fund as an alternative? Here's what the editors of Dow Jones' *SmartMoney* magazine had to say about how even the money managers are avoiding closed-end funds:

"When the managers at Deutsche Morgan Grenfell began to ask around about launching a new international investment product in late 1994, they knew one thing for sure: it wouldn't be a closed-end fund . . . a mutual fund whose shares trade on the stock exchange . . . brokers and planners wouldn't touch the idea . . .

"What's wrong with this $133 billion industry? Plenty. Investors are tired of getting burned by poor performance, and self-interested managers now have other ways to get into the sectors and foreign markets that closed-end funds exploit. Look around, and you can find a regular mutual fund, or a new breed of country fund launched this spring, that does the same thing better and cheaper . . .

"Are there any closed-end funds left that deserve attention? Yes, if they aren't going to be closed much longer."

SOURCE: Sam Jaffe, "It's Time to Bury Closed-End Funds," *SmartMoney* magazine (June 1996).

How and Where to Find All the Financial Data You'll Ever Need

Discovering the Best Online Mutual Fund Databases

Learn how to find the best databases online and on the Net. In step 5 we'll identify the important cyberspace databases for mutual funds, the same ones used by the pros. *These databases are run by the top print publishers who now have electronic editions online and on the Internet. We'll show you how to access them quickly and inexpensively in cyberspace.*

GET THE SAME INFORMATION AS THE PROS

Cyberspace is rapidly becoming the ultimate database for the new do-it-yourself investor. Out there in cyberspace—and that includes everything on the Net as well as all the online services, superpowered offline software tools, and private intranets with financial information services—is a massive database of financial information . . . the do-it-yourself investor's ideal research library.

Moreover, today's investors have access to the same information as the professionals—all those professional advisors, money managers, institutional investors, brokers, and others designated experts. And you can get it just as fast. Actually faster, because you don't have to wait for some expert to check his or her computer for the same sources you now have access to.

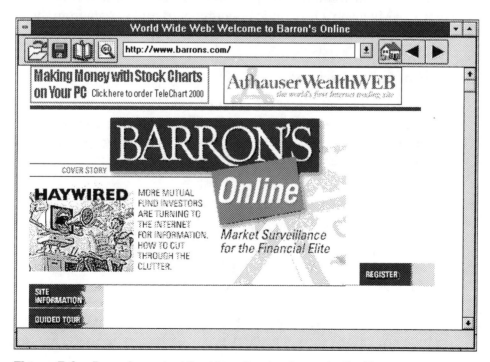

Figure 5.1   Barron's: mutual fund investors logging on to the Net.

Ten years ago these big guns of Wall Street had all the power; they created and owned cyberspace. Today, they're running scared; the playing field is definitely leveling; the individual investor now has an equal opportunity to compete.

THE SAME DATABASES USED BY THE PROS ARE NOW AVAILABLE TO ALL CYBERSPACE INVESTORS

When I first began exploring the new commercial cyberspace in the early days of its commercialization as the Web and Netscape exploded on the scene, I was amazed at the many new information resources available. This brief period was the transitional phase in the commercialization of the Internet. During this period, along with many others I was excited by all the free information offered by the following:

Educational Institutions

American universities were surprisingly active in the Wall Street world, including such Internet projects as the Edgar project at NYU, the University of Michigan's Economic Bulletin Board, full of data from the U.S. government, and MIT's stock charts and stock quotes.

Commercial Online Services

A substantial amount of information was also accessible from several of the recognized databases through America Online and the other online services, from Morningstar, Reuters, and *Money* magazine, for example, at prices considerably lower than their full services to the big institutions.

Internet's World Wide Web

And, of course, many small financial entrepreneurs responded rapidly to make information available on World Wide Web sites—at first free—from names like QuoteCom, NETworth, and PAWWS. Meanwhile, many of the established institutions were quite noticeably quiet, that is, until recently.

Well, the transition phase of cyberspace commercialization is over. Fortunately, however, while today's era of free cyberspace information is

CYBERSPACE DATABASES FOR MUTUAL FUND INVESTORS

AAII's Quarterly Mutual Fund Update
(800) 827-6364 http://www.aaii.org
Barron's Online/IDD Information Services
(800) 544-0422 htp://www.barrons.com
CDA/Wiesenberger Mutual Funds Update
(800) 232-2285 http://www.cda.com
Disclosure Incorporated
(800) 846-0365 http://www.disclosure.com
Lipper Analytical: Fund Profiles
(800) 221-5277 http://www.lipperweb.com
Micropal: Steele Systems and Kiplinger's Magazine
(800) 544-0155 http://www.micropal-us.com/~invest
Morningstar Research
(800) 735-0700 http://www.morningstar.net
Mutual Funds Magazine Online
(800) 442-9000 http://www.mfmag.com
TeleChart 2000: Mutual Fund Database
(800) 776-4940 http://www.worden.com
Tradeline/IDD Information Services
(800) 444-2515 http://nestegg.iddis.com/tradeline
Value Line Mutual Fund Survey
(800) 284-7607 http://www.valueline.com

rapidly disappearing, the *established* database giants now see the enormous buying power of the independent investor and are rushing in to plug this info gap in cyberspace, for nature truly does abhor a vacuum.

As a result, these database institutions are taking advantage of this cyberspace access to market and deliver information previously reserved for a select group of institutional investors willing to pay large fees. Instead of relying solely Wall Street institutions, they are selling their information to a whole new market: the individual investor on Main Street America, Main Street Singapore, Main Street Buenos Aires . . . on Main Street cyberspace!

Cyberspace—the Internet, online services, and offline electronic tools—is the delivery vehicle. Now the power tools are available to get the information to the small investor quickly, cheaply, and reliably.

DEADLY FUND MYTHS . . . WHY YOU MUST DO IT YOURSELF!

"Like the ancient Greeks, fund investors believe in myths. Here we debunk the biggest and give advice to make you a richer shareholder. . . . So what are the fund myths that can lead you astray? . . .

❏ Funds on a hot streak will give you scorching long-term results . . .
❏ Focus on performance and don't sweat the small stuff—like annual expenses . . .
❏ The more funds you own, the merrier your portfolio will become . . .
❏ If you want to score the really big funds, load up on small-cap funds . . .
❏ Aggressive growth funds will push your portfolio sky-high . . .
❏ Investing in junk bond funds is a sucker's game . . .
❏ Keep 5% or 10% of your portfolio in gold funds, which are a great inflation hedge . . .
❏ You can turn a load fund into a no-load fund these days . . .
❏ You should own a double-tax-free fund, whichever state you live in . . .
❏ Dollar-cost averaging increases your returns . . .
❏ International funds are a great way to make a quick killing . . .
❏ Virtually all investors should own an emerging market fund . . .

"A few general thoughts: If a fund category is extremely trendy . . . it's about to become a very bad idea. . . . If you're tempted to buy it, wait until it goes out of fashion. Always remember that you are investing in mutual funds not for today, not for tomorrow, but for a generation."

SOURCE: Jason Zweig, "12 Deadly Fund Myths—And How to Profit From Them," *Money* magazine (February 1996). For details, see the *Money* magazine's database, available on the Web at www.pathfinder.com/money.

ALL THE MAJOR DATABASE VENDORS ARE
NOW AGGRESSIVELY CHASING CYBERSPACE INVESTORS

As we move rapidly into this new phase of cyberspace development—the new commercial cyberspace—we also see the traditional database organizations in a process of rapid conversion to take advantage of this new delivery system and the new markets it has opened. In fact, almost all of these established fund databases—the ones that have built their reputations over the long haul as reliable mutual fund resources—are now in the process of conversion, of making their products and services universally available to the masses at reasonable prices. This trend is guaranteed to accelerate.

MORNINGSTAR: POWER TOOL FOR DO-IT-YOURSELF INVESTORS

"Morningstar No-Load Funds is for do-it-yourself investors who want the most complete coverage of no-load and low-load funds . . .

"Timely data, cutting-edge research tools (star ratings, styles boxes, tax analysis, derivatives coverage), and outspoken written evaluations make Morningstar's full-page reports the industry standard.

"You'll also get an updated performance index that tracks each fund—along with the latest ranking and industry averages."

SOURCE: Morningstar ad, *Investor's Business Daily* (March 1996).

A few years ago, when college students and individual entrepreneurs were providing information on the Internet, the timeliness and quality of information was anything but reliable. You got what you paid for. I remember seeing a note on one of the university Websites providing stock market information announcing to Web surfers that the graduate student in charge

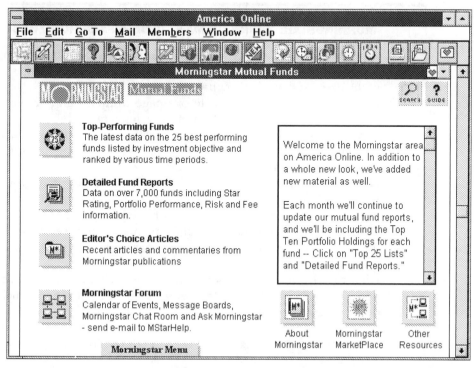

Figure 5.2   Morningstar mutual funds reports on America Online.

was on a holiday break . . . so market data was going to be delayed more than 15 minutes.

MORNINGSTAR: A SUPERSTAR
AMONG THE RISING STARS IN FINANCIAL CYBERSPACE

Quite in contrast, none of the commercial database competitors can afford even the slightest hint that they have any inconsistency or lack of reliability in the flow of their financial information. Morningstar, Value Line, Lipper, and their competitors must be a model of perfection.

Their customers won't tolerate any laxity, and they wouldn't be in business long if that were the case. The value they place on their integrity and reputation prevents them from being anything but darn close to 100 percent reliable.

MORNINGSTAR: RISING ON MANY CYBERSPACE HORIZONS

❒ **America Online.** At AOL's Personal Finance section, offering coverage of mutual funds and stocks. Mutual fund data is included as part of the basic AOL monthly subscriber's fee.

❒ **CompuServe.** Order complete one-page Mutual Funds report on any one of the 1,500 funds, electronically delivered.

❒ **INVESTools.** One of several Web-based newsstands for financial data publishers. Order Morningstar's one-page reports on funds, international stocks, and closed-end funds.

❒ **NETworth Internet Website.** NETworth is part of the growing Quicken Financial Network. You can access Morningstar information once registered. Registration is currently free.

❒ **Reuters Money Network.** One of the premiere online services specifically for investors. Prices are comparable to the competitive online services.

❒ **Charles Schwab.** The leader in online and Web-based discount brokerage, electronic trading software, and mutual fund services such as Schwab's *Select List* of the 50 top performers.

❒ **Quicken and Intuit.** Intuit imports Morningstar data for subscribers using most of the Quicken software products, including Investor's Insight.

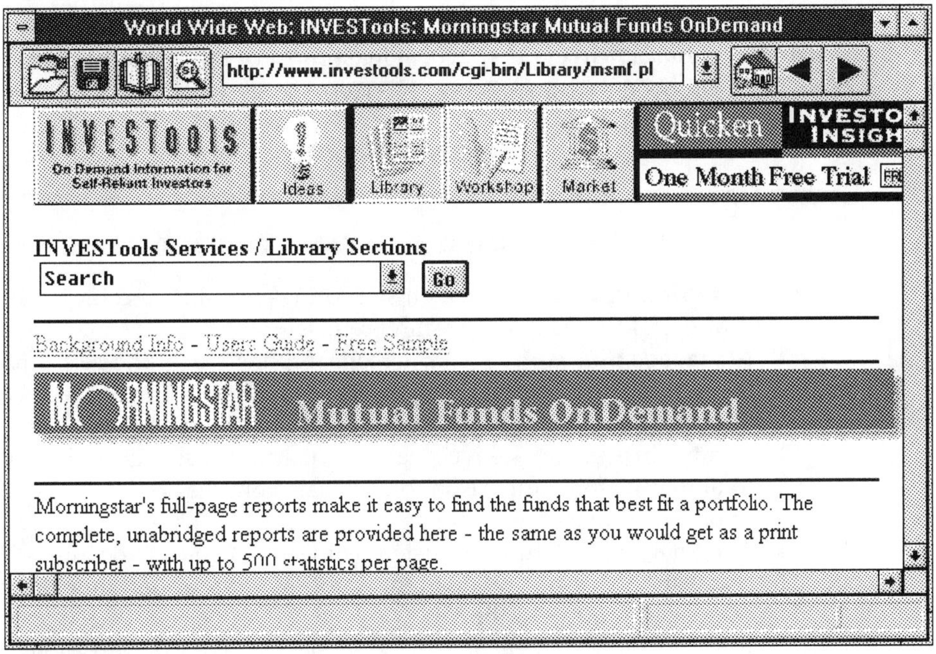

Figure 5.3 Morningstar reports at the INVESTools Website.

The new do-it-yourself investor will find these key databases in many different cyberspace locations. That's because they typically wholesale their information through multiple "retail" outlets, often leaving the impression to the neophyte investor that there are many more database resources for mutual funds than there in fact are. Before we move on to what you actually do with data, let's review the key fund databases.

MUTUAL FUND DATABASE #1: MORNINGSTAR TARGETS THE NEW CYBERSPACE DO-IT-YOURSELF INVESTOR

Morningstar is an excellent example of a traditional mutual fund database. Most of these mutual fund databases were originally designed more for the big-time professional and institutional money managers. Today most are becoming available to the individual investor, either directly or through many "retail" outlets.

Morningstar has already developed a solid reputation with many millions of investors, as well as many major institutions in the global financial community. In fact, today Morningstar is widely accessible from sources other than just cyberspace financial organizations. You'll find Morningstar virtually *everywhere* in cyberspace, at least most of the hot spots for investors: For example, AOL, CompuServe, NETworth, Schwab, and Quicken all use Morningstar's database.

DATA FORMAT FOR MORNINGSTAR'S PUBLICATIONS

❑ **Historical Profile.**   With their star ratings to help, fund investors see how each fund balances risk and return.

❑ **Manager's Biography.**   Key persons responsible for the performance of the fund: experience, education, salaries, and other funds being managed.

❑ **Fund Performance.**   Five years of quarterly returns with trailing total returns for comparison to peers; also graphs and analysis of the impact of management changes.

❑ **Tax Analysis.**   Returns adjusted, with capital gains exposure.

❑ **Analyst's Review.**   Evaluation of the reasons underlying the successes and failures of the fund.

❑ **Risk Analysis.**   Measures include beta, standard deviation, and Morningstar's risk analysis; each compares the fund's risk and volatility to the sector norms.

❑ **Fund History.**   Long-term comparison of key statistical benchmarks, including NAV quotes, total return to S&P 500 and Wilshire 2000, ratios of expenses, dividend income, return, ranking by sector, trading turnover, and other analytical processes.

❑ **Investment Objectives, Style and Strategy.**   An independent classification, including an analysis of the fund's consistency in its objectives and strategy through changing market conditions.

❑ **Portfolio Holdings.**   Analysis of major assets driving the performance of the portfolio, red-flagging whether the managers can invest in derivatives, complex or illiquid securities. Morningstar also analyzes historical changes in the percentages of asset categories, comparing norms and aberrations.

❑ **Sector Weightings.**   An analysis of the allocation of assets among sectors, examining portfolio diversification.

For many mutual fund investors, Morningstar has been the preferred print publisher years before their thrust into cyberspace. Their traditional print publications include a wealth of information. Morningstar packages and repackages its database in many different ways, both printed and electronic, for mutual fund investors. Here's a list to illustrate the information supporting this particular mutual fund database now being delivered alternatively in cyberspace:

Traditional Printed Publications

❑ *Morningstar Mutual Funds* (1,500 funds)

❑ *Morningstar No-Load Funds* (690 funds)

❑ *Morningstar Investor* (monthly newsletter)

❑ *Morningstar Mutual Fund 500* (annual directory)

❑ *Morningstar OnDemand* (individual reports by fax/mail)

❑ *Morningstar Closed-End Funds* (350 funds)

❑ *Morningstar Closed-End Fund 250* (annual directory)

❑ *Morningstar Variable Annuities/Life* (about 1,000)

Electronic Power Tools: Cyberspace, Online, and Software

❑ *Morningstar Principia for Mutual Funds* (7,000 no-load mutual funds, or 520 closed-end funds)

❑ *Morningstar Ascent* software (same database as Principia without their analysts' comments and only 70 of the 98 data categories available on Principia software)

❑ *Morningstar U.S. Equities OnFloppy* (software on 7,500 stocks)

❑ *Morningstar International Stocks* (software on 700 stocks)

❑ Morningstar online at AOL and other online services

❑ Morningstar Websites (NETworth, proprietary, and others)

**NEW CYBERSPACE FINANCIAL DATABANK PARTNERSHIP
NETWORTH, MORNINGSTAR, DISCLOSURE, AND INTUIT**

"Networth offers a lot of good information for free, and its 110,000 registered users attest to its popularity. And the site has become a powerful marketing tool for no-load families.... Given the warp speed of Web developments, don't be surprised if by next year you can screen hundreds of funds, order electronic prospectuses, place an order for shares, and pay for them online without parting company with your easy chair."

SOURCE: Wayne Harris, "The Web Gets Intuit," *Individual Investor* (January 1996).

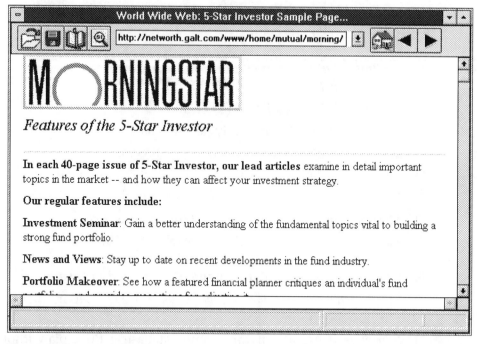

Figure 5.4   Morningstar: features of the 5-Star Investor.

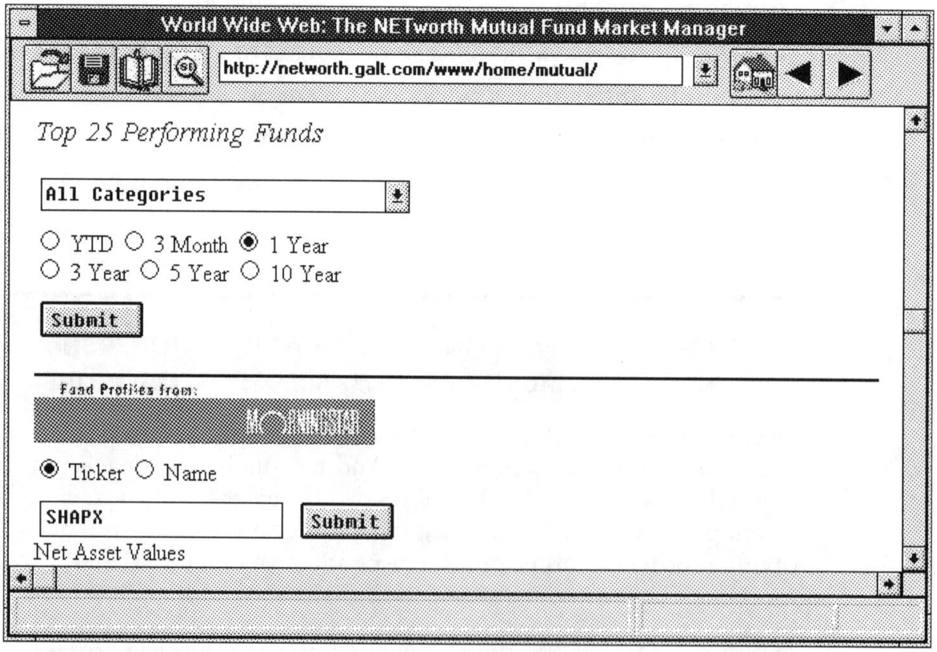

Figure 5.5   Morningstar on NETworth: online database screening.

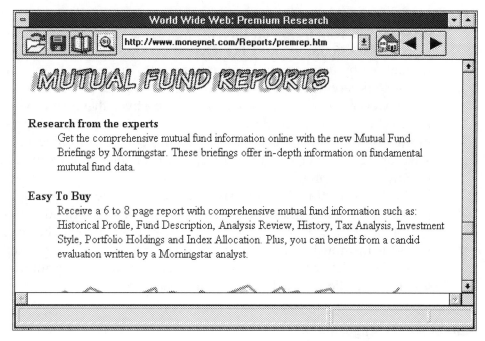

Figure 5.6 Mutual Fund Reports: Morningstar on Reuters Network.

You can check out Morningstar at their Website, www.mstar.com, for more detailed information about these products, services, and updates. As yet, their Website is not interactive. However, it is probably only a matter of time before Morningstar realizes that effective marketing in today's highly competitive cyberspace demands interactivity, building on the direct contact with investors in cyberspace, even if you have to charge for the information.

MUTUAL FUND DATABASE #2: MUTUAL FUNDS ONLINE MAGAZINE AND THE INSTITUTE FOR ECONOMETRIC RESEARCH

In contrast to the Morningstar organization, whose data is available through many retail outlets in cyberspace, the Institute for Econometric Research currently delivers its information through channels under its sole control, in print and in cyberspace. Think of Morningstar as a data wholesaler to many retailers, while the Institute is a one-stop shopping center for mutual fund data.

The Institute has been providing statistics and analysis on securities as early as 1978, with the publication of *Stock Market Logic,* the classic by Norman Fosback, founder and CEO. Over the years, the Institute has built a reputation by leveraging its databases into a collection of advisory newsletters serving stock and mutual fund investors.

However, from the press/media perspective, the magazine Mutual Funds Online and the Institute still exist in the shadows of old-timers in the mutual fund business: distinguished names such as Morningstar, CDA/Wiesenberger, Lipper, and Value Line. However, their relative anonymity is rapidly disappearing.

With the Institute's aggressive marketing strategy and high-profile positioning with its Mutual Funds Online Website, it is rapidly becoming one of the major power players in Wall Street cyberspace. In the last couple years the Institute has matured strategically. It has gone far beyond the traditional newsletter-publisher role, expanding in two significant directions that have positioned the Institute as a cyberspace leader.

Mutual Funds Magazine

The Institute is now the publisher of the only monthly periodical devoted exclusively to mutual funds. In a relatively short time its circulation has exploded to about half a million. More important for the cyberspace investor, you can access the content of the print magazine on the Internet at the Institute's Website before the print magazine reaches subscribers.

Mutual Funds Online Website

As one of the original advisory newsletters on the NETworth Website, the Institute was introduced to the potentials of cyberspace. Enough so to encourage the organization to leave and create its own Website. And last year the Institute confidently announced that "Mutual Funds Online contains the Net's best mutual fund browser," which includes the following:

- ❐ Fund advisory and information services
- ❐ Fund discount brokers
- ❐ More than 650 fund families
- ❐ Hot links to three dozen publications
- ❐ Plus 55 other mutual fund Websites

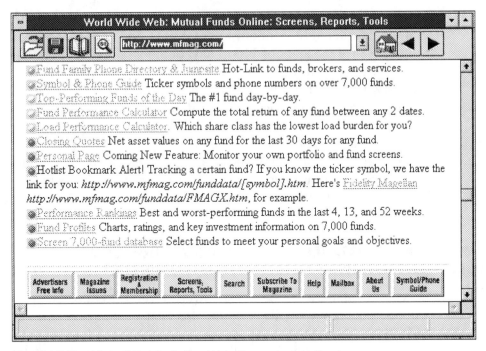

Figure 5.7 Mutual Funds Online Website: resource directory.

NEWSLETTERS OF THE INSTITUTE FOR ECONOMETRIC RESEARCH

Mutual Fund Newsletters

- ❑ **Mutual Fund Forecaster.** Profit projections and risk ratings.
- ❑ **Mutual Fund Buyer's Guide.** An investment scoreboard.
- ❑ **Fund Watch.** A chart service featuring high-performance funds.
- ❑ **Income Fund Outlook.** Bond funds and money market funds.
- ❑ **Mutual Fund Weekly.** Combination of the four fund advisories.

Stock Market Newsletters

- ❑ **Market Logic.** Full-service analysis of stock market and economy.
- ❑ **Investor's Digest.** Market advice from hundreds of services.
- ❑ **The Insiders.** Analysis and ratings of America's top investors.
- ❑ **New Issues.** The Institute's guide to initial public offerings.
- ❑ **Stock Market Weekly.** Combination of the four stock advisories.

The goal of Mutual Funds Online is to "give you the gateway to the world of mutual funds right from our Internet site." Today this Website is getting hundreds of thousands of hits a day, demonstrating its popularity with today's mutual fund investor. Because of its focus on the Internet investor, it is very likely that Mutual Funds Online will be the one to beat in cyberspace. Watch out, Morningstar and Value Line!

Obviously, a cyberspace investor using the Mutual Funds Online Website is getting the benefit of all of the proprietary database research and analysis that also supports the Institute's print publications, the 10 newsletters, and *Mutual Funds* magazine. As with Morningstar, it is the Institute's mutual funds database that creates and adds value for online and Net investors.

MUTUAL FUND DATABASE #3: THE DIGITAL DOW JONES GIANT AGGRESSIVELY TARGETING DO-IT-YOURSELF INVESTORS

Dow Jones, along with the other power players—Reuters, Knight-Ridder, and Bloomberg—virtually created financial cyberspace. And until the early 1990s, financial cyberspace was an exclusive club for members only, *the institutional investor.* The individual investor was empty-handed.

However, in the last few years, with the commercialization of Internet, the introduction of the graphics-based World Wide Web, and the exploding popularity of life in cyberspace, the massive size and potential of the new cyberspace market have forced Dow Jones and others to develop innovative products and services for this market.

In the past couple years, Dow Jones' strategy toward the do-it-yourself investor has been one of exploration and experimentation. The organization is so huge and decentralized, and the databases so massive, that at times the image Dow Jones projects in cyberspace has been fragmented, perhaps due to sibling rivalry among the various editorial fiefdoms.

Fortunately, this fragmentation appears to be calming down or developing a healthy synergism, and the image of a new, digital Dow Jones is now taking concrete form. Here are a few of the Dow Jones electronic database resources specifically focused on mutual funds:

Dow Jones News/Retrieval

DJN/R relies on other databases for information, as well as proprietary sources. Media General Financial Service provides performance statistics and background information on the major equity and bond funds. Historical prices are also available from Tradeline. At present, DJN/R is primarily a dial-up service for subscribers only.

The Wall Street Journal—Interactive Edition

The new, snazzier, Web-based electronic version of the old "bible of the gray-pinstripe investor," with news and reports on mutual funds. Subscribers are finding this new digital Journal a bargain for about $50 a year.

Tradeline Mutual Fund Center

Dow Jones is the controlling partner in IDD Information Services, since 1935 a leader in domestic and international securities data services. Their Tradeline service has provided price, earnings, and dividend data on 220,000 securities since the early 1970s. The Tradeline Mutual Fund Center is a Web-based resource with quotes and summary reports.

Figure 5.8 Tradeline Mutual Fund Center: daily performance data.

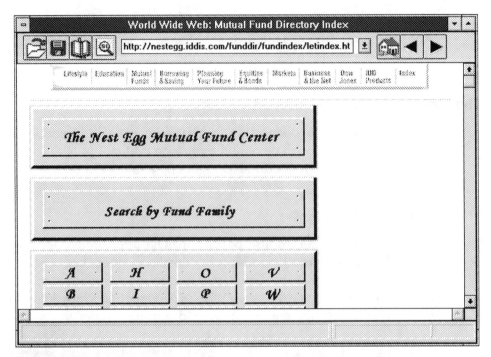

Figure 5.9   Tradeline Center: search engine to mutual fund families.

Barron's Online

An excellent new Web-based service developed in conjunction with IDD Information Services. The stated objective of Barron's Online is to provide readers with in-depth research, with fundamentals, performance data, and charts on 14,000 public companies and 5,800 mutual funds. Users will also be able to access current and past news items from *Barron's, The Journal,* and Dow Jones newswires.

Dow Jones is now coming on the Web with SmartMoney Online, the electronic version of their *SmartMoney* magazine. Given the glitzy style of the print version and their upscale audience, SmartMoney Online will be joining Barron's Online as a centerpiece for the new digital Dow's electronic services for the do-it-yourself investor in cyberspace.

SmartMoney covers more than mutual funds. However, it consistently adds a unique editorial slant on the funds it does cover. For example, the *SmartMoney* approach may be more selective than other online services, if their annual review of "Superstar Funds" is any indication. In the 1996 review, *SmartMoney* said that of "2,034 funds out there, only 7 passed our test." This kind of pinpoint bombing will be a welcome contrast to the usual mass-market global surveys in their competition.

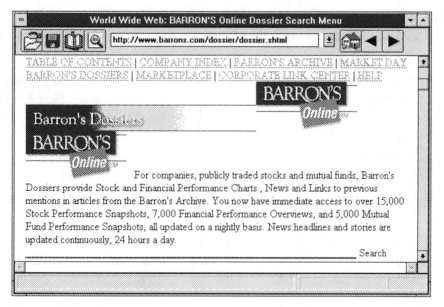

Figure 5.10   Barron's Online: dossiers on over 5,000 mutual funds.

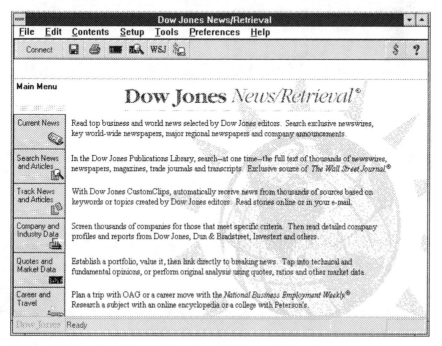

Figure 5.11   Dow Jones News Retrieval: new Digital Dow.

MUTUAL FUND DATABASE #4: VALUE LINE: AN OLD FAVORITE GETS AGGRESSIVE IN FINANCIAL CYBERSPACE

Value Line has been around for decades. The *Value Line Investment Survey* has been in the business of profiling stocks since 1931. Every self-respecting individual investor will recognize the *Value Line* name by its distinguished reputation, if not from frequent trips to the public library to research stocks.

Value Line proudly notes that their mutual funds products are backed by "disciplined, objective, analytic methodologies that have been proven over six decades, and by one of the world's largest independent research staffs, including over 100 analysts, statisticians, and economists."

Actually, Value Line waited until 1993 to expand into the mutual funds data arena, with its publication of *The Value Line Mutual Fund Survey,* just shortly before the Internet's Web craze ignited, and before the Institute for Econometric Research launched *Mutual Funds* magazine and Mutual Funds Online.

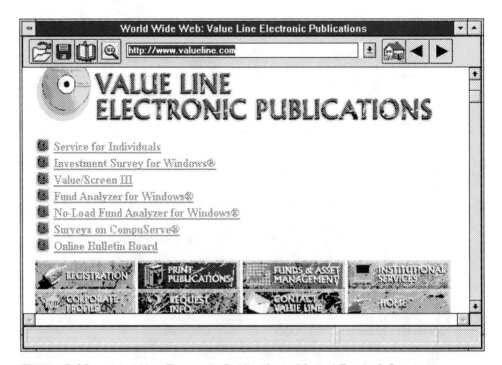

Figure 5.12   Value Line Electronic Publications: Mutual Funds & Stocks.

Value Line: Old-Timer Challenging Upstart Morningstar

According to *Worth* magazine's Andrew Gluck, "Morningstar wasn't pleased. In March 1994, the company alleged that Value Line had plagiarized the synopses of a fund's strategy prepared by Morningstar's analysts. 'That was a little surprising given that Morningstar's flagship product is so thoroughly predicated on a format' that Value Line has used for its stock profiles since 1931."

In a comparison between the databases included in the software systems each now has on the market—Morningstar's Principia and Value Line's Fund Analyzer—*Barron's* "Electronic Investor" columnist Howard Gold notes, "Both contain vast amounts of information—*maybe too much data*—on the total return, holdings, and risk characteristics of the thousands of funds they track."

FUND DATABASE GIANTS SLUGGING IT OUT FOR TOP HONORS

"The battle between Value Line and Morningstar may be generating most of the noise, but other companies are quietly fighting for their share of the data turf, too. Although Lipper Analytical Services, Micropal, and CDA/Wiesenberger primarily sell their fund information to institutional investors, each also provides data to a surprisingly large number of individual investors . . .

Lipper . . . performance data via Associated Press news service to many papers, including *The Wall Street Journal* and *The Washington Post* . . .

Micropal, a British financial publisher . . . appears on Prodigy . . . Kiplinger's . . . tracks 35,000 funds in 24 nations . . . software packages; such as Steele Systems Mutual Fund Expert and the AAII Quarterly Low-Load Mutual Fund Update . . .

CDA/Wiesenberger: provides data on returns, dividends, capital gains, risk, and yields on 7,000 funds."

SOURCE: Andrew Gluck, "Two Fund Data-Giants Square Off," *Worth* (June 1996).

Value Line is another example of the explosive interest in mutual funds. With an increase from less than $1 trillion in 1990 to over $3 trillion in 1996 and headed for the $6 trillion mark by 2000, it's clear that not only is the public vitally interested in funds, so are the press, media, and traditional financial information providers.

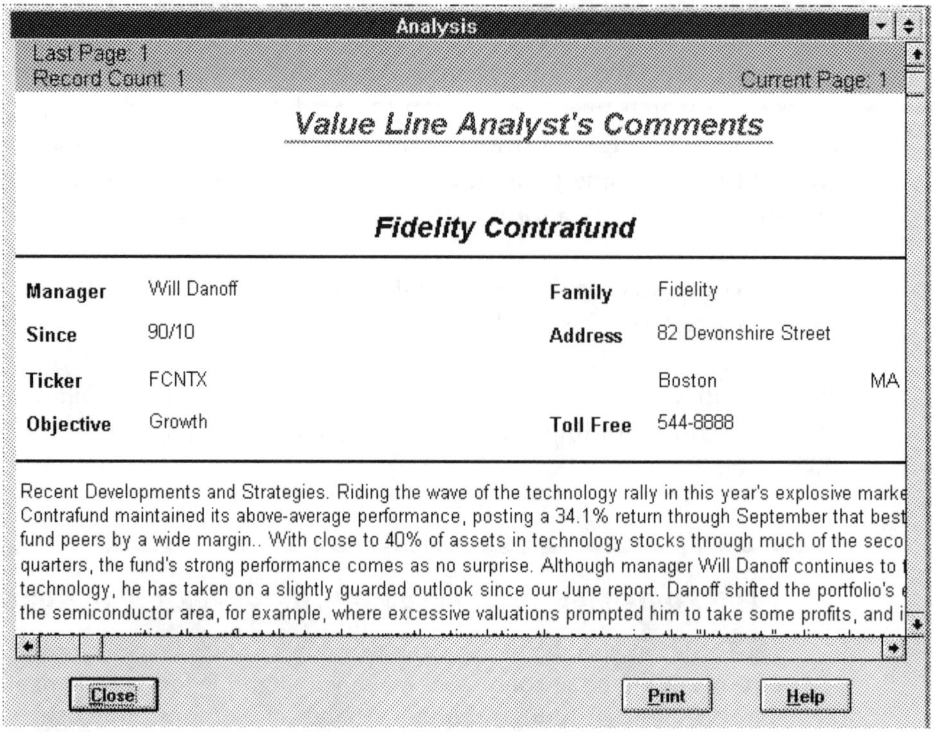

Figure 5.13   Value Line Fund Analyzer: Analyst's Comments.

The competition to deliver a mutual fund database is obviously not a game for fainthearted, undercapitalized entrepreneurs. Rather, the established firms now appear to be tooling up for battle. Indeed, the winning database providers appear to be already in the game with periodicals, online services, and electronic delivery systems.

Moreover, it is interesting to watch this scenario unfold, because these providers must simultaneously and aggressively go after much more than the mutual fund investor in cyberspace. This trend is forcing all of these database publishers to develop several delivery systems and products all at once—print periodicals, analytical software, online dial-up services, and Websites.

MUTUAL FUND DATABASE #5: CDA/WIESENBERGER FIRST CHOICE FOR 80,000 BROKERS AND FINANCIAL PLANNERS

CDA/Wiesenberger was the country's first mutual fund tracking service with a history going back over 50 years. Over the years they have become

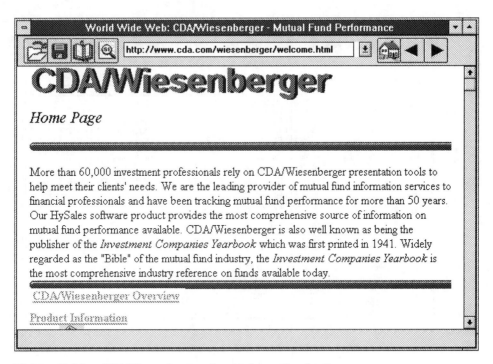

Figure 5.14 CDA/Wiesenberger: fund information for the pros.

one of the financial information powerhouses, building a solid reputation with the institutional investors, money managers, and brokers.

The company is a division of CDA Investment Technologies, which in turn is owned by the Thomson Corporation, a $7 billion international company with headquarters in Canada: "Our vision is to become the foremost information and publishing business in the world." An obvious challenge to Dow Jones and Reuters.

Thomson's business includes cyberspace investor resources such as First Call, Securities Data Company, Investext, *American Banker, The Bond Buyer,* and many other financial information firms comparable to CDA/Wiesenberger. The company also owns more than 100 U.S. newspapers, as well as the *Toronto Globe and Mail.*

CDA/Wiesenberger is one of Morningstar's chief competitors for the "lucrative brokerage-information" business, according to *Worth* magazine. In fact, its HySales software system is in use with 80,000 brokers, as a quick reference to explain mutual funds to customers, with some classy charts and graphics to illustrate investment plans. The company also provides brokers with demographic information on wealthy individuals. Its fund databases include the following:

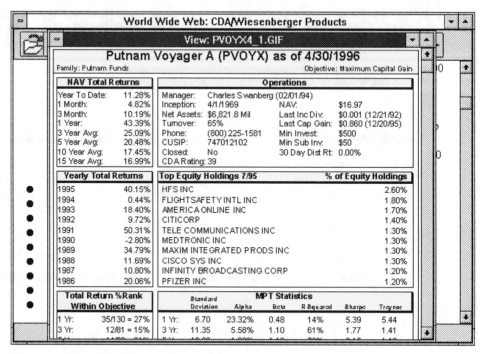

Figure 5.15 CDA/Wiesenberger Website: fund data report.

❐ 7,100 funds
❐ 500 closed-end funds
❐ 3,000 variable annuities

And their databases include 15 years of performance history and other key statistics, including 150 market indexes. CDA/Wiesenberger's print publications include two popular resources within the brokerage community:

❐ *The Investment Companies Yearbook*
❐ *Mutual Funds Update,* a monthly resource

As already noted, the CDA/Wiesenberger database is currently a service for brokers and independent financial advisors rather than individual investors. In fact, its literature specifically notes that "Current subscribers rely on HySales presentations to help 'close the sale' at nearly all meetings with clients" where the client is an individual investor.

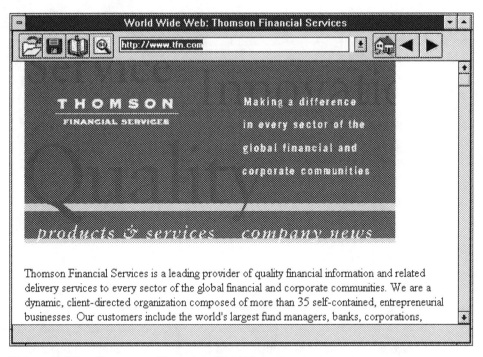

Figure 5.16 Thompson Financial: CDA/Wiesenberger parent.

In other words, if you're not a do-it-yourself investor yet, and you're using a broker or financial advisor for investment planning, there's a high probability that the broker or advisor's presentation to you was prepared using an information system from CDA/Wiesenberger and Thomson.

Given the dramatic transformation resulting from the cyberspace revolution, the trend to do-it-yourself investing, and the fact that CDA/Wiesenberger and its parent Thomson are savvy technology companies, it is highly probable that sometime in the next year or so they will also be marketing a version of their products directly to the individual investor, most likely on the World Wide Web.

MUTUAL FUND DATABASE #6: MICROPAL
BRITISH NEWCOMER COVERS U.S. AND INTERNATIONAL FUNDS

Like most other business and financial magazines, *Kiplinger's Personal Finance Magazine* buys its data from one of the major mutual fund databases.

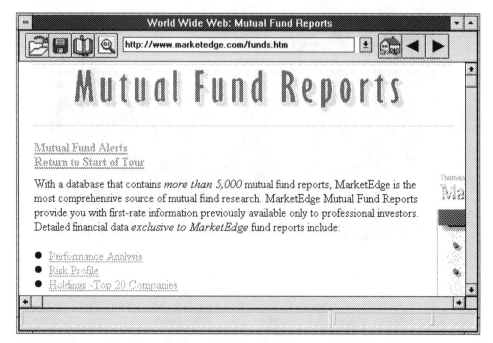

Figure 5.17   Micropal: British-based U.S. and global mutual fund data.

Kiplinger's data vendor is Micropal, Incorporated, a financial information services company headquartered in Great Britain, with U.S. offices in Boston.

Micropal is a recognized international vendor of mutual fund information. As a result, it's likely that Micropal will become an even bigger player among U.S. competitors in the near future, as global investment opportunities become a more accepted slice of the Main Street investor's portfolio.

Micropal was formed in 1985, first building a database on British mutual funds. Today they offer data and software serving clients in 24 countries, including U.S. funds, and appear well on the way to creating the number one global fund databank.

Kiplinger's used the Micropal database in publishing their annual survey of mutual funds, *Kiplinger's Mutual Funds '96*. In addition, the *Kiplinger's* annual included a free, introductory software product from the Steele Systems, called the Mutual Fund Expert, which also uses the Micropal database. The Mutual Fund Expert is a new offline cyberspace power tool designed for do-it-yourself investors, to help them screen, analyze, select, and monitor a portfolio of mutual funds.

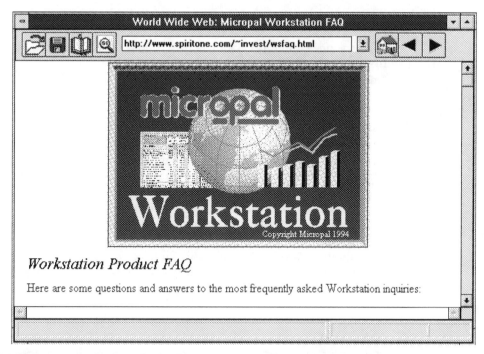

Figure 5.18 Micropal Workstation: fund management for professionals.

Generally speaking, it looks like Micropal will become one of the major competitors for Morningstar, Value Line, and other established U.S. mutual fund information companies. Expect to see much more of Micropal in the funds information, and welcome the competition. The cyberspace investor can't help but win, as competition encourages alternatives while presumably improving quality and decreasing costs.

MUTUAL FUND DATABASE #7: LIPPER ANALYTICAL SERVICES DATA SOURCE FOR NEWS MEDIA AND INSTITUTIONS MOVES TO WEB

Lipper Analytical Services is the primary wholesaler of mutual fund data to your favorite newspaper, distributed over the international newswire services of Associated Press. Mutual fund quotes in *The Wall Street Journal, The Washington Post,* and *San Francisco Examiner,* for example, are from Lipper databases. In fact, there's a high probability that every investor who's *ever* looked at mutual fund quotes and surveys in a newspaper was looking at Lipper's fund data.

STATISTICS INCLUDED IN LIPPER MUTUAL FUND PROFILES

❒ **Performance summary:** Includes NAV quote, objective, yield.
❒ **Investment policy** of the individual fund.
❒ **Advisor and manager:** And start date.
❒ **Historical data:** YTD and last five years.
❒ **Major investments:** Totals and percentages.
❒ **Portfolio assets:** By type of security.
❒ **Expense and turnover ratios.**
❒ **Volatility:** Measure of fluctuations in monthly returns.
❒ **Market phase rating:** Lipper's unique rating of relative performance in prior bull and bear markets, and current market phase.
❒ **Performance evaluation:** Compared to peer category.
❒ **Current value:** $1,000 invested five years ago, to S&P 500.
❒ **Significant events:** Changes in managers, policy, etc.
❒ **Investment information:** Symbol, initial offering, fees, minimum investment, 12b-1 charges, shareholder services, address, phone.

Figure 5.19   Lipper: new cyberspace standard for fund investors.

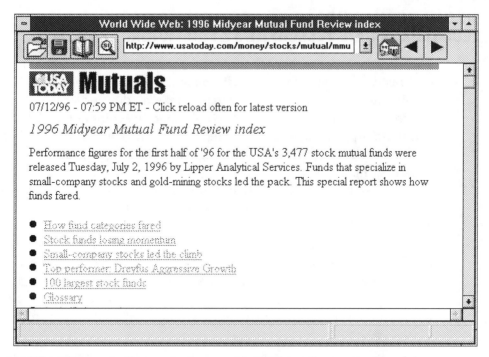

Figure 5.20   *USA Today:* Lipper analytical midyear mutual fund review.

Lipper tracks about 20,000 mutual funds worldwide, including the primary set of more than 7,000 U.S. funds managed by the 600 key fund families. Many individual investors are familiar with Lipper's *Mutual Fund ProFiles,* which is published in association with Standard & Poor's, a subsidiary of McGraw-Hill.

Until recently, Lipper appeared content in its niche as a behind-the-scenes wholesaler of mutual fund information to the news media and to the 600 mutual fund families, which strategically and historically have been Lipper's primary clients. If you want backup for the Lipper/AP data you see regularly in your local newspaper, you should consider buying a copy of *Mutual Fund ProFiles.* Check it out; the book's a valuable reference for professionals and individual investors.

Lipper is now aggressively positioning itself to establish a niche in the growing market of do-it-yourself investors in cyberspace as well as on Main Street. And they are guaranteed to be a major cyberspace challenger to Morningstar, Value Line, and the other fund databases. The net result of this increased competition should work out very favorably for the individual investor, in data quality, price, and availability.

MUTUAL FUND DATABASE #8: TELECHART 2000
TECHNICIANS RATE TELECHART #1 FOR MUTUAL FUND DATA

The average investor may be unfamiliar with TeleChart 2000, but not the experienced investor familiar with technical analysis. TeleChart 2000 is a highly rated and relatively inexpensive data vendor and charting software service from Worden Brothers. Not only that, the company picks no bones about running full page advertisements in the *Investor's Business Daily* telling us that they're "the world's #1 selling stock charting and data service by a large margin."

Worden Brothers built their reputation among active stock market traders and investors who use various technical analysis methodologies. Their starter kit is only $29, and the updates depend on the amount of data downloaded. One very active investor who carries his laptop around says that he uses TeleChart 2000 to follow over 100 stocks for about $30 a month, switching to Reuters Money Network for his fundamental research.

Worden Brothers began offering Mutual Fund Data in 1993 and since then have received the "Best Mutual Fund Data" award from *Technical*

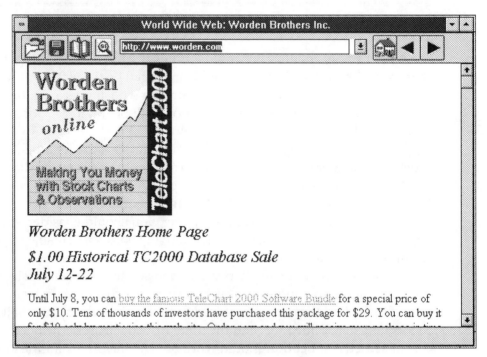

Figure 5.21   TeleChart 2000 for mutual fund data: CD-ROM and disk.

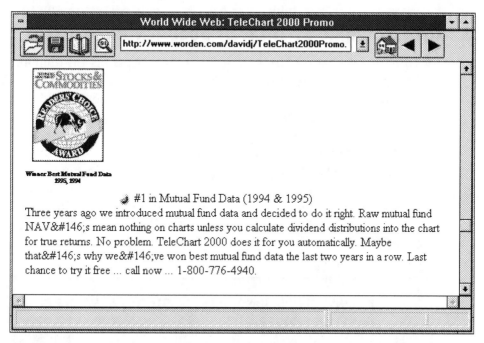

Figure 5.22   TeleChart mutual fund data: awarded #1 by technicians.

Analysis of Stocks & Commodities magazine several times. And when the upscale *Barron's* went online, TeleChart 2000 was right there as a pioneering advertiser to *Barron's* elite readers.

As they put it, "We decided to do it right. Raw mutual fund NAVs mean nothing on chart unless you calculate dividend distributions into the chart for true returns. . . . TeleChart 2000 does it for you automatically. . . . Our commitment to you is to provide the most innovative charts, the highest-quality data, the most professional support, and the lowest rates in the industry." However, Worden is mum about how they get the data.

If you're technically oriented, already past the novice investor's stage of the game, and looking for a reasonable alternative, contact Worden. The TeleChart 2000 system may not be a starter kit for the average do-it-yourself investor, but Worden Brothers has built a solid reputation for delivering accurate, quality databases at *rock-bottom prices* to the cost-conscious, active, independent investor. Remember the name *TeleChart 2000;* file it away for future reference. It's first class, and it'll be even better by the time you're ready for it.

MUTUAL FUND DATABASE #9: EDGAR AND SEC FILINGS
INSTANT ELECTRONIC DELIVERY OF DOCUMENTS

Mutual funds are required to give you a prospectus on demand. Many already have Websites from which you can download the electronic version. But many funds are still in the pre-Internet stone age and lack a Website, so you can't download the data. If you're in a hurry and need the prospectus right away, you now have several other alternatives, thanks to the Wall Street cyberspace revolution.

Beginning May 1996 all U.S. companies, including mutual fund managers, were required by law to file disclosure documents *electronically*. As a result, every investor in the world has access to prospectuses and all the other required legal/financial documents online and on the Internet within 24 hours of the filing.

REAL INVESTORS: IGNORE THOSE GLOSSY FUND REPORTS;
GET FREE PROSPECTUSES ON THE WEB FROM SEC.ORG

"Real investors don't rely on annual reports or glossy company handouts. They read the documents that companies file with the Securities and Exchange Commission, and anyone with Internet access can get them free through the SEC's Edgar Web site . . . professionals have been paying private services hundreds of dollars to get copies of a single SEC document. The Internet service is designed to give ordinary investors the same edge."

SOURCE: Jamie Heller, "Digital Investor: Get the Real Story from SEC Filings for Free," *SmartMoney* magazine (June 1996).

The new system of electronic filing—Electronic Data Gathering Analysis and Retrieval, known by its acronym EDGAR—has been under development for a few years and takes investors light-years beyond anything you'll ever see in your newspapers and rating reports, such as Lipper's half-page summary.

A total of 15,000 companies file 10 million pages annually with the SEC, averaging 42 pages a document. You'll discover all kinds of details about how much they're paying the bosses, nasty lawsuits, oddball expenditures, and a list of every darn investment, not just top 10 or so. The lawyers and accountants add their spin to blunt any negatives, but the SEC has a way of forcing them to expose their dirty laundry, and sometimes the boring becomes a mystery thriller.

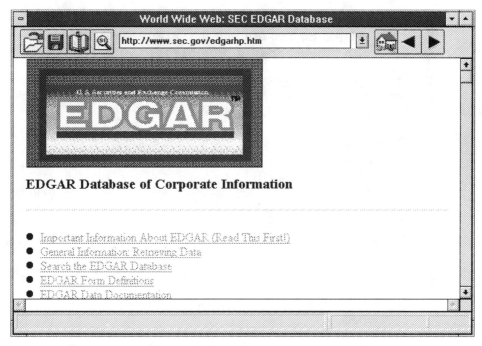

Figure 5.23　SEC/EDGAR Website: database for securities filings.

Investing is serious business. It's your hard-earned money and your future we're talking about here. You wouldn't buy a car without driving it around the block. Or a house without getting engineering and title reports. So never buy a fund until you've read its prospectus.

NEW COMMERCIAL SYSTEMS FOR DOWNLOADING PROSPECTUSES

The new world of instant EDGAR is perfect for today's do-it-yourself investor. If you are too anxious to wait for a snail-mail delivery to get a prospectus, and if the fund doesn't have a Website with a downloadable prospectus, get out there in cyberspace and access www.sec.org. Equally important, you will want to log on to this system in the future to follow up and track new developments in some of your existing fund investments.

Warning: You will quickly discover that the large EDGAR files download in slow motion; very time-consuming and often crudely formatted. Moreover, prospectuses are not posted until about 24 hours after the actual filing. Fortunately, there are some commercial resources that will help you get the information sooner, if time is critical:

REQUIRED SEC DOCUMENTS: ELECTRONICALLY FILED
AND DOWNLOADABLE DIRECTLY INTO YOUR COMPUTER

"Some common filings by public companies and mutual funds that you can find at the Securities and Exchange Commission's (SEC) Edgar site on the Internet global computer network:

- ❏ **S-1:** Registration of stock, includes financial tables . . .
- ❏ **DEF 14A:** Definitive proxy statement . . .
- ❏ **DEFC14A:** Someone is trying to gain control of the company . . .
- ❏ **8-K:** Recent events . . . acquisitions, change in control, resignations . . .
- ❏ **10-K:** Year-end annual report . . .
- ❏ **10-Q:** Quarterly report . . .
- ❏ **497:** Mutual fund prospectus. . . . Form 485BPOS contains changes and updates.
- ❏ **N-30D:** Annual and semiannual reports mailed to mutual fund shareholders.
- ❏ **N-30B-2:** Periodic and interim reports mailed to mutual fund shareholders.

SOURCE: Sandra Block, "SEC's Dull but Detailed Edgar: On-Line Site Cumbersome but a Wealth of Information," *USA Today* (May 24, 1996).

Disclosure Incorporated

For practically immediate delivery in a user-friendly format, check out the Disclosure Website. They have 4 million filings from 27,000 U.S. and international companies, and have accumulated SEC filings dating back to 1968. For $5 you can get any filing at the Disclosure Website as well as Intuit's NETworth Website, and online at AOL, CompuServe, and Microsoft Network.

EDGAR Online

Here's another early pipeline to the electronic SEC filings. The fee even includes e-mail alerts on key companies and mutual funds. If time is not critical—and you don't mind the long download times or the 24-hour delay—and the document is not available from the fund itself in a timely manner, you can always just wait until tomorrow and get the information free from the SEC.

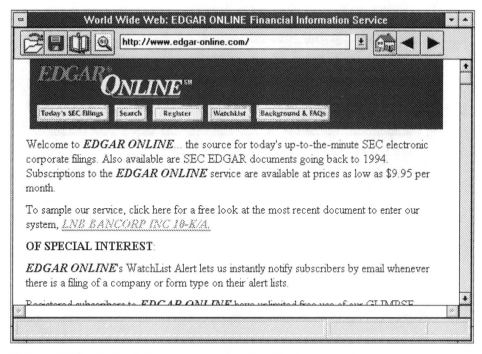

Figure 5.24   Edgar Online: current securities filings and alerts.

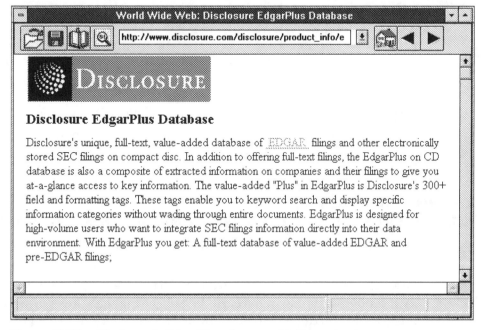

Figure 5.25   Disclosure's EdgarPlus: formatted full-text database.

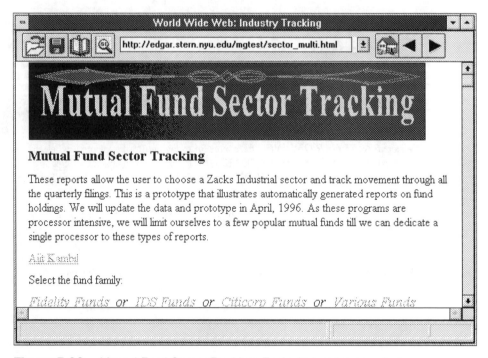

Figure 5.26   Mutual Fund Sector Tracking: Zacks industrial groupings.

One final note on EDGAR and prospectuses: The EDGAR system is not a fund-screening tool. As yet, EDGAR won't help you compare and select one fund over another. That you must do first with the kind of power tools discussed in Chapter 6. EDGAR will, however, supply you with the backup data on specific funds, once you have screened a database and have one or more funds to investigate further.

Spend the money and do the research. With today's brokerage commissions costing almost as little as a couple of research reports, it might be easy to skip paying for the right analytical reports. Don't fall into that trap.

BOTTOM LINE: CYBERSPACE IS THE PERFECT RESEARCH LIBRARY FOR MUTUAL FUND INVESTORS

Cyberspace is indeed transferring power to the individual investor. Remember: Almost all of the information in this survey of the key mutual fund databases was *not* electronically available to the do-it-yourself investor until very recently, beginning in the early 1990s. The big Wall Street firms, money managers, and brokerage firms controlled all the data and had all the power tools.

READ THE PROSPECTUS . . . EVEN THE FIVE STARS AND TOP GUNS!

You have direct access to one of the most important databases available, the legal prospectus the fund must file with the SEC. They're also required by law to send you one, and you'll get one eventually, or sooner if you want.

However, in this age of fast food, 30-second commercials, and quick fixes, it's easy for a busy investor to conclude that if a fund's got five stars from Morningstar and favorable write-ups in *Fortune* and *Kiplinger's* magazines—hey, that's enough reason to buy now.

Download the prospectus and read it anyway.

Compare all the boring legalese with the summaries prepared by one or two of the independent rating agencies. And how does it fit with the asset allocations in your plan?

Here's a checklist of the key points to look for in the prospectus. Remember, the key facts are usually right up front with the turgid details filling the rest of the document.

❑ **Investment objective and policies.** Determine for yourself what kind of fund you're investing, and don't be misled by its name and the buzzword it uses to categorize itself. Is it what it says it is? Is that what you're looking for?

❑ **Performance history.** Read the descriptive text for a broad picture and explanation of its performance. Review the financial data for distributions, yield, total return, turnover, income ratio, and its net asset value over time. How's it doing versus market indexes?

❑ **Expenses.** Check the transaction fees, management and other annual operating costs, and how the expenses compare to its peers in the same class.

❑ **Risks and restrictions.** Here's where the hype is filtered out, and they tell how they can lose your money, depending on various types of risks—market, credit, interest, economic, management.

❑ **Management.** Who are these people, and how are they doing? How long have they been with the fund? Are they the actual managers responsible for the fund's performance? What's their career track record?

❑ **Taxes:** For sure, check when they distribute dividends and capital gains.

❑ **Portfolio assets.** Check out the diversity. How well do they match the fund's stated objective and your asset allocation needs?

Do your homework. Make it a habit. Yes, most of the time it's just a dull, mechanical exercise. But every now and then it'll pay off by revealing an exceptionally good deal or protecting you from a big loser.

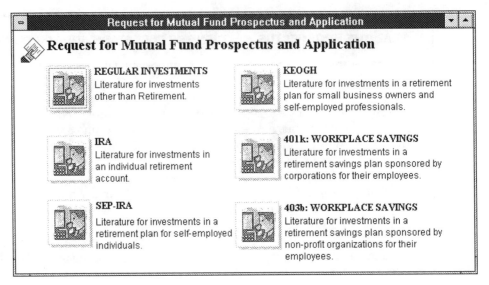

Figure 5.27 Request for Mutual Fund Prospectus on AOL.

It has been only in the past few years that Main Street investors have had the same access to information as the professionals. Today the playing field is leveling, because technology is advancing so rapidly that *everyone*—individual investors and institutional money managers—has access to the same information, instantly.

In fact, mutual fund investors in cyberspace now have a definite edge in the game, simply because almost all of the key databases can now be accessed electronically, online, and on the Net. It's no longer necessary to use antiquated delivery systems to access essential data. For example, do any of the following old practices sound familiar?

- ❐ Wall Street brokers still charging big commissions for common knowledge

- ❐ Financial and business magazine surveys hyping top guns and five-star winners

- ❐ Advisory newsletters loaded with ambiguities and delivered by snail mail

- ❐ Newspapers reprinting endless columns of raw, cryptic data in small type

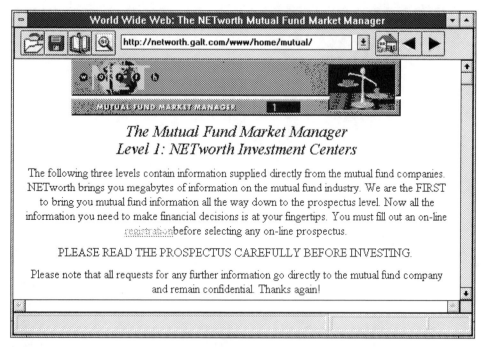

Figure 5.28   Please Read the Prospectus Carefully Before Investing.

Of course, some of the information received through these pre-Web, telecommunications delivery channels is still helpful. However, today, the *exact same* information from the *exact same* sources is available almost *immediately* online and on the Web, at prices any investor can afford. And the reason is very simple: *competition.* As we've seen in this chapter, the key mutual fund databases are now giving you a choice by offering you instant cyberspace delivery of the data you need for successful investing directly into your computer terminal. So take time to explore the database alternatives identified here.

Very soon, *all* investment decisions will be made in cyberspace, using the exploding array of new electronic investing technologies coming on the market in the past couple years. And to make it real easy, you can get ahead of the curve now by knowing who has the key data you need and how to get it into your computer quickly, easily, and cheaply. After that, successful mutual fund investing is just a mouse click away.

Using the Best Power Tools:
Software, Online, and Internet

How to Pick the Right Cyberspace
Technologies and Build a Portfolio of Funds

Working with the right software and online services is crucial to building a successful portfolio. In step 6 we focus on the major power tools that will help you sift through 8,000 mutual funds to find the ones that best fit the asset-allocation strategy in your personal financial plan. These computerized power tools include commercial online services, Internet Websites, and offline software.

INFORMATION OVERLOAD! THE PARADIGM SHIFTS FROM TOO LITTLE INFORMATION TO TOO MUCH INFORMATION!

Today's independent investors now have virtually unlimited instant access to all of the principal databanks covering the mutual fund industry. Moreover, you can easily get the information by downloading it from commercial dial-up services, by linking to hundreds of Internet Websites, or by having CD-ROM updates mailed to you monthly. Moreover, the price of the data is relatively cheap, thanks to the intense competition among database publishers.

In less than a decade, do-it-yourself investors have gone from having *too little* information from online, electronic, and cyberspace sources to being overloaded with *too much* information! And yes, it's a common complaint I hear from most of today's investors, even those with extensive online and Internet experience.

YES, YOU CAN BEAT WALL STREET'S BIG-MONEY MANAGERS

"Think like an amateur as frequently as possible. . . . You don't have to invest like an institution. If you invest like an institution, you're doomed to perform like one, which in many cases isn't very well. . . . If you're a surfer, a trucker, a high school dropout, or an eccentric retiree, then you've got an edge already.

SOURCE: Peter Lynch, *One Up On Wall Street* (Penguin, 1989).

"Fund managers' records aren't all that impressive: fewer than 30% of all U.S. diversified equity funds beat Standard & Poor's 500-stock index, the best measure of large-stock performance, over the past year. . . . When you become your own portfolio manager, you're in control and can take satisfaction in your investing prowess."

SOURCE: Gregory Spears, "Ready to Buy Your Own Stocks?," *Kiplinger's Personal Finance Magazine* (November 1995).

NEW SOLUTIONS:
NEW TECHNOLOGIES EMERGING TO HANDLE DATA OVERLOAD

However, most serious cyberspace investors actually welcome this new problem of cyberspace information overload. Why? Because along with the high-tech delivery systems that link you to these established databases, there are also currently available many new technologies—powerful analytical software designed for your computer—to manipulate the electronic data and manage your portfolio.

Today, using these incredible new power tools—previously available only to the elite Wall Street institutional money managers at substantially inflated costs—any investor can easily sift through mountains of raw data, reduce it to valuable information, filter out the junk, and quickly target the right funds that will best fit into his or her portfolio strategies.

THE WORLD'S BEST SOFTWARE AND ONLINE POWER TOOLS
FOR MUTUAL FUNDS . . . RIGHT ON YOUR COMPUTER

Today the competition is so fierce that the individual investor can't help but profit substantially from the resulting improvements in analytic software, not to mention the substantial cost reductions. After decades of neglecting the individual investor in favor of the Wall Street institutions willing to pay big bucks for data, the World Wide Web and the PC have opened a major new gateway *from* the major financial data vendors *to* the Main Street investor.

Not only the database vendors, but also offline software developers, commercial online services, discount brokers, Internet Websites, electronic magazines, investors associations, and other organizations are jumping into the competition. In the process, prices are being driven down, and the analytical software is now becoming so powerful that much of it is superior to what was available to the large institutional investors less than a decade ago.

In the remainder of this chapter our goal is simply to identify the top cyberspace power tools available specifically for mutual fund investors. We will review their main features and give you a general editorial evaluation of how each of these software tools ranks among their peers.

While it's possible we may have overlooked some excellent products, we believe that the ones included in this collection represent about 95 percent of the online and software resources actually purchased and now in use by individual do-it-yourself investors.

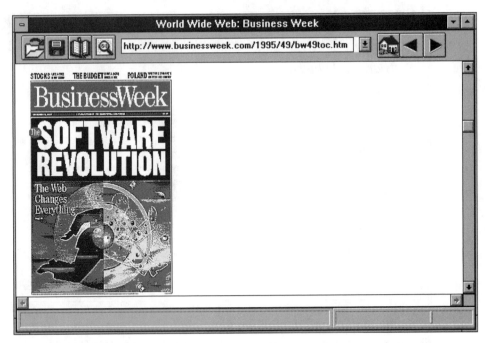

Figure 6.1 *BusinessWeek* online: financial intelligence leading the curve.

EVALUATION CRITERIA:
FIVE TIPS TO HELP YOU EVALUATE THESE NEW SYSTEMS

When you "look under the hood" and compare the pros and cons of these various power tools, there are five basic analytical functions that are important to keep in mind:

1. **Database Coverage**
   The database should include information on all stock and bond funds, now around 8,000. For limited purposes you may choose to work with a smaller, more select database, such as a Fidelity-only program; there are some such systems online and on the Web that offer very narrow databases. Just be aware that they may limit your research and your opportunities.

2. **Fund Information Available**
   The number of data fields provided by the system is important. The fewer line items of data available, the more restrictive your opportunities in the actual screening of the total database. Sample schedules are included later. Data fields will include management and objective, fund performance for key periods from year-to-date (YTD) to 10 years

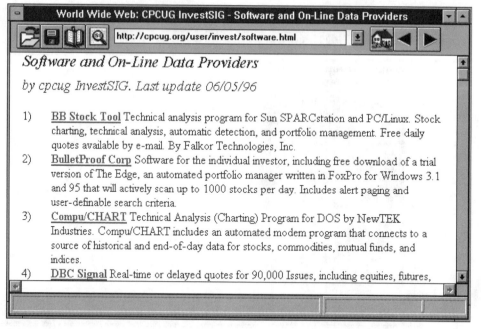

Figure 6.2 InvestSIG Directory: Software and On-Line Data Providers.

or more, risk measures, major holdings in portfolio, costs, load and management expenses, and so forth.

3. **Screening Criteria Power**

   The best systems and programs allow you to set your own particular variables and criteria for screening. For example, you may target only a particular sector of no-loads with specified minimum annual returns and maximum expenses. The screening function will then isolate the ones that fit your set of criteria, so you can do more detailed research. Check the maximum criteria handled on one screen.

4. **Portfolio Management**

   In addition to screening the database and analyzing specific funds, the program should have the power to monitor at least one portfolio of assets, including reevaluating the assets in your portfolio to current market value, distributions, and so forth. It should also include some basic performance benchmarks comparing your portfolio with various market indexes.

5. **Integrated Navigational System**

   The better systems currently being developed and marketed either perform all the essential tasks of investing from a single navigator on your computer or, better yet, are so well designed that they are seamlessly integrated with other components of an integrated system, with ease of importing and exporting information for trading, market updates, and inputting current quotes.

There are still some DOS-based programs available. However, the Windows-based programs now dominate this software market. One old DOS favorite, *BusinessWeek Mutual Fund Scoreboard,* was retired in the first quarter last year. Today's independent investors are now being offered some truly exceptional software packages to help them build successful mutual fund portfolios.

NEW COMPETITION FROM POWERFUL OFFLINE SOFTWARE SYSTEMS

When upstart Morningstar bolted onto the mutual fund scene in the early 1980s, Value Line had been around for over 50 years helping individual investors analyze securities.

MONEYMAG.COM: THE TOP-FOUR FUND-SCREENING PACKAGES CAN HELP YOU AVOID PAYING BROKERS FOR THE SAME ADVICE

"What these programs do, with varying degrees of success, is let you search for funds that meet your personal criteria ... two from Morningstar, the Chicago-based firm that supplies mutual fund data to *Money:* the top-of-the-line **Principia Plus** and a cheaper alternative, **Ascent.** The third contender, **Fund Analyzer,** is put out by rival mutual fund data warehouse Value Line. The independent challenger is **Mutual Fund Expert,** from the financial-software firm Steele Systems."

None of the competitors "adequately address such basic concerns as what a reasonable expense ratio might be, the merits of no-load versus load funds of allocating money among different funds. . . . Though it lacks that online capability, Morningstar's Principia Plus is still the best performer . . .

"If you are mainly interested in no-load fund data, you will probably prefer the no-load version of Fund Analyzer. . . . Choosing no-loads, of course, makes all the more sense once you've invested in software to help you do the choosing. Otherwise, you may be paying a broker or financial advisor merely to consult the very same program that's loaded on your machine."

SOURCE: Eric Tyson, "These Programs Can Help You Pick The Best Funds to Squirrel Away," *Money* magazine (August 1996).

Morningstar proceeded to carve out a niche in the fledgling mutual funds market. As recent as 1984, the total assets invested in mutual funds was less than $500 billion, smaller than the total currently invested in the combined Fidelity and Vanguard funds.

In 1993 Value Line finally decided to get in the game and compete with Morningstar for the explosive mutual funds data and rating service business. The battle is becoming very heated.

Last year, both organizations introduced new software programs—Morningstar's Principia and Value Line's Mutual Fund Analyzer. Fortunately, both are now making do-it-yourself investing much easier. In separate reviews comparing the two in *Barron's* and *Individual Investor,* two financial journalists who follow the cutting edge of cyberspace on a regular basis came to the same conclusion.

ROUND ONE: MORNINGSTAR VERSUS VALUE LINE SOFTWARE
FINANCIAL EXPERTS DISCOVER A "CLEAR WINNER"

Barron's columnist Howard Gold recently noted, "Both contain vast amounts of information—maybe too much data," and concluded that "Morningstar's package is user-friendly, but Value Line's gives more for the money . . . when price is considered, Fund Analyzer is a clear winner. For $395 a year, you get monthly CD-ROM updates, online access and Value Line's reports. For the same price, you get Principia, but not Morningstar's reports, which are *$400 more!* Morningstar's reports are better, but twice as good? I don't think so."

SOURCE: Howard Gold, "The Electronic Investor," *Barron's* (March 4, 1996).

Wayne Harris, the cyberspace technology columnist for *Individual Investor* magazine, observed that "New CD-ROMs from Morningstar and Value Line help the individual investor make sense of fund investing . . . both offerings sort and screen according to countless criteria and compare the results against dozens of indexes. They can even determine the risk/reward profile of a portfolio of funds. . . . Principia looks better, but Fund Analyzer's easier navigation system makes it the clear winner."

SOURCE: Wayne Harris, "Investors Online," *Individual Investor* (May 1996).

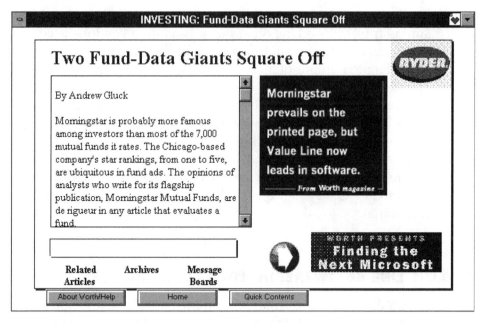

Figure 6.3 *Worth* online: Two Data-Fund Giants Square Off.

Interestingly, both of these experts concluded that Value Line's Fund Analyzer was the "clear winner." In reality, we could say that both systems are clear winners, because both are light-years ahead of previously available software packages. Better yet, in the final analysis, the ultimate clear winner is the do-it-yourself investor, with all this new technological firepower right there at the click of a mouse.

COMPETITION UPGRADES MUTUAL FUND SOFTWARE: DO-IT-YOURSELF INVESTORS GET MORE POWER, FASTER, CHEAPER

What we have here are two superior mutual fund data/software vendors, Value Line and Morningstar, who are engaging in an intense competition that, within a brief year or two, will result in the cyberspace investor having a choice between the second or third versions of these two fine software systems.

By then we'll probably discover that the two systems are remarkably similar in functions to satisfy investor needs. And by then both are likely to be discounted even further from current prices, particularly when the pressure is applied by all the other major fund data vendors listed below who are hungry and also want *their* piece of the market, all chasing a market exploding to millions of investors going online and on the Web in the next couple years.

New cyberspace technologies are rapidly providing the Main Street do-it-yourself investor with all the power tools necessary to make them truly independent of the Wall Street Establishment. Meanwhile, Wall Street firms remain tradition-bound, locked in an old paradigm, focused on keeping investors dependent on their advice, a working model that's no longer valid today as we enter a period that John Naisbitt calls the "Age of the Individual."

1. VALUE LINE SOFTWARE: NO-LOAD FUND ANALYZER

Both Value Line Fund Analyzer and Morningstar's Principia operate from a spreadsheet format. When initially confronted with the two programs—at 123 and 98 columns of information, respectively—even the more experienced investors may feel overwhelmed and intimidated. However, you'll quickly discover that with a couple mouse clicks, both systems allow you to customize their layouts to fit your special set of screening criteria, which should help you graduate quickly from confused novice to an in-charge, top-gun fund analyzer.

Not surprisingly, both organizations have also developed less expensive, scaled-down versions of their high-powered systems by removing some of the bells and whistles, making them either add-on extras or part of the upgrade to the full-service product. You will find screen and sort functions, performance evaluation and tracking, profile reports on funds and groups of funds, graphic comparisons, and some online updates and news.

The Value Line's budget product is the No-Load Analyzer. The price is so low that AAII and other organizations may have a hard time competing. The No-Load Analyzer starter kit is only $29 a month and $95 for quarterly updates or $195 for the monthly updates. The systems has limits, however. The No-Load Analyzer is limited to a database of 1,800 no-load and low-load funds. One major advantage: "unique ratings of both funds *and fund manager* performance."

	Value Screen.Funds - C:\VALUELIN\JPMORGAN.UNV					

File   Edit   Select   Tools   Portfolio   Reports   View   Help

Go-To [ ]   Dbl Clk [$10,000 Growth ▼]   View [Show All Columns ▼]   Filter [All]

	Fund Name	Obj	Objective Description	Ticker	Inception Date
1138	Fidelity Asset Manager: Income	AA	AssetAlloc	FASIX	1992-10-01
1139	Fidelity Balanced Fund	BA	Balanced	FBALX	1986-11-06
1140	Fidelity Blue Chip Growth Fund	GR	Growth	FBGRX	1987-12-31
1141	Fidelity CA Insured Muni Inc Fund	MC	Muni CA	FCXIX	1986-09-18
1142	Fidelity CA Muni Income Fund	MC	Muni CA	FCTFX	1984-07-07
1143	Fidelity Canada Fund	FO	Foreign	FICDX	1987-11-17
1144	Fidelity Capital & Income Fund	CH	Corp-HY	FAGIX	1977-11-01
1145	Fidelity Capital Appreciation	AG	Agg Growth	FDCAX	1986-11-26
1146	Fidelity Congress Street Fund	GR	Growth	CNGRX	1960-08-12
1147	Fidelity Contrafund	GR	Growth	FCNTX	1967-05-17
1148	Fidelity Convertible Securities	CV	Converts	FCVSX	1987-01-05
1149	Fidelity Destiny I	GR	Growth	FDESX	1970-07-10
1150	Fidelity Destiny II	GR	Growth	FDETX	1985-12-30
1151	Fidelity Deutsche Mark Performance	IB	Intl Bond		1989-11-16
1152	Fidelity Disciplined Equity Fund	GR	Growth	FDEQX	1988-12-28

Database view	Monthly data as of 2/28/1996	Weekly data as of 3/6/1996	4667 Funds

Figure 6.4   Value Line No-Load Fund Analyzer: database screen.

Fund Profile	

Last Page: 1
Record Count: 1   Current Page: 1

Fidelity Contrafund

	Ticker	Objective	NAV
	FCNTX	GR	$37.11

Ranks

Overall	2
Risk	3
1 Year Growth Persistence	3
5 Year Growth Persistence	1

Management Style Correlations

Large Value	-.21
Large Growth	-.04
Small Value	.31
Small Growth	.52

Latest Performance %

Yield	.02
Year-to-Date	2.89
1 Month	.60
3 Months	3.54
6 Months	6.24
12 Months	36.72
3 Years	17.40
5 Years	20.64
10 Years	18.48
Bull Market	232.12
Bear Market	-11.76
1987 Crash	-34.16

Current MPT Statistics

3 Yr. Beta	
5 Yr. Beta	
10 Yr. Beta	
3 Yr. Alpha	
5 Yr. Alpha	
10 Yr. Alpha	
3 Yr. R-Square	
5 Yr. R-Square	
10 Yr. R-Square	
3 Yr. Standard Dev.	
5 Yr. Standard Dev.	
10 Year Standard Dev.	

Annual Performance

	1986	1987	1988	1989	1990	1991	1992	1993
Total Return %	13.31	-1.90	21.02	43.16	3.93	54.91	15.90	21.42
NAV $ (Adjusted)	7.11	8.46	7.60	8.77	11.44	14.52	20.23	22.93
Beta	1.04	1.09	1.09	1.11	.90	1.00	1.00	1.08
Alpha	-7.70	-5.30	-2.59	1.27	7.29	11.78	11.30	11.55
R-Square	.83	.91	.91	.92	.90	.90	.87	.78
Standard Deviation	16.83	23.80	23.38	22.48	13.51	16.67	15.86	13.10

[Close]   [Print...] [Help]

Figure 6.5   Fund Profile in Value Line No-Load Fund Analyzer.

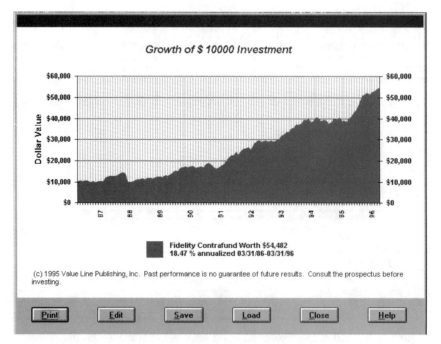

Figure 6.6   No-Load Fund Analyzer: historical performance.

Fund Holdings Report

Last Page: 1
Record Count: 1   Current Page: 1

Portfolio Holdings Report

Fidelity Contrafund

Data as
1995-06-

Name	Shares	Value ($ 000's)
INTERNATIONAL BUSINESS MACHS COM	3,800,000	364,800.00
INTEL CORP COM	3,495,000	221,277.00
GENERAL MTRS CORP COM	3,899,819	182,804.00
MICROSOFT CORP COM	1,850,000	167,194.00
PHILIP MORRIS COS INC COM	2,145,000	159,534.00
HEWLETT PACKARD CO COM	1,750,000	130,375.00
LSI LOGIC CORP COM	3,250,000	127,156.00
MICRON TECHNOLOGY INC COM	2,000,000	109,750.00
SCOTT PAPER CO COM	2,175,000	107,663.00
PHILIPS ELECTRS N V NEW YORK SHS	2,510,000	107,303.00
CHRYSLER CORP COM	2,149,200	102,893.00
MERRILL LYNCH & CO INC COM	1,911,000	100,328.00
FEDERAL NATL MTG ASSN COM	1,025,000	96,734.00
TEXAS INSTRS INC COM	718,400	96,176.00
SUN MICROSYSTEM INC COM	1,904,600	92,373.00
SILICON GRAPHICS INC COM	2,250,000	89,719.00

Figure 6.7   Value Line No-Load Fund Analyzer: portfolio assets.

2. MORNINGSTAR SOFTWARE: PRINCIPIA AND ASCENT

Morningstar's new Ascent is "the personal mutual-fund software program that's as simple as it is powerful," which makes the Ascent system a great starter kit for the individual mutual fund investor, a modified version of their superpowered Principia software. Morningstar's ads make it sound almost too easy, because it is.

> "Zero in on the funds you're looking for. If you'd like to see all 5-star, small-cap value funds that had an average total return of 20% *and* the same manager for the past five years, your list is a few mouse clicks away . . ."

> "Really understand what a fund is all about—Morningstar's star ratings show you how each fund balances risk with return. And our revealing style boxes show you each fund's true investment approach."

> "You can create graphs that compare fund performance and illustrate volatility . . . then print them out [with] detailed one-page summary reports for each fund, and custom summary reports for any group of funds."

With Ascent you get the first Windows-based platform designed specifically for individual investors, with the complete Morningstar database of about 8,000 funds and the ability to screen on 70 variables.

Seventy! That's overkill, many will say. But as the state of the art advances, and as more and more of the universe of 42 million mutual fund investors with improved skills begin researching online and trading on the Web, the investors with the edge, the winners, are likely to begin using more sophisticated screening criteria on a regular basis.

Ascent's cost is reasonable: just $45 for the initial disk or CD-ROM database and software, only $95 for quarterly updates, matching Value Line's budget system, but with more coverage, and $195 for the monthly updates. Compared to the full-scaled program, Principia, a large part of the savings comes from making the famed Morningstar Reports on individual funds an add-on charge that actually doubles the cost of Ascent. Given time, Morningstar is likely to get more competitive on price.

One final note: Make sure you have an extra 25MB on your hard drive—you'll need it. And remember, like most other initial promotions of software systems today, you can get Ascent on a 30-day trial offer.

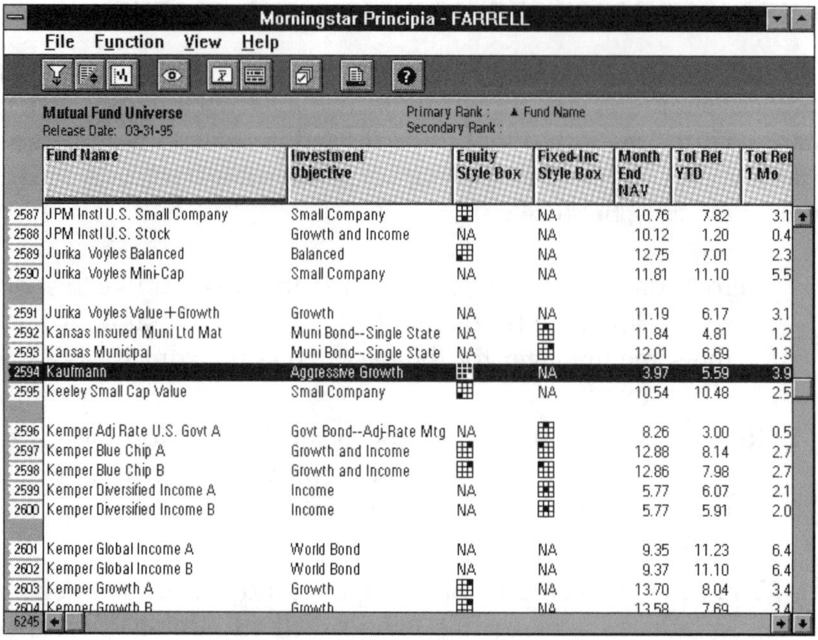

Figure 6.8 Morningstar Principia: screening total database.

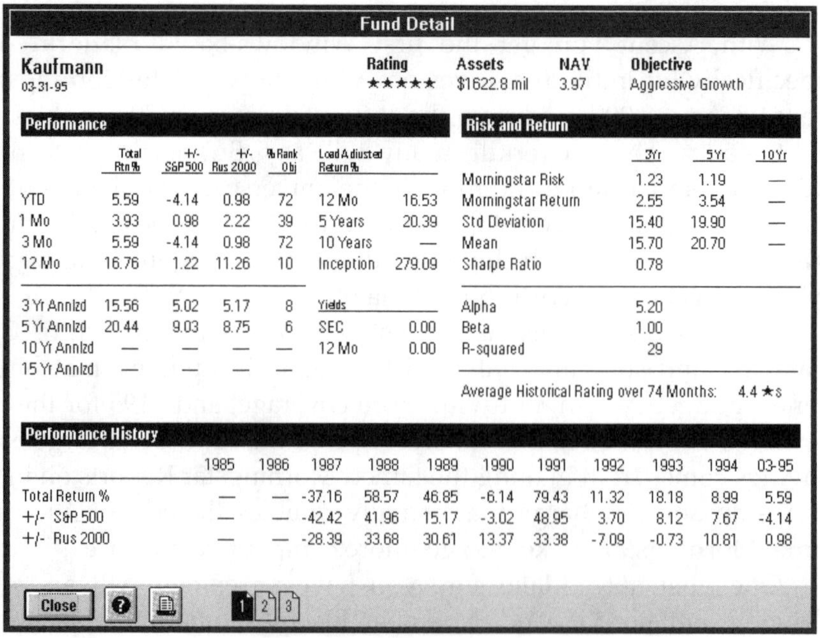

Figure 6.9 Morningstar fund details: performance and risk/return.

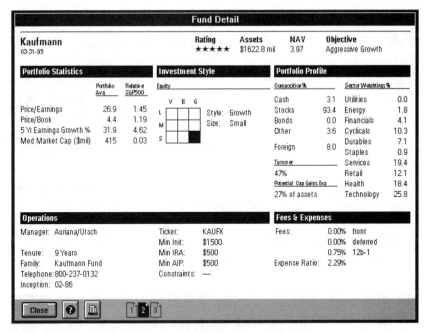

Figure 6.10   Principia fund details: statistics, profile, style.

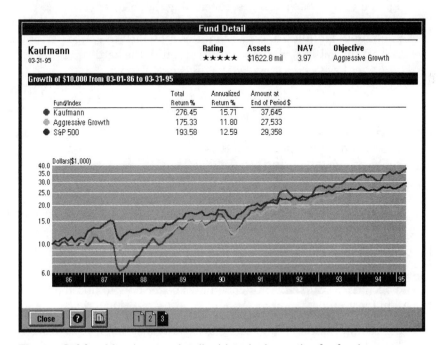

Figure 6.11   Morningstar details: historical growth of a fund.

3. STEELE SYSTEMS: MUTUAL FUND EXPERT SOFTWARE

Steele Systems Mutual Fund Expert software is solidly grounded in the Micropal database, the same database used by *Kiplinger's Personal Finance Magazine, U.S. News & World Report,* and the American Association of Individual Investors. Steele's Expert software is in wide use among many professionals at Merrill Lynch, Smith Barney, Dean Witter, PaineWebber, Prudential, Chase Manhattan . . . and the list of satisfied clients goes on. Micropal is an international leader in mutual fund information with a strong U.S. following.

In Kiplinger's annual, *Mutual Funds '96,* Steele Systems gave away the personal version 4.5 of its software package, which includes:

❐ 10-year performance track records of more than 7,400 funds, including stock, bond, and money market funds

---

BUSINESSWEEK: STEELE'S EXPERT IS "HANDS-DOWN WINNER"

Before Value Line debuted with its new system, *BusinessWeek* compared eight other software packages, concluding that Steele Systems Expert was "the hands-down winner. . . . Compared to Principia, Expert has stronger graphing capabilities, and more indices by which to gauge performance. And at 3 megabytes, Expert requires one-fifth the hard-drive space."

Other key systems reviewed by *BusinessWeek:*

❐ **AAII's Quarterly Mutual Fund Update** . . . Good value, but clunky interface. $50/year for quarterly updates . . .
❐ **Schwab's FundMap** . . . $25 . . . will recommend an asset-allocation plan and even specific funds.
❐ **Morningstar's Principia** . . . $395/year . . .
❐ **Quicken's Mutual Fund Selector** . . . replaced by its Mutual Fund Finder program in Deluxe 6.0 and Investor Insight online service.
❐ **Investors FastTrack** . . . $288/year; DOS, technical analysis for timers.
❐ **Manhattan Analytics' Monocle:** $149 plus $240/year; more timing . . .

"When it comes to choosing a mutual fund, you now have more tools to decide for yourself. And who knows better how to find the fund that's right for you?"

SOURCE: Amy Dunkin, "Using Your PC to Pick a Mutual Fund," *BusinessWeek* (August 28, 1995).

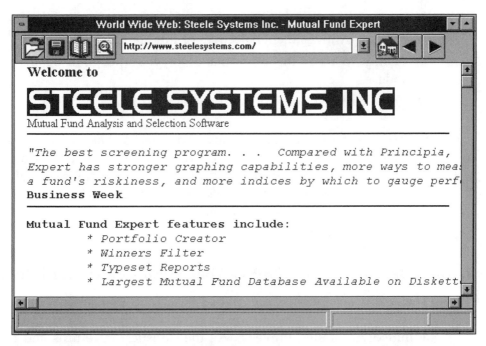

Figure 6.12   Steele Systems Mutual Fund Expert: Micropal database.

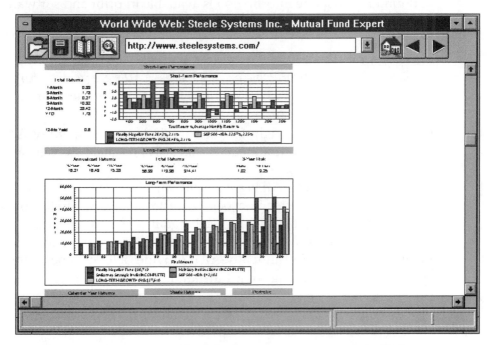

Figure 6.13   Steele Mutual Fund Expert: sample screens on the Web.

❏ Search and screening functions to help you select and rank the top performers by investment objectives or fund family

❏ Ability to track the performance of your portfolio against market indexes

❏ Test alternative strategies and model portfolios

Expert's database is updated monthly or quarterly on disks. *BusinessWeek* has rated the Expert software a "hands-down winner" over Morningstar and several other power hitters in this ball diamond. Check out Steele's Expert. It may be just what you need. It's definitely a winner with the pros, the press, and 4,000 satisfied customers.

4. AAII SOFTWARE: LOW-LOAD MUTUAL FUND QUARTERLY UPDATE

The AAII *Guide to Low-Load Mutual Funds* and its *Low-Load Mutual Fund Quarterly* both provide information on less than 1,000 mutual funds, admittedly a limited universe. All the statistics on returns and risks are provided by Micropal. Fund information is extracted from prospectuses and fund reports. The information is available in print and software. *BusinessWeek* concludes:

> On price alone—$50 for four quarterly updates (and just $39 for AAII members), vs. $100 for Principia or Expert—AAII's program is a bargain. The tradeoff, a clunky interface written in the FoxPro database program.

Clunky, but the price is right for the bargain hunter. Hopefully, AAII will be coming out with an updated version soon, on their Website, and with other software services.

Keep in mind that AAII is a *nonprofit,* members-only organization supporting the small investor in cyberspace. It operates with absolute integrity. If anyone is going to uncover bargain-basement services, you can count on AAII to do it. And while you're at it, join the organization. Full membership is only $49 annually. AAII provides a lot of benefits for cyberspace investors, including some outstanding publications:

❏ *The Guide to Computerized Investing,* covering every system in cyberspace

❏ *Computerized Investing,* a bimonthly newsletter on the cutting edge

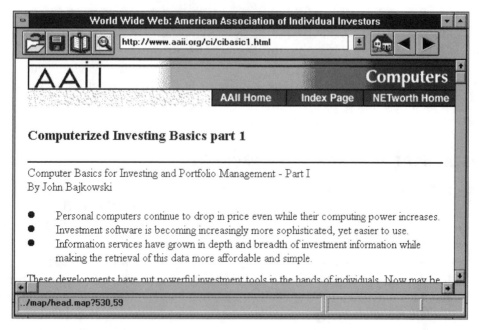

Figure 6.14   American Association of Individual Investors on the Web.

Figure 6.15   AAII's Personal Finance Software Center on America Online.

Bottom line: If you're content with a limited universe of funds and a clunky format, contact AAII in cyberspace, on the Web, and at America Online. The price is right, and the benefits are enormous for the independent investor. In fact, every individual investor in the world should be a member of the American Association of Individual Investors, in spirit *and in fact.*

5. TELECHART 2000 SOFTWARE PACKAGE

Over the years, the Worden Brothers' TeleChart 2000 organization has carved out a special niche with the technical analysts' crowd. And lately, one of its key periodicals, *Technical Analysis of Stocks and Commodities,* has awarded TC 2000 top honors for mutual funds data.

And yes, you might wonder quite rightly: Is an analytical software system that's oriented toward technical analysis and *short-term* market timing right for a mutual fund investor committed to building a *long-term* portfolio. Obviously, there is a fundamental, and possibly even ethical, conflict underlying these two strategic approaches. Moreover, the comparative performance of technicians has been frequently questioned. *BusinessWeek* has this to say:

> *Academic researchers have cast doubts on whether timing outperforms a buy-and-hold strategy. But many disciples of technical analysis—as much a religion as a cold science—swear by their individual success, particularly over the short run.*

Nevertheless, putting aside this dilemma, the fact remains that there is clearly a sizable share of the investment community who, for many reasons, prefer to use technical analysis. For many, technical analysis is their primary and even sole method of decision making. For others, it is an alternative perspective, a second opinion, a way of double-checking the results of some fundamental research. In either case, this market must be respected and will be served by TC 2000 and other organizations.

Besides, TC 2000 is a bargain: The initial CD-ROM has historical data on 14,000 stocks, funds, and averages—all for $30, and updates are less than $1 a day for unlimited charts. At that price, it may be worth it just to get a second opinion, even if you're not a believer in market timing and technical analysis.

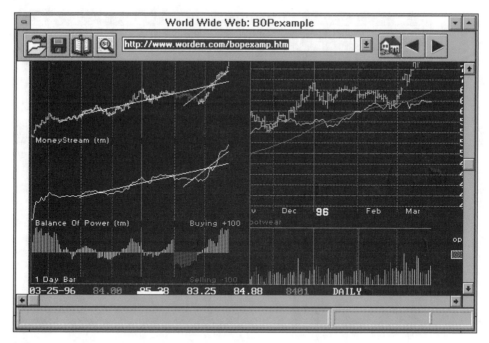

Figure 6.16 TeleChart 2000: sample screen on its Website.

THE NEW ONE-STOP NAVIGATORS
ARE INTEGRATING ONLINE SERVICES WITH OFF-LINE SOFTWARE

Until recently there appeared to be a consensus among reviewers suggesting that *offline* software packages were superior to *online* and Website systems. That may have been true with the earlier cyberspace systems. They performed limited tasks and chugged along with long download times. By comparison, the software systems were definitely more powerful, with more features, more data-manipulation power, and all designed to operate on high-speed computers.

However, that consensus may be dissolving soon, as online and Web technologies advance. The decision confronting the cyberspace investor is no longer an either-or choice between software systems on one hand and online/Website packages on the other. The reason is very simple: The emerging new generation is supplying investors with *integrated* packages specifically designed to use the *best of both worlds,* complementing one another. For example, consider the combination of Reuters Money Net-

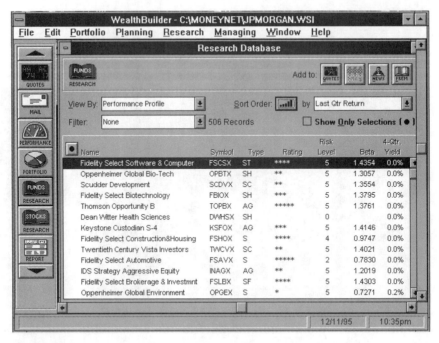

Figure 6.17   Reuters Money Network: screening mutual funds.

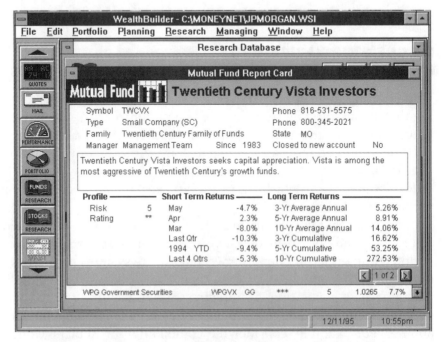

Figure 6.18   Mutual Fund Report Card on Reuters Money Network.

work for financial planning and portfolio management, Quicken Deluxe with their Mutual Fund Finder and its Morningstar database, and Schwab's StreetSmart package for trading the market.

Today's advanced systems are either plug-and-play modules that integrate and work with other major products . . . or they're history. Let's look at the key players that have emerged in the market for the do-it-yourself cyberspace investor.

6. REUTERS MONEY NETWORK AND WEALTHBUILDER: NEW, TOTALLY INTEGRATED NAVIGATIONAL SYSTEM

The mutual fund analytical tools in Reuters navigational system use the Morningstar database. In a few short years, Reuters International, a $3.5 billion information giant and pioneer in financial cyberspace, has made several rapid moves to penetrate the individual investor market. Consider these strategic actions by Reuters since 1994:

Fundamental Analysis Online and Websites

Acquisition of Reality Online, a commercial online service targeting the do-it-yourself market with market quotes, financial news updates, fundamental analysis, and a portfolio manager.

Personal Financial Planner

Along with Reality Online, Reuters also acquired WealthBuilder, the personal financial planner originally developed in conjunction with Time Warner's *Money* magazine, a software product for retirement planning, asset allocating, stock and mutual fund analysis, and portfolio strategizing.

Electronic Discount Trading

The newly named Reuters Money Network began expanding by customizing, "private labeling" as they called it, its investor software for several discount brokers who were expanding online and on the Web as *full-service electronic brokers*. This move may well make the Reuters Money Network software the standard for the brokerage industry and the most popular investor's cyberspace navigator.

REUTERS MONEY NETWORK: INTEGRATED ONE-STOP NAVIGATOR

- ☐ **Morningstar mutual funds:** Database of 7,000 mutual funds.
- ☐ **Investment portfolio management:** WealthBuilder and others.
- ☐ **Financial and market news:** Reuters, Dow Jones & other newswires.
- ☐ **S&P Comstock quotes:** Major exchanges domestic & worldwide.
- ☐ **Standard & Poor's company research:** Over 10,000 stocks & bonds.
- ☐ **Personal financial planning:** WealthBuilder and Quicken.
- ☐ **Investment newsletters:** Zacks Analyst Watch, S&P Outlook, etc.
- ☐ **Discount trading:** Schwab, PCFN, QuickWay, AccuTrade, and others.
- ☐ **Instant data retrieval:** Access on total 24-hour availability.

Reuters base charge is $25/month. And several of the services include additional subscriber fees and one-time charges. However, all are integrated into this one single software platform, operating online and on the Web.

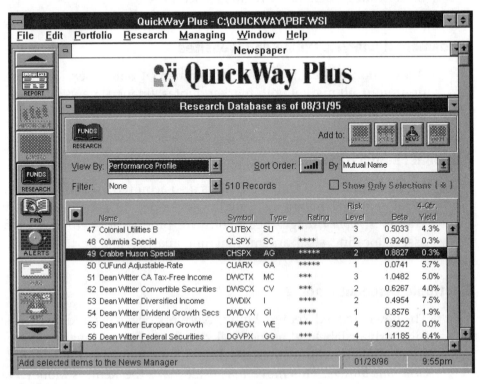

Figure 6.19   Quick & Reilly's version of Reuters Money Network.

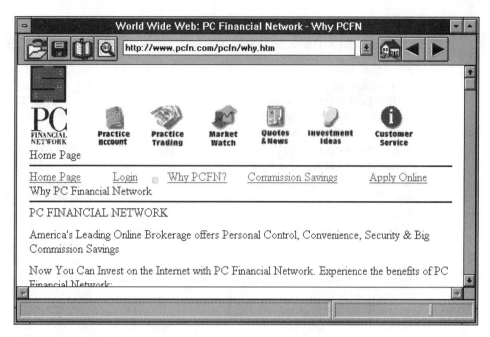

Figure 6.20   PCFN: online trading plus Reuters Money Network.

Technical Analysis Software

Recently, Reuters acquired Equis, the software developer of MetaStock, the world's most popular *technical analysis* system, thus beefing up the *fundamental* research power of Reuters Money Network.

And perhaps more important for our mutual fund investor, Reuters Money Network is cyberlinked to the Morningstar database of 7,000 mutual funds, with 40 data points on each fund, including returns, risk, and fees, plus their five-star rating system so you can quickly search, identify, and analyze the high-performance funds by category (growth, income, small cap, etc.) and tap into their individual fund reports.

Of course, one of the biggest advantages for the mutual fund investor using the Reuter's system is that you're cross-linked to all of Reuters other cyberspace tools in a single operating platform, one that is guaranteed to improve with age. In fact, Reuters seems destined to become the cyberspace investor's navigator of choice, in much the same way that Netscape emerged the Web surfer's browser of choice.

NEW CYBER-BROKERS: ONLINE AND ON THE WORLD WIDE WEB

AccuTrade (http://www.accutrade.com)	800-598-2635
Aufhauser (http://www.aufhauser.com)	800-368-3668
Bull & Bear (http://networth.galt.com)	800-847-4200
E*Trade (http://www.etrade.com)	800-786-2575
Fidelity Online Xpress (http://www.fid-inv.com)	800-544-5235
R.J. Forbes Group (http://www.rjforbes.com)	800-754-7687
Howe Barnes (http://pawws.com)	800-638-4250
Investex (http://pawws.com)	800-210-5496
Lind-Waldock (http://www.ino.com)	800-445-2000
Lombard (http://www.lombard.com)	800-566-2273
National Discount Brokers (http://pawws.com)	800-888-3999
PC Financial Network (www.pcfn.com)	800-825-5723
Quick & Reilly (http://www.quick-reilly.com)	800-634-6214
Charles R. Schwab & Co (http://www.schwab.com)	800-372-4922
Muriel Siebert & Co. (http://www.msiebert.com)	800-535-9652
Max Ule's Tickerscreen (http://www.maxule.com)	800-223-6642
Jack White & Company (http://pawws.com/jwc)	800-753-1700

---

7. NEW FULL-SERVICE DISCOUNT CYBER-BROKERS ON THE WEB

When the history of Wall Street is written, four trends will be identified as significant in shifting the center of the financial community *away from* traditional institutions of Wall Street in New York City, and out to the individual investors on Main Street cyberspace. And all four of these trends will be linked to Charles Schwab as a leading force in creating the new electronic world of finance that is giving the do-it-yourself investor freedom from dependence on the advice and decision making of the Wall Street Establishment. These four trends are as follows:

❏ **Discount brokerage:** Low commissions and minimal contacts.

❏ **Electronic trading tools:** Personal computers and trading software.

❏ **Full-service content online:** Comprehensive research and analysis tools.

❏ **One-stop mutual fund supermarkets:** Single-source access to mutual funds.

Figure 6.21   Schwab software: investing and portfolio management.

Figure 6.22   PATH On-Line from Jack White & Company: number one discounter.

Today's new brokerage world is being increasingly dominated by the "cyber-broker," with the more advanced, such as the Schwab organization, being a unique amalgam of all four trends: *full-service electronic discount brokers offering mutual funds.*

These new brokerage firms provide the do-it-yourself investor with discounts, operate primarily online and on the Net, and deliver all the necessary research, analytical tools, and advice directly into the investor's computer, without branch office visits and telephone contact.

Today's new mutual fund investors are freely capable of working through these cyber-brokers to process all of their investing tasks *from their computers at home*—independent of the Wall Street Establishment with its high commission structure.

8. TELESCAN INVESTOR'S PLATFORM: TOTAL-SERVICE NAVIGATOR

Telescan is David in the arena with Goliath, and a winner. Telescan has an extremely powerful navigational tool for cyberspace investing, with a special mutual fund search engine. In fact, company president David Brown wrote an excellent book, *Cyber-Investing,* about the Telescan system. Telescan, like many other cyberspace services, relies on the Morningstar database for basic information.

Although Telescan's system is supersophisticated, being heavily grounded in technical as well as fundamental analysis, it is also user-friendly and comprehensive enough that a new cyberspace fund investor can master it quickly, although perhaps with a slower learning curve than the less sophisticated mutual fund services on America Online, for example. Today's do-it-yourself investor can tap into various levels of Telescan's mutual fund resources in several ways:

❒ **Telescan Investor's Platform.**   An online dial-up service including some powerful analytical software. This system has a mutual fund search and screen function that competes favorably with the best out there today.

❒ **TipNet on the Web.**   The Internet version of Telescan Investor's Platform.

❒ **Wall Street City.**   Telescan's bold new Website has a directory called Mutual Fund Tower, providing you with NAV quotes, top-performing funds, and other fund data.

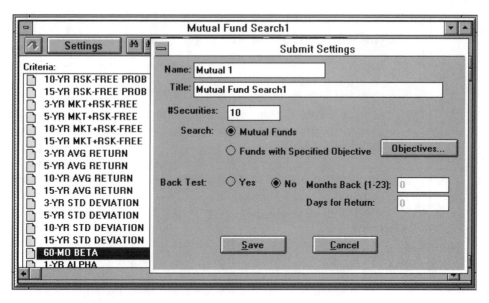

Figure 6.23 Telescan: mutual fund search and screening.

Telescan is totally integrated as an investor's navigator, both internally and externally. With Telescan the investor can do the following:

❐ Investment portfolio management: stocks and funds.

❐ Screen and identify new fund and stock opportunities.

❐ Research and analyze specific prospects.

❐ Time trades: maximize buy and sell decisions.

❐ Link to key resources: interface with Schwab, Zacks, S&P.

Individual Investor's Wayne Harris said there's "enough information for an army of Fidelity analysts." And there is certainly more than enough for the average mutual fund investor investigating Fidelity *and every other mutual fund out there.*

9. QUICKEN SOFTWARE: MUTUAL FUND FINDER AND INVESTOR INSIGHT

The Intuit team is another bright spot in this fierce competition to provide financial power tools and cyberspace databases to the fund investor. Espe-

---

4 TOP FINANCIAL TECHNOLOGY COLUMNISTS RATE QUICKEN . . .

❏ *Barron's* "The Electronic Investor." 7/8/96

Howard Gold was positive: "Quicken is by far the most popular financial software package in history . . . this new product, aimed at serious investors, has now leapfrogged over the previous leader in general investment—and portfolio—tracking software, Reality Online's WealthBuilder . . .

"For the beginner to intermediate fundamentally oriented investor, Investor Insight combines just about everything needed in one program . . . all at a reasonable price . . . remarkably easy to use . . . read a portfolio set up in Quicken—no surprise—and then update its value . . .

"Until Investor Insight came along, Reality Online's Reuters Money Network was virtually the only place in town to collect research and news on investments all in one place, presented in an easy-to-view format . . . Investor insight has the edge because of its ease of use, clean and attractive display and, especially, value for the money."

❏ *SmartMoney* magazine, "SmartMachines." 6/96

Walter Mossberg was less than impressed: "Trouble is, while Investor Insight does a competent job at providing basis information, it has some serious lapses—that reduce its value to all but the most basic investors . . . while it does track mutual funds, it does a poor job, because you can't retrieve news on funds . . . The program doesn't design an asset-allocation strategy or suggest mutual funds . . . Investor Insight is not another Quicken . . . overpriced, and I think it needs more features and sophistication to compete with both print publications and with the barrage of new financial services to come on the Internet."

Note that columnists in two Dow Jones publications, *Barron's* and *SmartMoney* have quite opposite opinions, an obvious complement to their independence. Note also that neither mentions their own online service, Dow Jones News/Retrieval, as competitive with Quicken's Investor Insight.

---

cially with their *integrated* collection of software products. Viewed as a total navigational system, Intuit has the potential of delivering an enormous powerbase to the independent do-it-yourself investor, as we saw in the second chapter.

. . . A NEW LEADER THAT NEEDS FINE-TUNING . . . YOU DECIDE!

❐ *Individual Investor* column "Investors Online." 3/96

Wayne Harris was very favorable: "Tucked away in the Quicken Deluxe Version 5 is a powerful and time-saving module called Investor Insight. Intuit will let you sample it for free for a month, but investors beware: Investor Insight is highly addictive . . . It features stock quotes, Dow Jones News, and company information from Standard & Poor's. You'll be amazed after spending a month familiarizing yourself with Investor Insight's fluid sorting, charting, and reporting. Factor in Quicken's formidable portfolio management tools, and you won't likely go back to whatever you were using before."

❐ *Money* magazine's "money mag.com." 12/95

Peter Keating's mixed review: "Quicken, the world's best-selling financial software, just got swifter . . . taken a leap into cyberspace—and developed a new on-line portfolio tracker for Quicken users, *Investor's Insight* . . . competes both with commercial on-line services like CompuServe, America Online and Prodigy, and full-fledged on-line investment databases like Reuters Money Network . . . In my opinion, Investor insight leads the pack in one basic task; keeping you up to date on your stock and fund investments . . . None of the competition matches *Investor Insight*'s facility at organizing the data into useful formats . . .

"One thing the Quicken package doesn't do particularly well is screen securities. The new program allows you to sift through a mutual fund database for funds that match certain criteria, but to get beyond that—or to screen stocks at all—you need more robust on-line investing programs, such as Reuters Money Network or Telescan . . . and you can't use Quicken to trade stocks or funds—at least not yet."

The real question for Intuit (as well as Dow Jones and every other financial data/software vendor) is: Can the company create easy-to-use, totally integrated navigators for the average do-it-yourself investor out there on Main Street cyberspace? So far, they are doing a great job.

Last year Intuit created its new Investor Insight as an add-on to its Quicken Deluxe package, and along with Investor Insight came a wealth of investor resources:

❐ **Mutual fund finder.**   Tap into the Morningstar research database.

❐ **Historical fund and stock information.**   Download five years of data.

❏ **Analytical tools.**   Set up your criteria, screen and analyze charts.

❏ **Portfolio tracking.**   On-demand data updates of your favorite funds.

❏ **Market news and analysis.**   Dow Jones News Service and *The Journal.*

❏ **Analysts' recommendations.**   Ratings, market, and industry trends.

❏ **Company research reports.**   From Standard and Poor's.

❏ **Price/volume charts.**   QuickZoom tracks market-moving news.

❏ **Major indexes.**   DJIA, S&P 500, AMEX, NASDAQ, other indexes.

❏ **Internet Web access.**   Through Netscape to other databases.

Quicken clearly is taking strategic steps to stay on the cutting edge of the cyberspace revolution, with its online banking consortium and with its new Investor Insight package, an online add-on service to the Quicken Deluxe software.

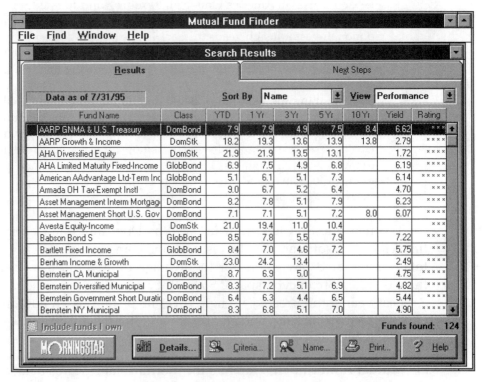

Figure 6.24   Quicken Mutual Fund Finder: database search results.

Quicken: Top Navigational System for Cyberspace Investors

The initial reviews of Quicken's Investor Insight have covered a wide gamut of opinions, suggesting the barriers to entry are becoming very high in this field—even for competitors with substantial capital. Nevertheless, the bottom line is that Quicken has a superior product and is in an excellent position to become *the* dominant force in the financial information industry, ahead of Reuters and Dow Jones.

In the final analysis, of course, when the chips are down, *your own personal evaluation* is the only one that counts, not some expert's opinion. Moreover, loyal Quicken users are likely to welcome the Investor Insight package, and to accept that it'll experience ongoing upgrades consistent with regular improvements in Intuit's other high-quality products.

Besides, software "experts" may be at least as fallible as the average stock market analyst. In fact, in reading these various software reviews you may even ask yourself if they were all reviewing the same software. In any event, we can conclude that, *even among experts,* the software decision is a

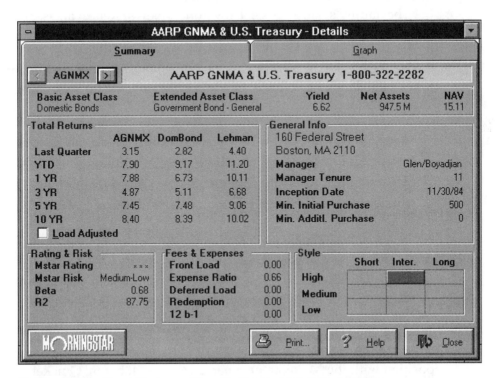

Figure 6.25 Fund Finder profile with Morningstar data reliability.

highly personal one. Nevertheless, their points are thought-provoking and deserve consideration. But, in the end, you must judge for yourself.

Bottom line: Like most new products, Quicken's Investor Insight needs some fine-tuning, and it is being upgraded. But overall, Intuit's grand assemblage of integrated software products—everything from the new Investor Insight and TurboTax to online banking, financial planning, and so much more—strongly suggests that in the immediate future Quicken and its Investor Insight will become one of the major cyberspace navigators for the do-it-yourself mutual fund investor.

10. THE NEW DIGITAL DOW JONES: SEARCHING FOR A NAVIGATOR

A new generation of individual investor products is emerging from the traditional, staid Dow Jones. All the recent competition from Quicken and Reuters, as well as StreetSmart and the cyber–discount brokers with new software platforms has Dow Jones on the counterattack, similar to Microsoft after Netscape rocketed past them.

The family's workhorse, Dow Jones News/Retrieval, is also going through an overhaul. The plain-vanilla product even got a facelift with the recent addition of the Windows on WallStreet software—an obvious step in the right direction. A new spirit is clearly emerging among the many Dow Jones publications that have an eye focused on the do-it-yourself, cyberspace investor:

❐ **Barrons Online.** Website detailed mutual fund and company research.

❐ **Tradeline Mutual Fund Center.** Quotes and data on mutual funds.

❐ **Interactive Wall Street Journal.** News delivered all day long into your PC.

❐ *SmartMoney* **magazine.** Going online with its unique perspective.

While Dow Jones News/Retrieval is the logical leader to spearhead the cyberspace do-it-yourself revolution, the more spirited teams at *The Journal, Barron's,* and *SmartMoney* seem less tentative and more adventuresome about taking full advantage of cyberspace and creating a new image.

Bottom line: The new digital Dow is moving rapidly to reestablish its position with the Main Street cyberspace crowd, before Quicken, Reuters, and the cyber-brokers lock down all the business. Barrons Online and

---

MUTUAL FUND WEBSITES REVIEWED IN *BARRON'S*

Here's the graduate course for mutual fund investing. Bookmark all of these resources on your Web browser, and return to them regularly.

Barron's Online (www.barrons.com)
Bloomberg/Mutual Fund News (www.bloomberg.com)
Data Broadcasting (www.dbc.com)
Eagle Wing Research (www.eaglewing.com)
IBC Financial Data (www.ibcdata.com)
Interactive Nest Egg—Mutual Funds (nestegg.iddis.com/depts/
    mutfund.html)
Internet Closed-End Fund Investor (www.icefi.com/icefi/index.html)
InvesTools (www.investools.com)
Investor's Edge (www.irnet.com)
Kiplinger's Online (kiplinger.com/mutualfund/fundhome.html)
Mutual Funds Cafe (www.mfcafe.com)
Mutual Fund Company Directory (www.sc.cmu.edu/~jdg/funds.html)
Mutual Fund Info Center (pawws.secapl.com)
Mutual Fund Research (www.webcom.com/~fundlink/)
Mutual Funds Magazine Online (www.mfmag.com)
Networth (networth.galt.com/)
Personal Finance Web Sites (www.tiac.net/users/ikrakow
    /pagerefs.html)
Stockmaster (www.stockmaster.com)
The Mutual Funds Home Page (www.brill.com)
TrustNet (www.trustnet.co.uk)

SOURCE: Eric Savitz, "Funds in Cyberspace: Some Online Resources for Investors in Mutual Funds," *Barron's* (July 8, 1996). This directory of major Web resources was featured in *Barron's* quarterly review of funds, and is likely to be updated regularly in print and at its Website.

SmartMoney Online are becoming surprisingly glitzy Internet storefronts for the new digital Dow. Meanwhile, the Interactive Wall Street Journal is growing at the rate of a million new cyber-readers a year, and, coincidentally, the print version also increases readership. Something's going right; this is no old gray dinosaur trapped in the tarpits.

Dow Jones controls what may be the single most powerful database available to the financial world. The News/Retrieval's recent addition of

Figure 6.26   Windows on WallStreet: DJN/R's new technical face.

the Windows on WallStreet navigator is a clear strategic move to reposition them as a leader in the new cyberspace revolution. Yes, Dow Jones News/Retrieval is back in the game.

However, they'll have to run hard to catch up with competitors like Telescan, Quicken, and Schwab, for example, or to match the sharp marketing moves Reuters has been making since they acquired Reality Online and transformed it into Reuters Money Network. Meanwhile, Barrons Online, Tradeline, and SmartMoney Online are also DJN/R competitors . . . all of which should work to the advantage of the new cyberspace investor.

THE MAJOR COMMERCIAL ONLINE SERVICES: COMPUSERVE, AMERICA ONLINE, AND PRODIGY

The traditional commercial online services—America Online, Compu-Serve, and Prodigy—are by their very nature one-stop navigators in cyberspace. However, in contrast to Reuters, Dow Jones, and Telescan (services solely designed for the investor), the commercial online services offer subscribers and their families many other services.

At America Online, for example, you'll find a wide range of information on movies, weather, and healthcare tips, as well as sports, travel, and relationships. All of this adds considerable value, especially if the whole family's fascinated with cyberspace.

The downside is that mutual fund investors will probably not find the same high-quality, high-powered tools available that you would on either of the prior two categories of resources: the software packages (Principia or Value Line's Fund Analyzer) or the integrated online/software systems (Reuters Money Network and Telescan). Nevertheless, each of the three leaders has a particular collection that many fund investors may find more than adequate, especially in the early years in cyberspace.

11. COMPUSERVE'S MUTUAL FUND RESOURCES: FUNDWATCH FROM *MONEY* MAGAZINE PLUS MORNINGSTAR AND VALUE LINE

CompuServe's FundWatch is managed by the editorial team at *Money* magazine, a publication of Time Warner. The FundWatch relies on the CDA/Wiesenberger database, and is comparable in scope to the other databases with the major online services. Detailed reports on funds are available. In addition, an investor can also screen on investment objectives, fees, expenses, and other variables.

While the number of screening fields and the combinations at FundWatch is limited (as with the other commercial online services), CompuServe's mutual fund search and screening function is more than adequate for most investors. However, as your portfolio grows, you may want one of the more sophisticated integrated systems previously discussed.

CompuServe is a triple threat in the funds arena. They provide subscribers with some major bonuses: Not only do you get *Money* magazine's FundWatch, with its access to the CDA/Wiesenberger database, but you also have access to both the Morningstar and the Value Line databases. So look beyond the *Money* magazine billboard; make sure you explore the resources of all three of these mutual fund databases when you check out CompuServe.

Figure 6.27 CompuServe: *Money* Magazine's Investor Center.

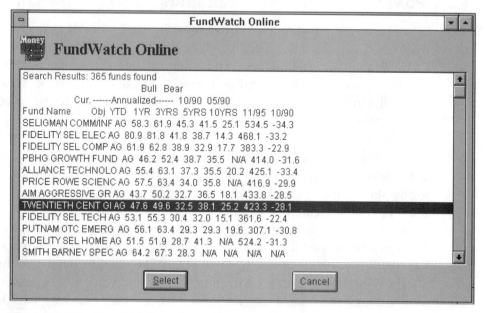

Figure 6.28 FundWatch on CompuServe: mutual fund screens.

12. AMERICA ONLINE'S MUTUAL FUND SUPERMARKET: MORNINGSTAR, FUNDS, QUOTES, NEWS, RESEARCH, AND MORE

Here is yet another major "retail" outlet for the Morningstar database. Moreover, AOL is a surprisingly valuable retail outlet when you realize that the Morningstar services are *not* an add-on extra charge. Plus there are many services specifically for mutual fund investors on America Online:

- ❐ **Mutual Fund Resource Center.** AOL's navigator for fund information.

- ❐ **Mutual Fund Center.** Access a group of participating fund families.

- ❐ **Morningstar Research.** Quotes, profiles, top-25 performers for major sectors.

- ❐ **Mutual Fund Graphs.** From the Prophet organization's database.

- ❐ **Fidelity Online Investor Center.** Prospectuses, planning, brokerage, and more.

- ❐ **Vanguard Online.** Education, planning, asset allocations, portfolio strategies.

- ❐ **Mutual Fund Account Transactions.** Trade, exchange, buy, and sell online.

- ❐ **American Association of Individual Investors.** Software, education, research.

- ❐ **Online magazines covering funds.** *BusinessWeek, Worth, Consumer's Reports.*

- ❐ **Links to key fund Websites.** Direct while on the AOL online connection.

- ❐ **Other mutual fund resources.** 401(k) strategies; Decision Point fund charts.

Some investors may conclude that access to the Morningstar database, with its fund profiles, NAV quotes, and top-25 screens for the 25-plus major categories of funds, is enough to justify AOL's subscriber fee.

Bottom line: As extensive as the AOL mutual fund information is, and as convenient as it is to have so many resources in one place, AOL's Mutual Fund Center is primarily a yellow-page directory with discrete, rather than integrated, listings, and the AOL/Morningstar's service, adequate though

MORNINGSTAR FUND PROFILE ON AMERICA ONLINE

- ❏ Profile of the fund
- ❏ Loading
- ❏ Yield per share
- ❏ Assets
- ❏ NAV quotes (net asset value)
- ❏ Top-10 holdings
- ❏ ROI (five-year and average)
- ❏ Management fees
- ❏ Family of funds
- ❏ Management salaries
- ❏ Investor contacts

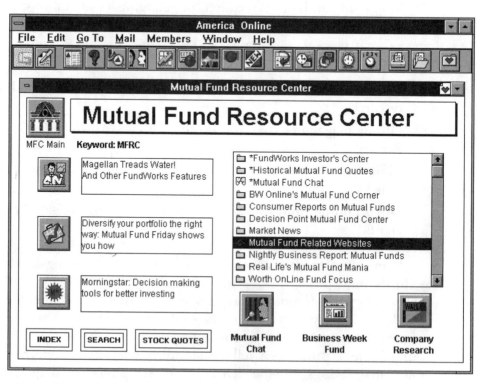

Figure 6.29 America Online's Mutual Fund Resource Center.

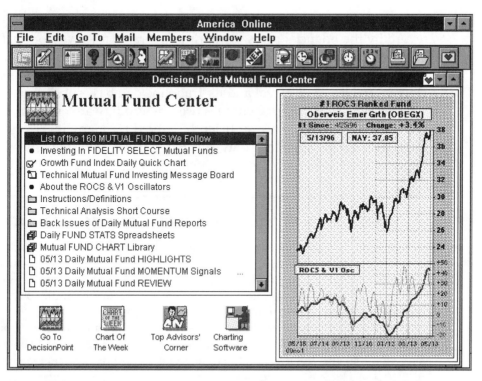

Figure 6.30   Decision Point Mutual Funds: AOL and Investools Website.

it may be, still lacks the screening firepower of either the offline software or integrated systems, and it lacks a solid portfolio manager.

13. PRODIGY'S ONLINE SERVICES FOR MUTUAL FUND INVESTORS: FEATURING WINNERS LIKE TRADELINE AND DOW JONES NEWS

Prodigy is currently going through a major reorganization, which appears to be affecting its services across the board. Prodigy was originally launched in 1984. After years of ownership by Sears and IBM, Prodigy's growth stalled in the last couple years, while CompuServe and America Online skyrocketed past it in shear subscriber numbers.

Finally, after pouring over $1 billion into Prodigy, last year the two money partners sold Prodigy for about $250 million. Hopefully, the restructured Prodigy will be able to recover and live up to its full potential as an equal competitor of CompuServe and America Online.

Meanwhile, in spite of this trauma, Prodigy is held in surprisingly high regard by the financial press, garnering favorable reviews from *Individual Investor* and *BusinessWeek,* for example. Moreover, from a content basis, its mutual fund and other financial input comes directly from the databases of Dow Jones News/Retrieval and its Tradeline database subsidiary.

Although the screening engines used by Prodigy are minimal, and the line items limited, they are sufficiently lasered for many investors. Hopefully then, Prodigy will not only survive, but rise from the ashes like the phoenix and emerge as a new cyberspace prodigy.

INDEX FUNDS: AN ALTERNATIVE TO NEW HIGH-TECH SOFTWARE

Although the new mutual fund software packages offer services other than screening databases, such as trading and portfolio management, from a purely analytical perspective, these new high-powered technologies add a note of hard realism to the scene and make it painfully obvious that the large majority of mutual funds are subpar performers.

Consider these facts: Over periods of one to 15 years only 15 to 32 percent of diversified stock funds have beaten the S&P 500; thus 68 to 85 percent fail to beat the indexes. Plus the best index funds have no loads and very low fees.

"One thing becomes clear as you track, chart, graph and plot the various funds you are choosing: A depressingly large number of them don't outperform the simple indexes against which they're benchmarked. Does it pay to spend hundreds of dollars and dozens of hours on software that will still give you about a one-in-five chance of topping a no-brainer index fund? Some people might want to keep the money and go to Aruba."

SOURCE: Howard Gold, "Fund Software: The Feeling's Mutual," *Barron's* (March 4, 1996).

"In the time it takes to read this article, you can devise a simple, low-cost, diversified investment plan that virtually guarantees that your returns will beat those of the vast majority of mutual funds. No exhaustive, exhausting research is needed, and you don't even need to know who runs the funds. . . . There are 133 index funds, and you can expect a lot more. . . . While you won't do better than the index your fund mirrors, you *will* do better than many, if not most, other stock funds."

SOURCE: Ken Sheets, "The Agony & The Index," *Kiplinger's* (October 1996).

14. SPECIALIZED MUTUAL FUND SOFTWARE PACKAGES FOR INVESTING AND PORTFOLIO MANAGEMENT

There are a few other specialized software products available to the mutual fund market that warrant examination. Manhattan Analytics FundPro and Monocle software systems are also designed for investors who are technical analysis–oriented. Both *PC Computing* magazine and *Technical Analysis of Stock and Commodities* have given these products high marks.

An early review in *PC Computing* magazine comparing Monocle with Reuters Money Network concluded that the latter was not only more versatile and less expensive, but RMN was designed to help the investor work with a much broader investment portfolio, including stocks and bonds. However, in another review, the American Association of Individual Investors said Monocle is "the most complete mutual fund investing package out." Check out their new Website, ManhattanLink.

Overlap is a unique software system for serious investors who want to "construct truly diversified portfolios, to fine-tune portfolios, and to maintain existing portfolios." Overlap is a special portfolio-balancing software program specifically designed to ensure that your portfolio maintains the

Figure 6.31   Manhattan's Monocle: technical analysis and market timing.

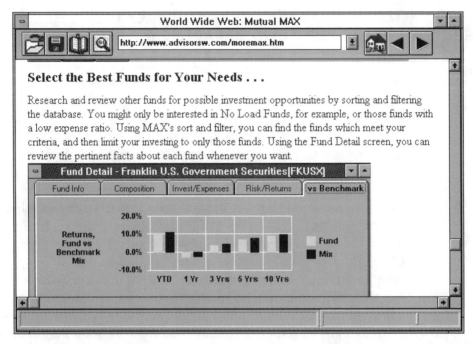

Figure 6.32 Mutual MAX: software selecting the best funds for you.

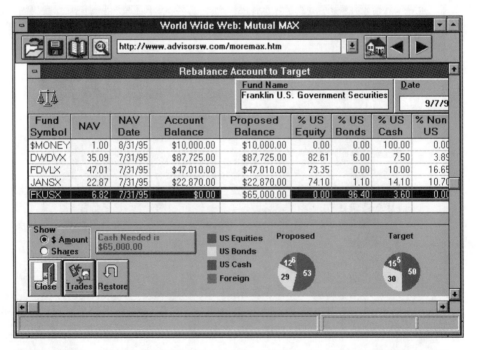

Figure 6.33 Mutual MAX: rebalancing to maintain your asset allocations.

important asset-allocation ratios developed as part of your personal financial plan. Until Overlap develops its Website, investors can reach them at (800) 683-7527.

Similarly, another mutual fund software developer, simply called the Advisor, has two software products designed to optimize your portfolio's asset allocation. Its Mutual Fund Advisor software product is for professionals. And they market an inexpensive version, Mutual Fund MAX for individual investors. You'll find information about both at Advisor's Website.

THE RAPIDLY APPROACHING MERGER OF OFFLINE SOFTWARE TECHNOLOGIES AND ONLINE/WEB SERVICES

Financial cyberspace is rapidly coming to the point where the lines between online services and offline technologies disappear. Sun Microsystems has reminded the computer-literate community for a long time that "the network is the computer." In fact, *the global cyberspace network is your computer.* And the Web is one massive database, a vast collection of power tools for investors.

Online services that serve only as billboards no longer attract repeat visitors. And many Websites are becoming interactive. Today we see more and more of the basic investment analyses right there on the Web as your computer, without special software.

NETworth, with Morningstar and Disclosure power tools, Mutual Funds Magazine Online, Telescan, and Lombard are just four excellent examples of the trend toward a merger of online and offline technologies on the Internet. All had powerful pre-Web technologies. Now all are retooling their content and offline technologies for online and Website use by investors. And the competition is guaranteed to intensify.

Obviously, financial cyberspace is in a transitional period that will continue for a period of time, perhaps a year or so. The speed of data transmission on the Internet and the limitations of current Web-oriented investment analysis technologies are clear obstacles. But not for long.

Even with these limitations, the pressure is so powerful to establish an early niche in this huge new cyberspace market that many financial information providers are rushing in where angels fear to tread. They are willing to fly into battle with a single-engine fighter, because waiting until a Stealth bomber version is perfected may mean missing the action completely.

From another perspective, you can bet that you'll see substantial improvements in Websites like Mutual Funds magazine, Telescan, Lombard, and NETworth in the near future. So keep your judgment of these pioneers in proper perspective. And start exploring the new Web resources for mutual fund investors.

BOTTOM LINE: INVEST LIKE THE PROS . . . IT'S EASY TO DO IT YOURSELF WITH THE NEW HIGH-TECH POWER TOOLS

The emerging new global financial cyberspace has rapidly become a level playing field. Until the 1990s, the Wall Street Establishment—institutional investors, professional money managers, and major stock brokerage firms—virtually owned Wall Street cyberspace. And they controlled all the electronic power tools. Average, individual mutual fund investors were unable to compete; rather, they had to depend on and be subservient to the Wall Street powerhouses.

No more. Today, with all these new power tools becoming available for the independent, do-it-yourself investor, the playing field is indeed leveling. The independent investors may be exposed to information overload; yet with it has come a host of new, inexpensive technologies to navigate through and manage the data. As a result, today's independent investors have all the power they need to use the information effectively, converting the overload into decision-making solutions.

The paradigm has indeed shifted . . . in favor of the Main Street investor.

STEP SEVEN

The Best Investment Strategies to Help You Beat the Pros

The Secret to Thinking Like a Mutual Fund Manager

Master a few basic strategies and you'll be thinking like a mutual fund pro. In step 7 we'll focus on a few key criteria used by professional money managers in picking mutual funds and building successful portfolios. These criteria include specific screening criteria, new computer technology, past performance, and the critical need to focus on selection of fund managers.

THINK LIKE A MUTUAL FUND MANAGER:
BECAUSE YOU ARE ONE, MANAGING YOUR OWN PORTFOLIO

In his book *Megatrends,* John Naisbitt refers to this decade as "the Age of the Individual." On Wall Street, this decade is rapidly becoming the Age of the Do-It-Yourself Cyberspace Investor. And that's doubly true with the mutual fund industry. Millions of investors are discovering the power of controlling their own financial destiny.

Why think like a fund manager? *Because you are one.*

Hey! It's your money, your portfolio, and your future. And there's no broker, no independent advisor, no professional manager in the world who will ever cover any of your losses, no matter how pushy they were about getting you *into* the particular security. The caveat, "past performance is no

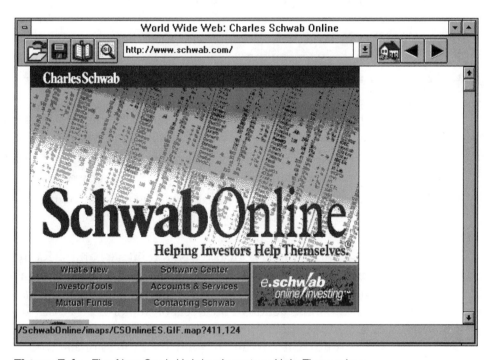

Figure 7.1 The New Goal: Helping Investors Help Themselves.

guarantee of future results," is there more to protect them, not you. Think of it. They're off the hook. You're stuck.

New Market Wizards author Jack Schwager reminds us, "Whether you win or lose, you are responsible for your own results. Even if you lost on your broker's tip, an advisory service recommendation, or a bad signal from the system you bought, you are responsible because you made the decision to listen and act . . . do your own thinking." Yes, it is your money, your portfolio, and your future.

Start thinking like the manager of a mutual fund . . . because you already are one.

STRATEGY #1: DO IT YOURSELF ON YOUR OWN COMPUTER

Here's the bottom line. Your number one strategy for investing in mutual funds from this minute forward is this: Do *everything* from your computer . . . research and analysis, news and quote updates, portfolio management and trading, screening and tax accounting . . . *everything!*

That's how the professionals do it—on their computers. In fact, here are the five primary strategies we'll present in the remaining chapters:

1. Do it yourself on your computer and the cyberspace network—offline analytical software, online services, and the Internet. Think like a pro.
2. Bet on the fund's manager, who is the comanaging partner of your portfolio.
3. In developing your screening and selection criteria, past performance does matter, in spite of the law and conventional wisdom.
4. Use the cyberspace network as your database and a primary analytical tool of equal importance to your offline software power tools.
5. Screen, analyze, and pick the best funds using your own power tools first. Then check out the best possible second opinions.

The term *strategy* has historical roots in military battles. Today, strategies are game plans and paths, blueprints and methods. They put a man on the moon, and they'll put you in a mutual fund. Strategies are *maps of the future* that guide your actions and decision-making processes until you actually reach your target in the future.

Books on mutual funds are written by professionals who describe strategies in complex, convoluted, and confusing terms. So you're left with

Figure 7.2 Investors' Top-Gun School at Mutual Funds Online.

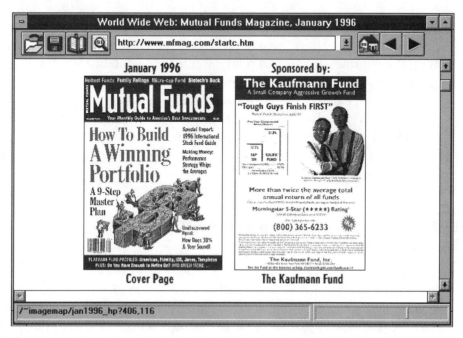

Figure 7.3 Mutual Funds Online: How To Build A Winning Portfolio.

Figure 7.4 Training manuals for the cyberspace investing battle.

the strange feeling that the professionals definitely have the edge on you. Until recently, investors have been *dependent* on Wall Street as the middle-man. These professionals had ready access to the databases and ownership of all the power tools. No more; there's a new game in town.

Today the rules of engagement in this war have changed. And today, the key difference that we continue to emphasize and reemphasize is that the new do-it-yourself investor, the independent small investor on Main Street, has all the necessary computer power tools online and in cyberspace to strategize like a professional.

CYBERSPACE INVESTING: HIGHWAY, MARKETPLACE, OR BATTLEFIELD?

Bill Gates says that a *centralized marketplace* is a better analogy for cyber-space than a superhighway. Actually, in the world of cyberspace investing, a battlefield is the best analogy. Investing is a serious war game. Win-win may work at the negotiation table, but not on the NYSE. Today's do-it-yourself investor is in a time zone that is rapidly assimilating the strategic energies akin to the high-tech, high-speed Desert Storm engagement.

Remember the Apache helicopter pilots with their night vision, the intelligence downloaded from AWAC reconnaissance aircraft miles up, the cameras in smart bombs pinpointing chimneys. . . . Today's cyberspace investor now has that kind of firepower. Until recently, the Wall Street Establishment—large brokerage firms, money managers, and institutional investors—controlled the high-tech weapons and owned the battlefield of cyberspace. Today's battles are waged on a level field.

THINK LIKE A PROFESSIONAL: GET STREET SMART

The single most important strategy for the new breed of cyberspace investor is to use *the new computer technology, not another set of rules in the latest book in print.* And the strategic *thinking* necessary for successful investing is learned in what Charles Schwab calls the "school of hard knocks":

"With StreetSmart's advanced features, you can invest like a pro. StreetSmart gives you trading and investment management capabilities that no other software provides.

"You can track the performance of your investments with reports and graphs *you* design. By trading online, you can respond to fast-moving markets—and cut your commissions. You're able to tap into investment news as it's happening—including news culled for your *specific* needs. Plus you have access to research databases from well-known information providers. Once you use StreetSmart, you'll see why I say 'it's the professional way to invest.' "

Translation: Get street-smart. You can do it yourself on your own computer.

In the old-fashioned mind-set that still dominates the strategic thinking of the Wall Street Establishment, investment strategies were anchored in a *dependent* relationship between the customer and the professionals, brokers, and financial advisors.

Under this scenario, Wall Street Establishment insiders possess some secret access to an inner sanctum of superior intelligence about the markets, and they alone understand the cryptic rules of engagement for the investing war. Last year an executive vice president of one of the largest Wall Street firms announced that "do-it-yourself investing is not a viable concept in the nineties." In his view, individual investors *need* Wall Street.

No wonder most books on mutual funds plod endlessly on with lists of rules: how to pick winning funds, how to select the types of funds for you, how to do this and that. Then they abandon you to pencil and paper and your local newspaper's stock pages, with the hope that somehow you can apply these cryptic strategies to endless lists of yesterday's data bits from almost 8,000 funds, until finally you become so exasperated you give up and call your broker for advice.

Strategy? There is only one clear strategy for investors today: *Do it yourself!*

Do-it-yourself investing in cyberspace is your number one strategy. Get out there and start *using* Schwab, Quicken, Reuters, Telescan, *something. . . . Any one of these packages is an improvement over using a broker and the quotes in your newspaper.*

HERE ARE THE THREE KEY CRITERIA PROS USE TO PICK WINNERS

According to a *Mutual Funds* magazine survey of 100 leading experts on mutual funds, the three most reliable criteria used by the professionals in picking a wining stock fund:

1. **Past performance.**
   A consistent 10-year track record of returns.
2. **Consistent management style.**
   Fund managers have clear and focused investment strategy.
3. **Tenure of portfolio managers.**
   The team has longevity, including bear market experience.

SOURCE: "How the Pros Pick Winners," *Mutual Funds* (November 1995).

And what about the secret rules of investing? If there really are any meaningful rules in this moving-target environment, the rules will become clear to you *once you get into this new high-tech game* and you develop your own rules. These rules can only be self-taught.

If you need a reminder about the basics, go back and read Charles Schwab's eight basic steps in the first chapter. Better yet, go online to the Vanguard University Website for a refresher course. . . . Do your graduate study in cyberspace.

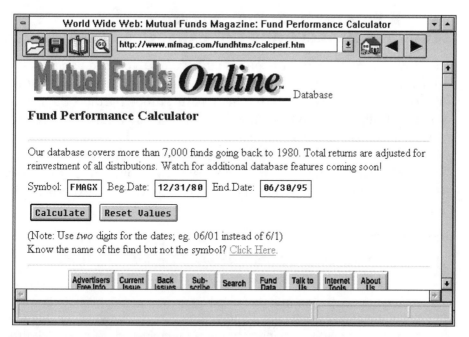

Figure 7.5   Online Mutual Fund Performance Calculator.

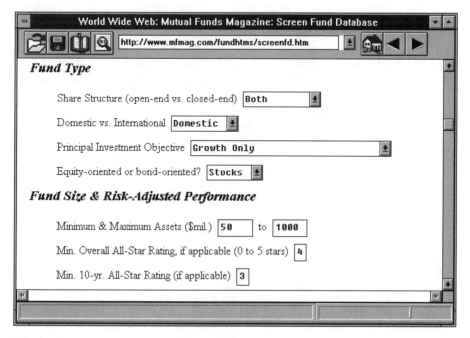

Figure 7.6   Input your fund-screening criteria on the Web.

STRATEGY #2: HOW THE PROS PICK WINNERS
THEY BET ON THE MANAGER AND THE MANAGER'S PERFORMANCE

You say you're not a professional manager, and you can't spend as much time on your portfolio as one of these pros. No problem. You can still *think* like one . . . and in effect "hire" them as full-time "partners" to comanage your portfolio. That's what you do when you buy a fund: You're hiring a comanaging partner.

So, what should you look for in picking the right fund manager? It's really quite simple. Let's see how the best pros—your new partners—think strategically. We already know the strategies used by the experts in picking mutual funds for clients.

WARNING: PAST PERFORMANCE IS NO GUARANTEE
(SO WHY DOES EVERYONE USE IT!)

"Late Twentieth Century definition of a nightmare: Wading through 7,000-plus choices in search of the perfect fund. You won't find it. Markets are fickle, people who manage funds are fallible, and it's absolutely true that 'past performance is no guarantee of future results.' "

SOURCE: Manuel Schiffres, "Fifty Funds With The Mark of Excellence," *Kiplinger's Mutual Funds* (1996).

"The reality is that there is virtually no relationship between the past, present, and future performance of an equity fund (aggressive growth, growth, growth and income, international stock, and global equities) or a long-term bond fund (corporate, foreign, government, municipal, or world). A number of studies support this view; in fact, I have never seen a study that disputes it. . . . According to Lipper, in each of the past four years, equity funds that were awarded five stars (the highest rating given by Morningstar) underperformed their respective asset class's average return over the twelve months that followed."

SOURCE: Gordon Williamson, *100 Best Mutual Funds* (Adams, 1995).

"Most investors know the fund industry's 'past-performance-means-nothing' warning. Few heed it. . . . For proof, look at fund family market share figures for 1995. It shows that past performance, however it may relate to future performance, matters a great deal to fund investors."

SOURCE: "Past Performance Matters," *Mutual Funds* magazine (May 1996).

Mutual Funds magazine surveyed 100 of the most respected mutual funds experts in America, asking them how they pick winners. Specifically, the *Mutual Funds* team asked the 100 experts to select the *three criteria* they found most reliable in picking winning stock funds. The top criteria used by a majority of these professional insiders are as follows:

1. Past Performance

"Consistently good returns over a long period of time" was far and away the most popular answer. Oddly enough, even though disclaimers and research studies cast doubt on past performance as a predictor of the future, this is in fact the key criteria the pros use.

2. A Clear Management Style

The problem with a vague and inconsistently applied management style is obvious. The fund managers are probably short-term gunslingers, doing whatever seems to work in the short run, without a solid, consistent long-term strategy.

3. Tenure of Portfolio Managers

Kiplinger's magazine hit the nail on the head: "Funds don't make money, fund managers do." A fund's past performance is hardly useful if the manager who did the job is gone. Moreover, past performance is at least questionable with young managers who lack experience in a bear market.

These 100 experts were asked about the criteria they'd use to pick a fund, and the *managers* and their *past performance* were the criteria of choice. Risk was also high on the list, along with other important criteria such as expenses, fund family affiliation, portfolio composition, and performance among peers. Down-market performance failed to register very high as selection criteria on the charts with these 100 fund professionals. But the managers make the investment decisions. In effect, they become your partners, so choose wisely.

Solution: If you want to think like the mutual fund manager of a winning portfolio, focus on *the manager*'s past performance, tenure at the fund, and experience over a variety of market conditions. *Bet on the jockey, not the horse, not the stable.*

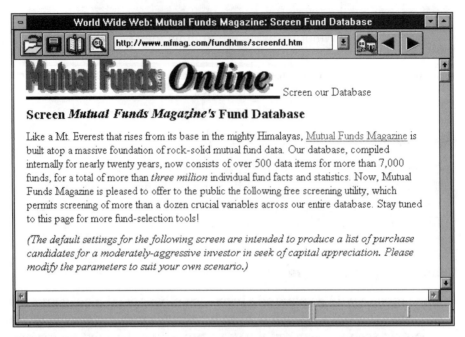

Figure 7.7 Mutual Funds Online: database screening on the Web.

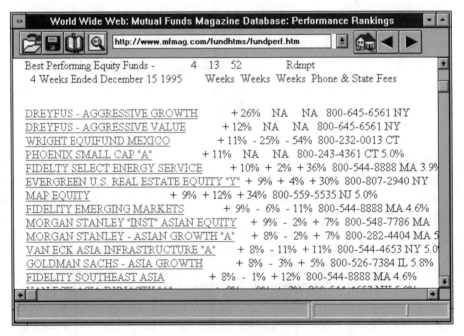

Figure 7.8 Online screening: best-performing funds by objective.

IS PAST PERFORMANCE REALLY NO GUARANTEE? PROFESSIONAL EXPERTS DISAGREE WITH CONVENTIONAL WISDOM

Before going much further, we need to confront this central issue of past performance. The extremes of this issue boil down to these two questions: Should you listen to the regulatory agencies and the independent researchers, and ignore past performance completely? Or is past performance really one of the main criteria that individual investors should use to pick winning funds?

The Securities and Exchange Commission has had a lot of experience that justifies attaching the disclaimer on every prospectus. And no less authorities than Lipper Analytical Services, *Kiplinger's* editors, and many other experts echo the same sentiments. Indeed, research studies indicate that winning horses often trip the next time on the track.

Yet, while you can't ignore these warnings, the fact is that the experts do focus on the managers, their performance, and tenure. That is their reality, in spite of the wisdom of the SEC.

NEW STUDIES: PAST PERFORMANCE CAN PREDICT THE FUTURE!

"Any mutual-fund owner has seen the grim warning in the literature: Past performance doesn't predict future results.

"Wrong says a New York University finance professor. Martin J. Gruber . . . argues that past performance does predict the future and that smart investors who favor hot stock funds are able to beat the market. Such evidence flies in the face of the 'buy-and-hold' investment precept, not to mention the widely held notion that it is better to buy low-cost 'index' funds that settle for just matching the market's returns . . .

"The extra kick is the result, he says, of—surprise!—the fund's superior management. That's the argument active managers have been making for years. . . . The managers have an edge."

SOURCE: Jonathan Axelrod, "A Case for Betting on Funds' Past Results," *The Wall Street Journal* (July 5, 1996).

"The past preformance of a fund is not a perfect guide to its future performance, but it is your single best guide."

SOURCE: Warren Boroson, *Keys to Investing in Mutual Funds* (Barron's Educational Series, 1992).

Perhaps the solution lies somewhere between the extremes of ignoring past performance completely and making it your number one fund-picking criteria.

Some new research even supports the idea that certain "hot" funds (a high performer in the past year) may actually continue hot, and may even outperform buy-and-hold strategies that favor index funds. While the research study specifically noted that the benefits of this kind of investment strategy would only accrue in an IRA or other tax-protected investment environment, it nevertheless supports the need to focus on the fund manager.

More important, however, this New York University research study concluded that the primary reason hot funds performed and continued performing was quite obvious: superior management. "The managers have the edge." In other words, investors are confronted with two apparently contradictory criteria here:

> **Criteria #1: The SEC says, "Past performance is *no* guarantee."** With most funds, including five-star performers, past performance does not guarantee future performance, and indeed, may even have a negative impact on price/volume patterns.
>
> **Versus**
>
> **Criteria #2: Experts say, "Past performance is your best criteria."** With many top funds, the past performance of the managers and the funds is a reasonably valid predictor of future performance.

And once again, as with so many of the most important strategies used in making investment decisions, the responsibility for the outcome of the decision is back in the hands of the individual investor. You must decide between two seemingly contradictory rules, because, in the end, you're stuck with the results.

Hopefully, some time in the near future there will be more research on the forecasting variables that favor the continued high performance of top-gun managers. Certainly one factor worth studying might be the effect of a rapid inflow of new capital following high star ratings, advisory newsletters' recommendations, and high-profile media coverage.

Meanwhile, it's clear that not only does past performance definitely have a positive impact on future performance, but also in fact, *most investors, as well as professionals, actually do use past performance as a major selection criteria.*

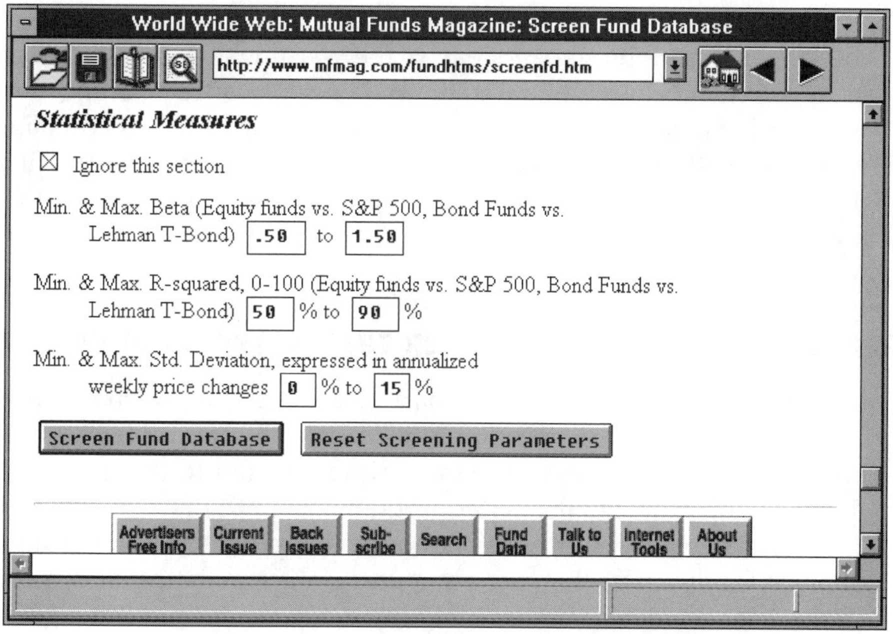

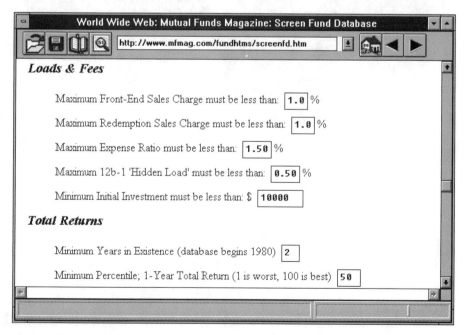

Figure 7.9 Mutual Funds Online: statistical screening criteria.

Figure 7.10 Online screening: wide range of criteria for investors.

Apparently, most investors pay about as much attention to the legal disclaimer as serious smokers pay to the warnings on cigarette packages. Fortunately, however, ignoring the past performance warning not only won't kill you, it may even *improve* your economic health as you target the winning portfolio managers. And with the help of the new financial databases and computer-based power tools now available to the new breed of cyberspace investor, you can test this important criterion yourself.

SCREENING FOR WINNERS IS FASTER THAN A SPEEDING BULLET

One of the primary—if not *the* primary—differences between the strategies used by the old-style noncomputerized investing and the new breed of cyberspace investing using the new high-tech computerized power tools is the screening power of the better programs.

This may seem obvious. Yet the ability to rapidly screen huge databases of 8,000 funds using the new computer programs is the most powerful strategy for the new investor. Not only can you screen out the gems and

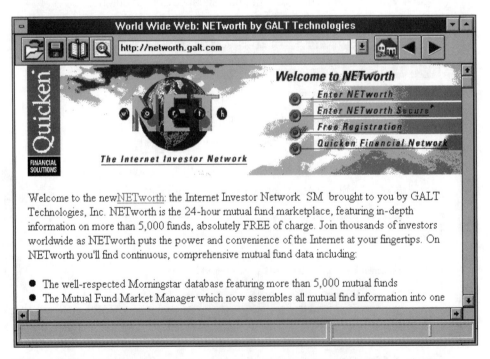

Figure 7.11   NETworth: the Internet investor's one-stop network.

Figure 7.12 Market Outlook from Benham/Twentieth Century Funds.

swiftly target them for more work, but you are also accelerating your learning curve—testing out the rules of engagement, discovering what works and what doesn't. Moreover, it's a self-taught course in the high-speed lane. Earn while you learn!

In other words, your number one investment strategy is solidly grounded in the screening power of your cyberspace software. And you can use it as well as any pro.

SCREENING FOR TOP-GUN MANAGERS AND WINNING FUNDS: A HIGH-TECH EXAMPLE FROM *MUTUAL FUNDS* MAGAZINE

As we've already seen, Morningstar, Value Line, Steele, and other software products are all designed to permit offline screening. Telescan, Mutual Funds Online, and others are racing to perfect Web-based versions.

This competition between various portfolio-screening and management tools is still in the early stages, changing rapidly, improving at an accelerating and unpredictable pace. The competition is between four types of services, and in many cases the vendors are testing all four systems:

1. **Off-line software** (Principia, Ascent, Expert, Fund Analyzer)
2. **Integrated offline software and online services** (Telescan)
3. **Traditional online services** (AOL, Prodigy, and CompuServe)
4. **World Wide Web-based services** that offer a mutual fund database as well as the analytical tools for screening (Mutual Funds Online, NETworth, and Telescan)

To date, the offline and the combination offline/online systems are the most powerful, but it is clear that there is a rapid movement toward Web-based systems, often in combination with offline analytical software.

Regardless of the computerized, technological system you use, *the investment criteria and process are the same.* You search with the same key criteria. However, you simply get to do more searches in a shorter period of time. Let's review one sample screening from the Institute for Econometric Research's *Mutual Funds* magazine, published in the November 1995 issue. Watch the step-by-step advance through a set of eight criteria. To quote the magazine:

> *With more than 2,100 stock funds out there, some investors feel they would have better luck plucking needles from a haystack than finding funds that are right for them. Pshaw! Finding funds that best suit your needs may take a bit of effort, but with all the resources at your disposal, it's hardly a mission impossible. [There are] thousands of viable approaches to selecting a fund, and each approach will yield a different set of buy finalists.*

Here's a sample of the screening process for a conservative investor with $25,000, looking for some solid stock funds:

❏ The candidates were 2,100 mutual funds and **targeted funds beating** their **peer groups** four out of six years in the 1990s; that narrowed it down to only 274 funds right away.

❏ Cut out **closed-end funds trading at a premium;** down further to 259.

❏ **Diversify by eliminating sector funds** and others with minimum investments over $5,000; this screen cuts the group to 208 funds.

❏ Now screen out funds with **safety ratings below the S&P 500;** only 79 left.

❏ Toss funds with **less than a 3 percent yield,** and any with down-market ranks below a "C" grade, and you're down to 18 funds.

MUTUAL FUND BUYER'S GUIDE: 18 KEY SCREENING CRITERIA

The Institute for Econometric Research publishes a *Mutual Fund Buyer's Guide* that covers 1,500 key funds. Their criteria are noted here because they represent the kind of information underlying the Mutual Funds Online Website. *More important, these criteria suggest the kind of information cyberspace investors need for the rapid screening necessary to make the best possible portfolio decisions:*

❑ **All-star ratings.** Distinguishing the very best funds.
❑ **Investment objective and style.** Fund goals and investment strategies.
❑ **Safety ratings.** For the risk-aversive conservative investor.
❑ **Up-market and down-market rankings.** With the best and worst funds.
❑ **Correlations.** How closely the fund follows the market cycles.
❑ **Yield.** Spots the highest returns adjusted to current price.
❑ **Performance scoreboard.** Winners and losers over months and 10 years.
❑ **Telephone switching.** You should know the cost of swapping funds.
❑ **Minimum investment.** Find the ones that fit your requirements.
❑ **Tax load.** Key estimate of tax liabilities reducing your return.
❑ **Closed-end funds.** Separate ones with premiums versus discounts.
❑ **Portfolio turnover ratio.** The amount of activity in the fund.
❑ **Net capital gains distribution.** When taxes hit the investors.
❑ **Annual expense ratios.** Identifies total fees and expenses charged.
❑ **Total assets.** Find the most popular big guns and the hidden gems.
❑ **Recent price.** NAV price of open-end funds and market for closed-end funds.
❑ **Sales load.** The cost of getting in and getting out, or redemption.
❑ **Worst-ever loss.** Unique criteria to evaluate your risk exposure.

Bottom line: these investment-screening criteria are commonly used by the serious mutual fund investor and are similar to those found in each of the major databases. They are integral to any successful cyberspace investing system for making portfolio buy/sell decisions, online and on the Net.

❑ Eliminate any fund with **less than 80 percent tax efficiency;** 15 left.
❑ Cut funds with **managers on board less than six years;** and that leaves only 12 funds.
❑ Finally, exclude funds with expenses above average stock fund.

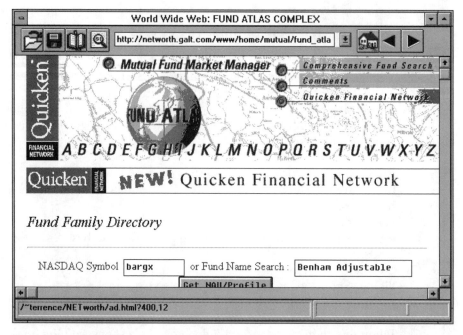

Figure 7.13   NETworth: screen fund families for profiles and NAV quotes.

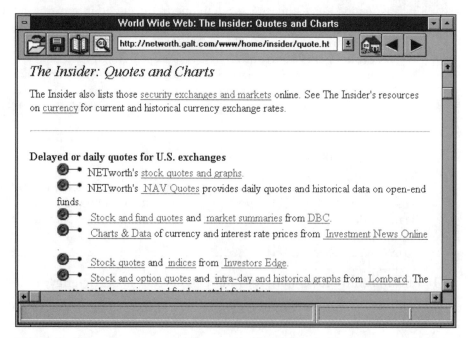

Figure 7.14   Insider links to other Websites for NAV quotes and charts.

In this example from *Mutual Funds* magazine, the screening process moves you quickly through your database, starting with over 2,000 stock funds and ending up with a manageable group of 10 winners that fit your criteria. Now you're ready to rerun and test for other criteria (if you want), or check the rating agencies, or get the prospectuses and read the details. Whatever your research calls for.

Some unique features of the Institute's information are their safety ratings, five-year projected returns, worst-ever losses, down-market ratings, and a risk-adjusted star rating system in which poor performers—over half the funds—receive no stars. There are more special features, but you get the idea.

And if you want detailed information, you can pick up a copy of the print magazine at your favorite newsstand. Or call and get a copy of one of the Institute's excellent mutual fund newsletters. Better yet, log onto its Website . . . and start screening funds. For $5 a month, you can get Mutual Funds Online, a fund watcher's dream.

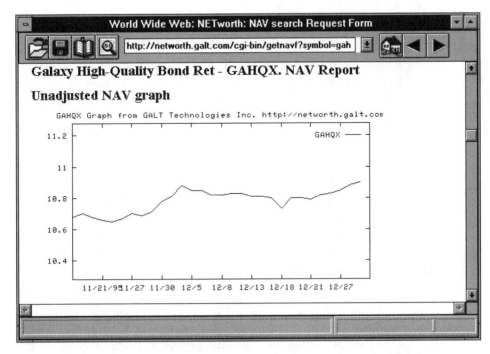

Figure 7.15   NETworth graphs: historical performance of a mutual fund.

TOP-GUN TARGET PRACTICE . . .
HOW THE NEW POWER TOOLS WILL HELP YOU SCREEN WINNERS

While the press is focusing on the contest among the traditional mutual fund database and software powerhouses—Morningstar, Value Line, Lipper, and CDA/Wiesenberger—newcomer *Mutual Funds* magazine and the Institute for Econometric Research is moving swiftly, like a Stealth bomber under the radar, toward the do-it-yourself fund investors' market. In fact, the Institute, with its *Mutual Funds* magazine, is turning out to be one of the next big players in the content market.

TEN OF THE BEST PRINTED GUIDES FOR PICKING WINNERS

BusinessWeek Guide to Mutual Funds (McGraw-Hill)
Handbook for No-Load Fund Investors (Sheldon Jacobs, *The No-Load Fund Investor*)
Investment Companies Yearbook (CDA/Wiesenberger)
Moneyletter's Mutual Funds Almanac (Agora Financial Publishing)
Investor's Guide to Low-Cost Mutual Funds (Mutual Fund Education Alliance)
Morningstar Mutual Fund 500 (Morningstar Publishers)
Mutual Fund Buyer's Guide (Norman Fosback, Irwin Professional Publishing)
Mutual Funds Encyclopedia (Gerald Perritt, Dearborn Publishing)
S&P/Lipper's Mutual Fund Profiles (Standard & Poor's, McGraw-Hill)
The 100 Best Mutual Funds You Can Buy (Gordon Williamson, Adams Publishing)

And just as Netscape took Microsoft off guard, the Institute's total package—including the Mutual Funds Online Website, its magazine, and its newsletters—is rapidly becoming a dominant force in the new cyberspace mutual fund industry.

Whether you as an electronic investor use the screening tools—Morningstar's Ascent, Value Line's Fund Analyzer, Steele's Expert, Telescan, Mutual Fund Online, or any other cybersystem—your investment decision-making process is the same. It does not matter which system you're using. Ultimately, you're merely using a tool to leverage the power of your brain and make it more effective.

Of course the *Mutual Funds* magazine example is only one of thousands of possibilities. That's right, thousands. Each investor must choose the rel-

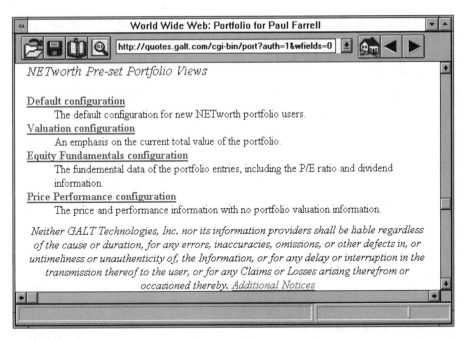

Figure 7.16 NETworth: Configure an online fund portfolio.

Figure 7.17 NETworth feature: Question fund experts online.

evant screening criteria and weight them accordingly. There are thousands of possibilities here, depending on your unique investment needs coordinated with your financial plan. Moreover, they may be different tomorrow or next year.

And that's exactly why the computerized power tools are so important; they do all the number crunching and allow the investor—through trial and error—to try many alternatives rapidly. *Mutual Funds* magazine called it "target practice," which is a great way to look at the screening process.

Practice makes perfect. And the new computerized tools are like having a rapid-fire automatic weapon rather than a single-shot pistol. With these new power tools you can get off a lot more rounds in the same amount of time during the screening process, improving your investment decision-making skills in the process. That's one strong reason why the Vanguard/*Money* quiz discussed in the first chapter favors the cyberspace investor.

THE 11 KEY SCREENING CRITERIA
FROM THE SEC'S NEW PROFILE PROSPECTUS

The format of the prospectus is about to change after 60 years. It turns out that most people never read it. So for the past few years the Securities and Exchange Commission has been exploring new ways to simplify the mutual fund prospectus. In fact, eight large fund families have been testing a more user-friendly profile prospectus, with very favorable results.

Arthur Levitt, the SEC chairman, calls it "an important step in the SEC's ongoing campaign to take the mystery out of the marketplace for public investors." Norman Fosback, CEO of the Institute for Econometric Research and editor in chief of *Mutual Funds* magazine believes that the profile prospectus "will represent the most significant change in mutual fund marketing since the enactment of depression-era securities law."

The structure of the new profile fund is important, because it can act as a structure for the investor's screening process by summarizing the key elements about a fund. The 11 key points in the new profile prospectus are as follows:

1. The fund's goal
2. Investment strategy
3. Significant risks

4. Investors appropriate for this fund

5. Fund expenses

6. Past performance

7. Investment manager and tenure

8. How to buy shares

9. How to sell shares

10. How distributions are made and taxed

11. What services are available

In addition to the SEC, the media, and investors, the Investment Company Institute (a trade organization for mutual fund managers) favors the new profile prospectus, and as a result, there's a high probability it will soon be the standard, as an alternative for the long-form, legalese-loaded prospectus.

The new user-friendly profile prospectus will be a welcome tool. However, it's only a tool; it can't be your only tool; and it definitely shouldn't be your first tool. Remember, it's a follow-up step, *after* your initial screening

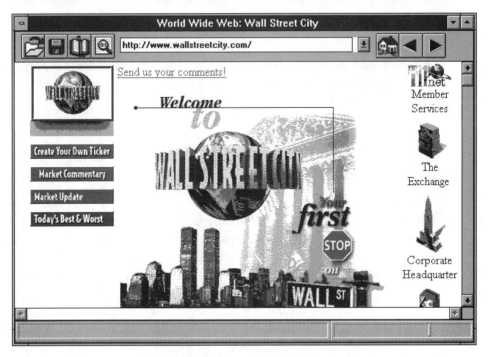

Figure 7.18 Telescan's new Wall Street City on the Internet.

Figure 7.19   Mutual Fund Tower: tools to find the best funds.

research and analysis. *First* you screen your favorite databases using your cyberspace power tools, and *then* you do more detailed research and check out the prospectus.

BOTTOM LINE: START THINKING LIKE A FUND MANAGER BECAUSE YOU ARE ONE, YOU MANAGE YOUR OWN PORTFOLIO

In reality, the first seven chapters are all about how to start *thinking* strategically like a pro. Our conclusion is that investment strategies are not merely another rehashed set of rules, more dogma printed on paper about how to asset-allocate, pick the right funds, and so on. There are far too many books like that. It's time to set all the books aside *and get into action.*

Strategic thinking like a pro requires *thinking* and *action.*

Today, strategic thinking is no longer a set of rules. In fact, you need to *forget all strategies.* Instead, *think* strategically: It's a process, a way, a path, an action verb, not a static noun. Today, the rules are not as important as the *process.*

If "the medium is the message," as Marshall McLuhan says, then clearly the new computer technologies have become the biggest strategic message for today's new breed of do-it-yourself investors.

WHEN TO CONSIDER SELLING A FUND: FIVE KEY GUIDELINES

"Buying a mutual fund is often the easy part. It's knowing when to sell that's difficult. Unless you hold your fund shares in a tax-deferred account, any sales are taxable events, so you want to make the right move. Here's a rundown on when it makes sense to sell.

- ❏ **Your investment objectives change.** This is probably the most important reason . . . retirement . . . daughter will enter college next year . . .
- ❏ **Management change.** Buying into a mutual fund is really hiring someone to manage your money . . .
- ❏ **Change in investment style.** A large-cap growth fund that has become a large-cap value fund should raise a question mark.
- ❏ **The fund's asset size has grown.** Growth of assets can affect performance drastically . . .
- ❏ **Underperformance.** The worst reason to sell. But if the fund has underperformed for two years, find out why. . . . If there's been some significant change at the fund, don't wait . . ."

SOURCE: Tom Siedell, "When to Sell a Fund," *Your Money* (June/July 1996).

Computerized cyberspace thinking has long been an inherent way of life for the professional money managers. Fidelity Investments spends $350 million and Merrill Lynch $925 million on computerized information systems annually. Computers are second nature for them, indeed a way of life, a totally integrated process of strategic thinking for these pros.

Now the same high-tech power tools are available universally, not just to the Wall Street Establishment elite. And it's time that every individual investor in the world made use of them.

Like a top-gun pilot, think of your computer as a high-tech weapons system in a very real war game. You can't afford to fly vintage WWII equipment. In order to win in the tough realities of the new global investment battlefield, strategic thinking must be done with new cyberspace technologies.

Figure 7.20   Zacks Analyst Watch: Research the fund's major assets.

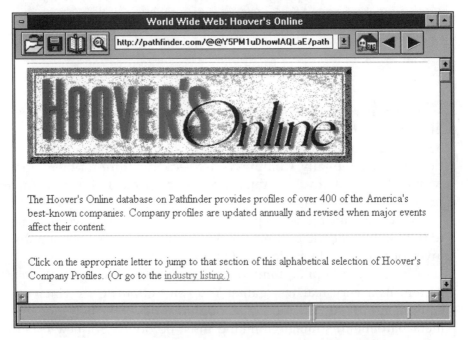

Figure 7.21   Hoover's Online: Fundamental research on key holdings.

In short, to start thinking strategically like a pro, computerize the process. Leverage your brain; capitalize on all the strategic thinking you are already doing naturally. Be a truly independent mutual fund investor and do all your investment thinking with your computer. Start thinking strategically . . . using the new cyberspace investment technologies.

HOW TO BUILD A WINNING PORTFOLIO: THE BIG PICTURE

"There's more to investing than picking a mutual fund. You need a master plan and a program to stick with it. This nine-point blueprint will ensure a solid foundation . . .

Point 1: **Establish your goals** . . . You establish two critical elements: When you'll need the money, and how much you'll need.

Point 2: **Assess your finances** . . . Determine what you have to work with . . . Experts advise that you earmark at least 10% of your income for retirement . . .

Point 3: **Determine your risk appetite** . . . Many experts say . . . is the single most important decision . . .

Point 4: **Make taxes work for you** . . . Whether taxable or tax-free investments best suit your bond fund and money market accounts.

Point 5: **Define your strategy** . . . A dollar cost averaging strategy . . . then moving on to a buy-and-hold strategy makes the most sense. . . . But no strategy works all the time.

Point 6: **Diversify** . . . The driving force in building a winning portfolio is getting the asset allocation right . . .

Point 7: **Education.** If financial experts agree on anything, it is this: Do your homework. Fortunately, we live in the information age . . .

Point 8: **Put your plan into action** . . .

Point 9: **Maintenance** . . . Maintaining your fund portfolio is as important as keeping up with the repairs and maintenance of your home. In both cases, you preserve the value of your investment."

ADAPTED FROM: Barbara Whelahan, "How to Build a Winning Portfolio," *Mutual Funds* magazine (January 1996). Fortunately, you can download articles from the Mutual Funds Online Website at http://www.mfmag.com. Try it the next time you're on the Internet.

Picking Superstar Funds and Top-Gun Managers

How to Screen for Top Performers Using the "Second Opinions" of Experts on the Web

Finally, in step 8 we'll outline a working strategy for picking the best mutual fund managers and the top-performing funds, the jockeys and horses with consistent, long-term track records, ones that regularly win the races. You'll discover resources available to help you identify them and keep track of them in the future.

SEARCHING FOR SUPERSTARS AND TOP-GUN HEROS: IS MEDIA SENSATIONALISM CREATING UNREAL EXPECTATIONS?

Eastwood and Cruise, Shaq and Magic, Montana and Palmer, Buffett and Soros, Rukeyser and Garzarelli, Captain Kirk and Luke Skywalker. . . . We love our stars! Why? Deep down, we *need* them. New mythic heros inspire us to rise above mundane realities of living in a *Dilbert* world. The press thrives on this tendency.

The popular press has been quite well aware of this fixation with stars and heros for a long time. And lately, the historically conservative financial press has succumbed, now looking like the tabloids, MTV, and Nintendo, with illustrations and stories bordering on the sensationalism of *People, The Hollywood Reporter,* and *The National Enquirer.* Many of last year's headlines from the top financial magazines reflect this new age of Wall Street glitz.

MUTUAL FUND SHOWBIZ: DOES STARPOWER CREATE WINNERS?

"There's a touch of showbiz in the mutual fund business today. Box office attractions? Their fame celebrated on the screen and in ink, fund managers like Jeffrey Vinik of Fidelity Magellan, Mario Gabelli of the Gabelli Funds and Michael Price of Mutual Series pull in the customers. What *novice* investor doesn't want his money handled by a star?"

SOURCE: Mary Beth Grover and Jason Zweig, "Capital Research: Steak, No Sizzle," *Forbes* (August 28, 1995).

The illustrations are equally titillating, competing with the best of Hollywood's movie posters: loud colors, high-concept photography, and classy art with engaging symbolism. Today's print journalism is in a universe parallel to cyberspace, where fact and fantasy overlap in a confusing, surrealistic hodgepodge.

As a former newspaper editor and head of a national financial-news cable network, I've watched this trend rapidly overtake the financial pub-

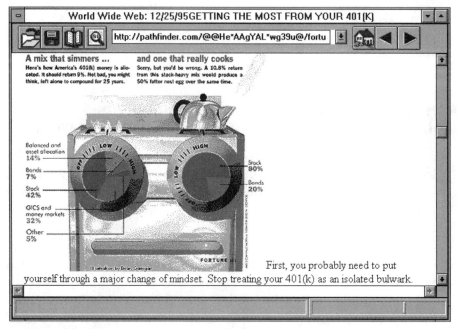

Figure 8.1　Red-hot returns: the financial press turns up the heat!

Figure 8.2　InvesTools financial newsletters on the Web.

lishing industry in the past few years. The worst of it borders on the very kind of promotional hype the securities laws were written to prevent. Even with the best, the entertainment spin and the sales hype often distract from valuable data and analyses.

Moreover, as new money continues pouring into mutual funds, this phenomenon is likely to get worse instead of better as the traditional media compete to outdo one another, throwing at us more and more articles with hot tips about the hottest funds. However, you can make it all amusingly tolerable if you keep in mind that the entertainment value of this material may well exceed the investment value.

HOT, GLITZY HEADLINES. . . . WALL STREET GOES HOLLYWOOD!

Recent headlines from America's leading business and financial periodicals.

America's Hottest Funds . . . For Pure Heat . . .
Today's Hottest Funds . . . Smokey the Bull says . . .
The Ultimate Guide to Mutual Funds 1996
Rookie of the Year . . . 5 Promising New Funds
Are These the Mutual Funds Stars of Tomorrow?
Top Guns . . . 5 That Blow the Competition Out of the Sky
The 7 Best New Mutual Funds That Beat the Market
The 8 Most Dependable Funds
9 Funds That Deserve to Be in the Spotlight
9 Undiscovered Stars
9 Sturdy Funds to Get You Over the Bumps
The 10 Most Popular Funds
12 Deadly Fund Myths and How to Profit from Them
America's Wildest Stars
Mutual Fund Stampede
Betting on Funds . . . Tips to Picking the Right Pony
Funds Fit for a Guru
Macho Managers

In a recent *Time*/CNN poll, 75 percent of those interviewed agreed that the news media is getting too "sensational." However, under the B-movie headlines, the hype, the drama, and the tabloid sensationalism, disciplined investors will usually find a lot of solid statistics and research. Just be patient, methodical, and *stay focused on your own game plan.*

WARNING: THE NEW FINANCIAL PRESS MAY BE DANGEROUS TO HEALTH OF YOUR PORTFOLIO

The investing public has already been preprogrammed by the magic of Hollywood, MTV, and Madison Avenue, where reality and fantasy overlap. Rather than miss the ride when the latest "hot tip about the hottest funds" flashes in the financial press, many give in to the impulse to react quickly. They run out and buy a ticket, and become the first in line to watch the "superstar of the month" play the hero in the latest thriller. *Consciously or unconsciously, the financial press is now cheering this game on!*

You can hardly fault the financial publishers for this new marketing glitz. They're just doing their job, under enormous pressures to sell their product. Besides, they wouldn't be doing it if it didn't work. After all, the public *does* have a strong fascination with superstars, heros, and villains. The media is merely catering to the public's latest addiction.

In addition, the press is faced with intense competition from so many other forms of entertainment: television, videos, sports, CDs, electronic games . . . and now the Internet loaded with Websites and cheap elec-

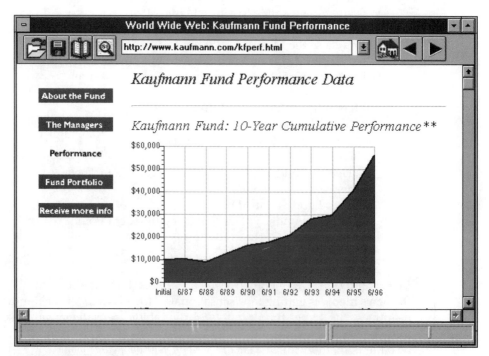

Figure 8.3   Kaufmann Fund: number one performer since the crash.

Figure 8.4 Robertson Stephens: Mutual Funds Contrarian.

tronic publishing. All of which is forcing the financial press to abandon their historically conservative editorial values in favor of the kind of glitz and pizzazz that sells for Hollywood—stories of heros and stars.

The solution: Double-check everything you read in your computer. . . . The new financial press may be dangerous to your investment health.

You have no choice if you're going to be a successful independent investor in this emerging new world of cyberspace mutual funds. As Jack Schwager said in *The New Market Wizards,* "Don't get caught up in the mass hysteria . . . *by the time a story is making the covers of the national periodicals, the trend is probably near an end* . . . never listen to the opinions of others." And today this principle is becoming even more important as the number of funds increases.

Remember, you're not buying a five-buck ticket to Magic Mountain or *Star Wars* (it only seems like it). You're making major investments in your future with your hard-earned money. You must stay focused, remain disciplined, and stick to your plan.

Methodically go about doing your homework on your favorite online/ software system from Reuters, Quicken, Schwab, Telescan, Steele, Value Line, or Morningstar. Otherwise you'll end up trapped in a vicious cycle as a perpetual victim of the hottest rumor from today's glitziest financial periodical . . . and that's not just old news, that's a disaster scenario.

YOU KNOW BEST, TRUST YOURSELF
AND YOU WILL ACHIEVE YOUR FINANCIAL GOALS

Okay, so you must be *very* skeptical about betting on all those top-gun managers, five-star funds, and the hottest of hot families of funds. After all, we've already learned that once their success hits the mass media, these winners often do stumble and come in second or middle-of-the-road next time around the track . . . *after* they take your money.

In fact, as we've already seen in earlier chapters, studies clearly show that all the media attention apparently inflates egos, distracts them from their game, and as a result, they just can't run as hot a race when all the new money starts pouring in.

Nevertheless, there are still some consistent, high-performance marathon runners in the fund business, some Michael Jordans and Arnie Palmers. And we'll help you with some tools you can use to find them and yardsticks to measure them by.

KIPLINGER'S SECRET OF SUCCESS: PICK TOP-GUN MANAGERS

"There's a malady loose. It's called, 'Find This Year's Hot Fund'. . . . You'll go insane playing this game. . . . The secret of success as a mutual fund investor is to find talented stock pickers and invest in them rather than the fund. To state it another way, funds don't make you money but people do, and you've got to give them time."

SOURCE: Editorial by Fred W. Frailey, *Kiplinger's Mutual Funds* (1996).

The cyberspace investor has a working database that's now approaching 8,000 funds, with more than 500 new ones added annually. Unfortunately, the following alarms have sounded:

❏ *SmartMoney* recommended only seven of the latest new funds for buying.

❏ *Forbes* warns that our country has "100 times" as many funds as it needs.

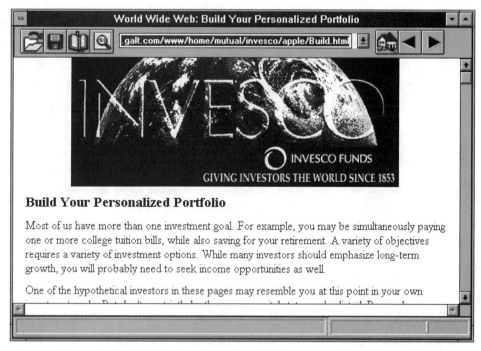

Figure 8.5 Invesco Funds: 100-year track record investing worldwide.

In addition, a mere 62 fund families control 80 percent of the total $3 trillion invested in mutual fund portfolios today. Yet *nobody* knows better what you need in your portfolio than you do . . . not *Barron's,* not *Forbes,* not *Kiplinger's,* not *Mutual Funds* magazine. You know best, only you. Trust yourself.

SUCCESS TACTIC #1:
SEARCH FOR THE WINNERS ON YOUR OWN COMPUTER
USING YOUR OWN SCREENING CRITERIA

Charles Schwab, Jack Schwager, and other leading investment wizards universally and emphatically advise investors to "take all advice with a grain of salt and do your own thinking." Some go further: *Investors should never listen to anyone, not even the experts.*

Why? The so-called experts are often wrong. Besides, today's mutual fund investors have all the computer power tools, software, and online services necessary to operate in cyberspace as independent investors:

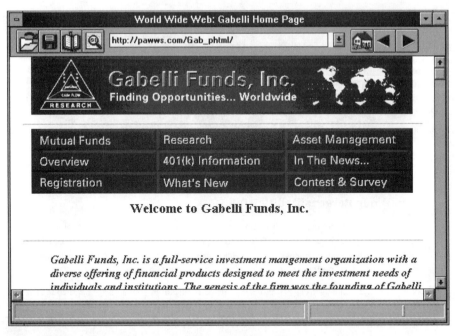

Figure 8.6 Gabelli Funds at the PAWWS World Wide Web site.

Figure 8.7 Strong Funds: top-performing family of funds.

❏   *without ever talking to another broker,*

❏   *without listening to the advice of another financial "expert,"*

❏   *without subscribing to any more advisory newsletters, and even*

❏   *without reading another print financial publication!*

That's right, under this alternative you can forget all those magazines and spend your time in a more valuable pursuit: preparing your own lists of stars and top guns. In the early chapters, we discovered that most experts agree that you probably only need 8 to 10 stock funds to achieve your goals anyway. We also saw that fund investors already have available the best possible cyberspace technologies, power tools, and methodologies for creating winning portfolios and achieving financial independence.

In other words, you already have all you need to win at this game now . . . all the computer software, databases, online services, and Web resources. All you have to do is get into action and use the power tools you have; just review Chapter 7.

THE OTHER 10 PERCENT OF A SUCCESSFUL PORTFOLIO: PICKING THE RIGHT FUNDS

"90% of your investment success comes from picking the right type of funds, and only 10% from picking the right funds."

SOURCE: William Donohue, *Mutual Fund SuperStars, Invest in the Best, Forget about the Rest* (Elliot & James, 1994).

Morningstar, Value Line, Quicken, Schwab, and their principal competitors constantly remind us that today's power tools are loaded with the same information the professionals use. Today, Main Street is playing the game on a level playing field with Wall Street. And every investor can become a do-it-yourself fund investor in cyberspace. It's easier than you think; it's less expensive; and it's more profitable.

SUCCESS TACTIC #2:
USE ONLINE BEST-FUNDS LISTS FOR "SECOND OPINIONS"

Most of us will continue reading the print editions of *Money* and *Mutual Funds, Forbes* and *Fortune, Barron's* and *The Journal.* Perhaps it's an addic-

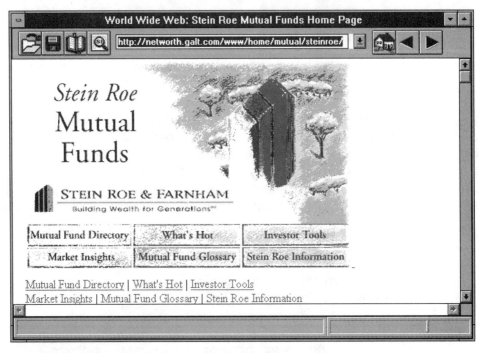

Figure 8.8   Stein Roe Mutual Funds: building wealth for generations.

tion, but many of us do enjoy reading. Sensationalism is here to stay. Hopefully, you are aware enough to filter it out. But that's not the real problem.

The single biggest problem in the minds and computers of most investors today is information overload!

It's driving us nuts! There's so much information in the financial press. And there's now too much information in cyberspace. There's just too much information everywhere. Every serious investor knows exactly what I mean if you're also trying to keep up with every one of the leading 15 to 25 financial and business publications. No wonder the press resorts to sensationalism to get your attention in the sea of noise.

The difference, however, is that if you're operating in cyberspace, with Reuters Money Network, StreetSmart, or similar power tools, you are in control.

❐ *You control the screening process right at your computer.*

❐ *You have direct access to the best databases.*

❐ *You set the criteria to fit your special needs.*

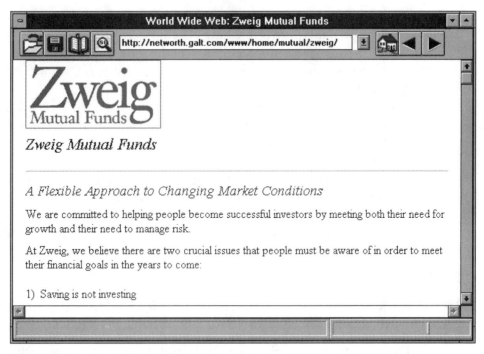

Figure 8.9 Zweig Mutual Funds: Remember, saving is not investing.

❐ *You can quickly test many alternative scenarios.*
❐ *You can interact live with your own investment portfolio.*

So, what value are the major financial publications with their hot lists of top-gun managers and star funds? Here are four reasons to use their pre-screened lists of the best funds and managers:

❐ **Educational tools** (new technologies and new methods)
❐ **Idea generators** (to trigger new thoughts)
❐ **Uncover hidden facts** (revealing facts you have missed)
❐ **Second opinions** (double-checking your own conclusions)

In other words, although we're constantly stressing the need to do your own independent research, analysis, and decision making in cyberspace, the financial press is and will remain an important element in your investing system . . . assuming you can also control the information overload—technologically, psychologically, and timewise.

Perhaps even more important, most of today's leading financial magazines and newspapers are publishing electronic editions online and in cyberspace, so you can access more and more of the right information directly into your computer, and these best-funds lists can be great second opinions, along with your own screening.

So let's review these key mutual fund resources. How can you locate them? What are their screening methods and criteria? How valid are their methods and criteria? Can you transfer some of their wisdom to improve your screening procedures?

After all, these editors and publishers are all competing and screening for the same superstar funds and top-gun managers you want. Discover how they do it. Then, the next time around, do it *before* they publish their results and before the noncyberspace masses can react . . . and avoid information overload in the process.

HOW TO PICK WINNERS: LESSONS FROM 16 TOP PUBLICATIONS, EXPERTS ARE ALREADY SCREENING THE WINNERS FOR YOU!

In the near future, as the new Web and online/software technologies develop, it's quite likely that all of today's financial and business publishers will come to realize the powerful position they're in. In cyberspace, the old model of the static one-way print magazine model is dead. Today's cyberspace resembles interactive television and video games. And the financial press is rapidly waking up to this fact.

When this reaches a critical mass, financial publishing may then go the next step into the new cyberspace world and compete directly (or by merger or joint venture) with investing systems like Principia, Ascent, Fund Analyzer, Mutual Fund Expert, Investor Insight, and other power tools—a very likely scenario.

We're in an incredible new era of cyberspace opportunities, where editors, analysts, and publishers can interact directly online with their readers and, in effect, jointly write "articles" about the top-performing funds and managers. This is happening as the lines continue to blur between writer, reader, and written, between content, software, and cyberspace.

Interestingly, the print publishers are leading this latest trend in the revolution. Apparently, it's an extension of their historic, detailed coverage of large financial databases, such as the familiar stock tables of *Barron's, The Journal,* and virtually every local newspaper.

TOP-16 FINANCIAL MAGAZINE WEBSITES. . . . BOOKMARK THEM!
THESE EXPERTS PRESCREEN WINNING FUNDS FOR YOU

Barron's	//www.barrons.com
Bloomberg Personal	//www.bloomberg.com
BusinessWeek	//www.businessweek.com
Financial World	//www.financialworld.com
Forbes	//www.forbes.com
Fortune	//www.pathfinder.com/fortune
Individual Investor	//www.individualinvestor.com
Kiplinger's	//www.kiplinger.com
Money	//www.pathfinder.com/money
Mutual Funds	//www.mfmag.com
SmartMoney	//www.smartmoney.com
USA Today	//www.usatoday.com/money
U.S. News & World Report	//www.usnews.com
The Wall Street Journal	//wsj.com
Worth	//www.worth.com
Your Money	//www.consumerdigest.com

Investors are also encouraged to check the http://www.mediainfo.com for leads to other publications, as well as general research for new publications on the nine search engines in Chapter 4.

BARRON'S ONLINE: SUPERSTAR FUNDS, MANAGERS, AND FAMILIES

In much the same way that *Barron's* weekly print edition is eagerly awaited by its loyal fan club, the new Barron's Online Website is also eagerly awaited. Barron's Online is becoming a "real cool" site in cyberspace, and the company is now building an even bigger fan club throughout the known world, at least the known cyberspace investment world.

As any regular reader knows, *Barron's* regularly covers mutual funds. Of special interest are its quarterly and annual reviews, as well as special reports, which investors can access at the Barron's Online Website. Of special interest are two winners written by Eric Savitz, one of *Barron's* mutual funds experts:

❏ **Rating the major fund families**
  "It's all in the families . . . the first-ever ranking of America's mutual-fund families," which *Barron's* prepared from the Lipper database in

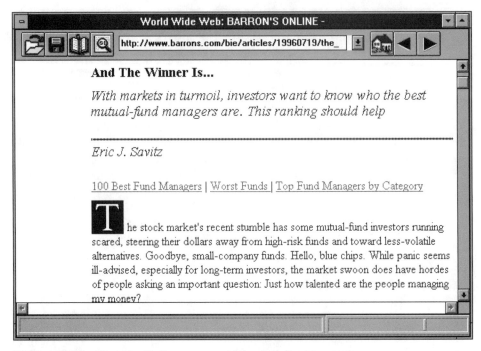

Figure 8.10   Barrons Online: survey of the top fund managers.

February. Ranking the 62 major families, and also ranking them by fund category for various performance periods. In calculating overall family returns, Lipper weighted individual fund returns to maintain integrity of the study.

❐ **Mutual fund managers rated**
"And the winner is . . ." *Barron's* midyear survey of the 100 best fund managers and the top fund managers by fund objective and category.

In addition, investors can also access fund "dossiers" (profiles and quotes) at any time on this Website. These fund dossiers tap into the highly respected Tradeline/IDD database, which is another key member of the Dow Jones editorial family, along with various print publications: *Barron's*, *The Wall Street Journal*, and *SmartMoney* magazine, all of which are now on the Web.

If Barrons Online continues developing superior products, they'll upstage their siblings at Dow Jones, as well as the Dow Jones cyberspace pioneer, Dow Jones News/Retrieval, at least in the mutual funds arena.

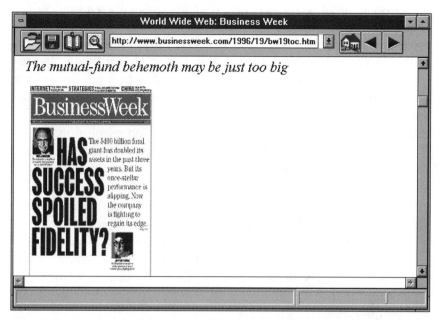

Figure 8.11   BusinessWeek Website: regular analysis of fund industry.

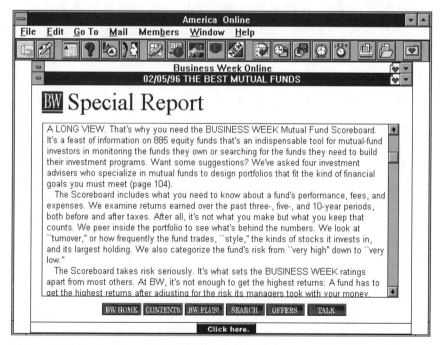

Figure 8.12   BusinessWeek Mutual Funds Scoreboard: best funds list.

BUSINESSWEEK: THE MUTUAL FUNDS' SCOREBOARD

BusinessWeek is one of the many McGraw-Hill publications, and clearly one of the most influential publications in the world, with a global readership in excess of 7 million. Its exceptional coverage and feature stories on new telecommunications and software technologies, online services and cyberspace, intranets and the Internet have been extremely helpful chapters of the rapidly unfolding history of the information revolution.

The same high level of journalism extends to *BusinessWeek*'s coverage of the mutual fund business. As with many in this emerging new generation of financial Websites, investors can search their archives and retrieve articles on a specific topic—the economy, technology, mutual funds— whatever your research path demands. America Online subscribers are already familiar with these search provisions and archives.

As with many other key financial publications, *BusinessWeek* often features special reports on funds, managers, families, and performance ratings soon after the major rating organizations, such as Lipper and Morningstar, release their quarterly data.

For example, in February last year, *BusinessWeek* titled one of its special reports, "The Best Mutual Funds . . . All You Need to Pick the Ones That Fit Your Needs." The 885 equity funds selected for the survey were screened using these criteria against the Morningstar research database:

❐ Returns over the prior 3-, 5-, and 10-year periods
❐ Both pretax and after-tax returns analyzed
❐ Portfolio turnover or frequency of trades
❐ Style or kinds of stocks invested in
❐ Largest holdings
❐ Risk level

And using these criteria, 48 of the 885 equity funds, or roughly 5 percent, earned the magazine's highest rating for their performance in the first half of this decade. *BusinessWeek* also noted that while the average diversified equity mutual fund realized a 32.1 percent return the prior year, *the S&P 500 index itself beat over 80 percent of the funds*, with a hot 37.5 percent return. *BusinessWeek*'s surveys are also available on AOL, where investors also have quick access to the Morningstar database for more current details.

Given the rush of the competition to the Web, and *BusinessWeek*'s leadership position in reporting on the information-technological-cyberspace revolution, and the predictions of massive growth in the mutual fund industry, you can be sure that the BusinessWeek Online Website will undergo some major upgrades in the next year, thanks to the intense competition from *Barron's, Worth, Kiplinger's, Money,* and *Mutual Funds* magazines, all of whom are becoming very aggressive in cyberspace.

FINANCIAL WORLD MAGAZINE: TOP PERFORMERS AND BEST BETS

The mutual fund information at *Financial World*'s Website is an excellent indication of how this trend is heating up. Clearly, more and more print publishers are reading the handwriting on the wall. The vast majority of cyberspace investors are mutual fund investors, and most are very independent-minded do-it-yourself investors.

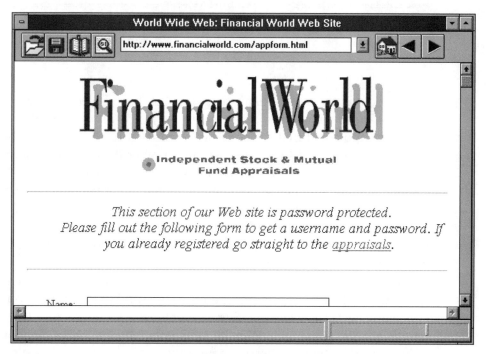

Figure 8.13   Financial World: independent mutual fund appraisals.

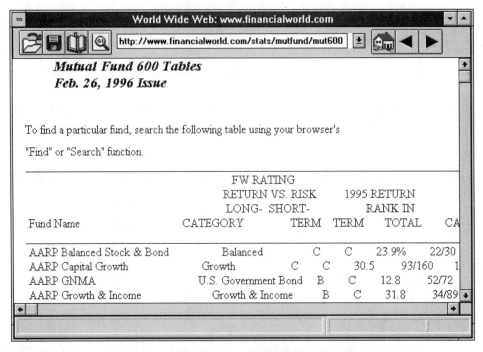

Figure 8.14 Financial World: best bets and appraisals of 600 funds.

Consequently, we regularly see the Web-based electronic editions of these financial magazines feature mutual fund information. It takes no genius to figure out that the coverage of mutual funds in print versions is on the increase. And they now use the same editorial content to capture and attract return cyber-visitors. It all makes logical sense.

Financial World should be complimented for their insight in adding some rather extensive fund information for Web users. At the *Financial World* site investors will find a listing of the "20 Best Bets" for the coming year, as well as a full listing of 600 top-performing funds, ranked by category, returns, and other criteria.

In addition, *Financial World* provides you with a search engine so you get a more detailed "appraisal" of any special fund that captures your interest. Morningstar is *Financial World*'s database. Although rapid improvements are likely at this Website, *Financial World*'s Website should be bookmarked by every cyberspace fund investor.

FORBES: CHAMPION OF NO-LOADS AND DO-IT-YOURSELF INVESTING

Forbes is currently developing its new Website, and cyberspace mutual fund investors are likely to be one of their major target audiences. *Forbes* has been a champion of no-load funds and is likely to keep up the pressure in cyberspace. Maybe *Forbes* will even add some new features, such as the "*Forbes* 400 Best Funds for 401(k)s" and the "*Forbes* 400 Richest Mutual Fund Investors." Don't knock it, *Forbes* brings a very special editorial perspective to everything.

Cyberspace publishing demands a different editorial and marketing approach, so the probabilities are very high that mutual fund information will start appearing more often at the *Forbes* Website in order to attract return visits by the fickle cyber-investors. Besides, articles about the "Best 401(k) Funds" are appearing with such boring frequency (and increasing our information overload), that a fresh slant on mutual funds would be welcomed . . . and *Forbes* has the power and panache to do it.

Forbes has a rich editorial tradition of covering trends and trendsetters in the world of business and finance, and is likely to become more aggressive on the Web. So expect the unexpected. Cyberspace is a world of surprises.

FORTUNE: THE BEST FUNDS FOR BUILDING WEALTH

The print edition of *Fortune* magazine regularly runs feature articles on mutual funds. In fact, *Fortune*'s intense coverage of funds is somewhat surprising, considering that both *Fortune* and *Money* magazines are owned by the Time Warner media giant. Fortunately for fund investors, this sibling rivalry appears to be not just tolerated, but encouraged in a very healthy way by the parent company, both in print and on its Pathfinder Website.

For example, *Fortune*'s year-end issue had several articles on funds, including "The Best Funds for Building Wealth." In the article, *Fortune* detailed the criteria used to screen the Morningstar database and came out with a list "designed to make your search easier and more rewarding." Here are the criteria *Fortune* used to screen its database and identify the top-performing funds and managers:

❑ **Total returns:** After taxes and after adjusting for sales loads.
❑ **Turnover:** An indicator of trading activity and taxes.

Figure 8.15   Forbes Website: regular mutual funds surveys.

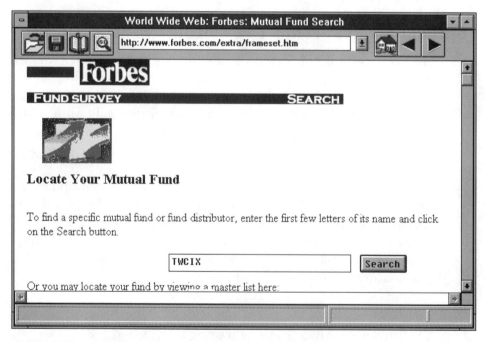

Figure 8.16   Forbes search engine to funds and fund families.

Figure 8.17 The Forbes directory of mutual funds and fund families.

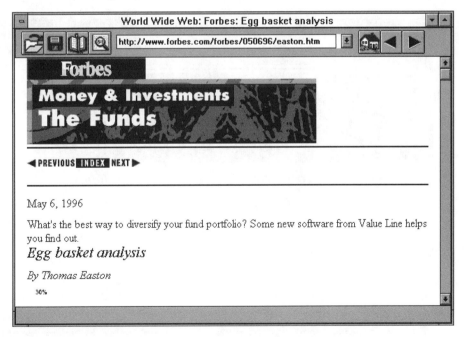

Figure 8.18 Forbes on funds: diversification strategies and more.

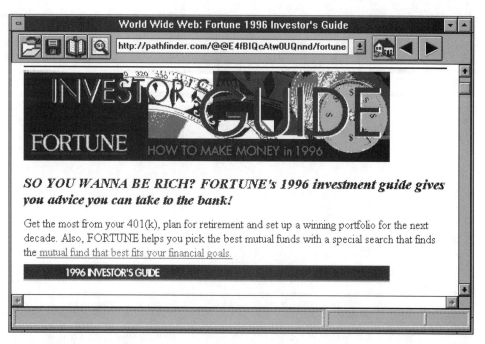

Figure 8.19 Fortune Investor's Guide: how to make money.

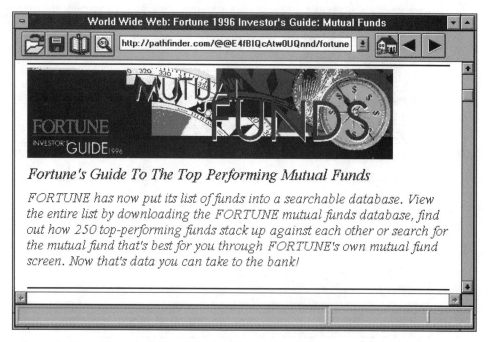

Figure 8.20 Fortune Guide to the Top Performing Mutual Funds.

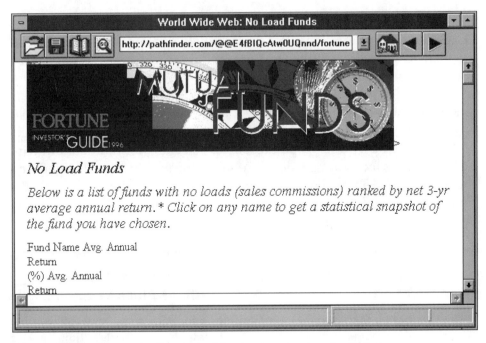

Figure 8.21   Fortune's directory of the best no-load mutual funds.

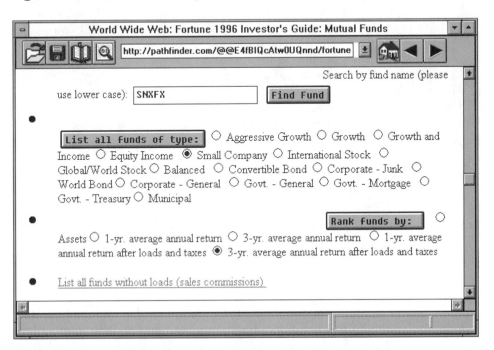

Figure 8.22   Fortune search engine: access best funds by objective.

❑ **Management:** Responsible performers are still managing.

❑ **Other criteria:** No long lock-ins, available nationally, initial invest-ment less than $10,000, no start-ups, and no single sector, country, state, or security funds.

And with that selective set of criteria, "the 280 stock, hybrid, and bond *funds* we wind up with offer a short list of *money managers* worth considering." Note that like many other expert resources screening for mutual fund win-ners, *Fortune* is focusing as much or more on the managers as the funds, on the jockeys as well as the horses. This is a repetitive theme through the financial press today, one you should take to heart in developing *your* spe-cial criteria and in doing *your* screening.

FORTUNE: THE TYPICAL FUND MANAGER ADDS "VIRTUALLY NOTHING TO THE PERFORMANCE OF HIS PORTFOLIO BY HIS STOCK SELECTION."

Fortune brings us back to the basic principle of focusing on asset allocations (90 percent of your portfolio's success) rather than using funds to time the market and pick stocks (only 10 percent of your portfolio's success):

"A sophisticated measurement of risk helps tally the value managers add to funds with their stock-picking ability. That's important, because picking a mutual fund is a bet on the jockey as well as the horse . . .

"*Fortune*'s analysis allowed for allocation into seven types of equities and six types of fixed-income assets. The results essentially compared the funds' performances with what they would have achieved if they had simply gone unmanaged.

"The results were not entirely inspiring. While some managers clearly exceeded their benchmarks, the typical fund manager on *Fortune*'s list added virtually nothing to the performance of his portfolio by his stock selection. In many cases, the funds managers actually lower returns by poor stock selection. Does this mean that you should ignore the Best Mutual Funds list? Not at all. But be mindful that some of the funds are riskier than others, even if they are in the same category."

SOURCE: Terence Pare, "A New Way to Rate Funds and Their Managers," *Fortune* (December 25, 1995).

Like every other of these top-performing periodicals, *Fortune* regularly covers the mutual fund industry: funds and managers, retirement plan-ning and 401(k) plans, boomers and Gen Xers, fund networks and their brokers. *Fortune*'s year-end issues are especially valuable, filled with many excellent articles on topics for the fund investor, a virtual *primer* on mutual fund investing.

More important, you can track and uncover all of *Fortune*'s mutual fund articles on the Web, especially the quarterly articles rating and screening funds and managers. Included are search engines that help you screen *Fortune*'s archives for valuable information buried in past issues.

And although the text and data are often abbreviated (on the current Web editions of most publications), you should expect that this condition will improve as future Web technology improves; then the new electronic magazines will become not only as inclusive as the print editions, they will also be interactive. Meanwhile, explore the new electronic *Fortune,* right next to the electronic *Money* on Pathfinder.com.

INDIVIDUAL INVESTOR MAGAZINE: MAGIC STOCKS AND HOT FUNDS

The editorial focus of *Individual Investor* magazine is definitely more on stocks than funds, especially small caps, new issues, and the fastest-

---

THE SEVEN DEADLY SINS OF MUTUAL FUND INVESTORS

"Countless mutual fund investors chronically commit small mistakes. Individually, these mishaps won't make much of a dent on a portfolio. But together, they'll ravage your returns. . . . Here's a look at the seven worst mistakes mutual fund investors commonly make—sins, hopefully, you'll learn to avoid.

1. Selecting a mutual fund because it was one of last year's best performers . . .
2. Investing in mutual funds with high portfolio turnovers . . .
3. Buying load funds if you really don't need help from a broker . . .
4. Failure to invest aggressively enough . . .
5. Waiting for a market decline to invest . . .
6. Selling funds for the wrong reason . . .
7. Buying a fund and forgetting about it."

"Most people commit these errors from time to time, and then forget. That is probably the biggest mistake of all." Not learning, and making the same mistake twice.

SOURCE: Steven Kaufman, "Seven Deadly Sins of Fund Investors," *Individual Investor* (August 1995).

growing companies, securities with higher return/risk profiles. Nevertheless, *Individual Investor* magazine does cover funds on a regular basis, and periodically they do extensive features.

The magazine tends to be quite selective in their recommendations, that is, approaching its job with a rifle, like *SmartMoney,* rather than with a shotgun, like *Kiplinger's* or *BusinessWeek.* In last year's March issue, for example, *Individual Investor* narrowed its focus to a mere 18 funds in six categories: aggressive growth, growth, equity growth, international and global, sectors, and fixed-income funds.

They created weighted averages for select criteria: total returns over various performance periods, by sector, and other proprietary analyses of portfolios compared to *Individual Investor's* forecasts for market sectors most likely to outperform in the coming year. *Individual Investor* also noted that 11 of the 15 stock funds from the prior year beat their peers.

In print, *Individual Investor* is already a near-perfect magazine for today's do-it-yourself investor. With their electronic edition, they are becoming a major new resource for the cyberspace investor in mutual funds, as well as stocks. Watch out *Barron's.*

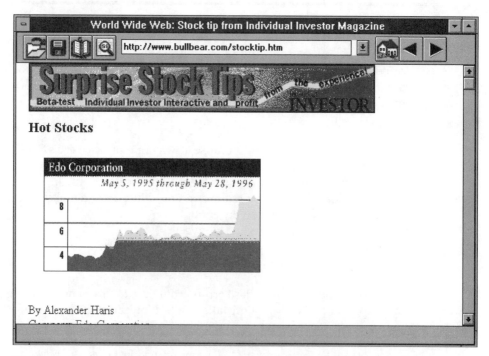

Figure 8.23   Individual Investor: bulls, bears, and hot mutual funds.

KIPLINGER'S: THE ULTIMATE MUTUAL FUNDS ANNUAL GUIDE

There's absolutely no question about it, the monthly print magazine, *Kiplinger's Personal Finance Magazine,* is a winner with individual investors. And now their new annual, *Kiplinger's Mutual Funds,* is a must-buy. And fortunately for all cyberspace fund investors, *Kiplinger's* new Website will be the home for all this same high-quality research and analysis.

As with almost all these Websites from the financial magazines, some of the information will be available free, while investors will have to pay for the full service (usually, a subscription to the complete text of the current issue). Other possible subscription services that may or may not be optional include news, quotes, retirement planning, company and fund profiles, and archive searches, for example. Fortunately, the new Kiplinger Online Website is still delivering a super selection of free services.

Here's a suggestion you might consider as one of many more lessons in your ongoing education in this new cyberspace mutual fund investing. Compare the "Best Funds" lists for *two or more* of these Websites and see how much (if any) overlap exists. For example, in *Kiplinger's Mutual Funds '96,* the editors included a list of 50 superfunds, which they identified as

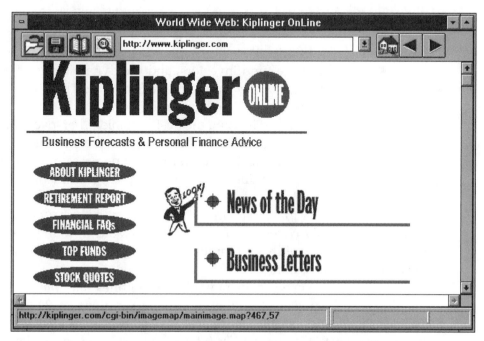

Figure 8.24   Kiplinger Online Website: top-rated funds information.

"consistently good . . . and deserve your attention." Note, however, that only 2 of the 18 funds recommended by *Individual Investor* about the same time were among *Kiplinger's* 50 superfunds.

Both lists are loaded with winners. Yet because the lists are so narrow, they may give the subtle—and obviously false—impression that all funds *not* on a particular list are not "consistently good," and therefore don't merit your attention. Wrong.

Viewed another way, if *each* magazine had to pick a broader top 250 (rather than 18 or 50), the combined total of 68 funds from both magazine lists just might be included in the new top-250 list. Yet there's no guarantee. With different criteria, two sets of editors or experts will always come up with different best-funds lists, no matter how big. And so will you.

In any event, you will always get some valuable tips from these best-funds lists prepared by experts and editors. But in the end, if you need only 6 to 12 funds to diversify a portfolio, and the experts can't agree, the decision (as always) falls squarely back in your lap (or rather your laptop or desktop computer). And Kiplinger Online can help you. It's a must-see site for every independent fund investor.

MONEY MAGAZINE: PATHFINDER INTO THE NEW CYBERSPACE

Time Warner's Pathfinder Website is emerging as one of the truly great resources for cyberspace fund investors, and the dynamic duo of *Fortune* and *Money* magazines is a big part of the reason why. They have a clear edge in leveraging the whole Time Warner database.

Moreover, Time Warner is using the best possible cyberspace technologies to continue delivering established content providers in this new electronic form. On top of all this, Time Warner's experience in the film and television industries is proving to be a major asset in attracting the new cyberspace crowd.

We already know that *Money* magazine is one of the best *print* resources for regular monthly coverage of mutual funds. And now the Pathfinder edition of *Money* is rapidly becoming one of the top electronic publications for mutual fund investors.

In fact, because cyberspace now gives monthlies like *Money* and *Fortune* the delivery power of a daily newspaper, and even a 24-hour news channel, *Money* and its siblings are now giving the digital Dow Jones family (*Barron's*, *SmartMoney*, and *The Interactive Journal*) a spectacular run for

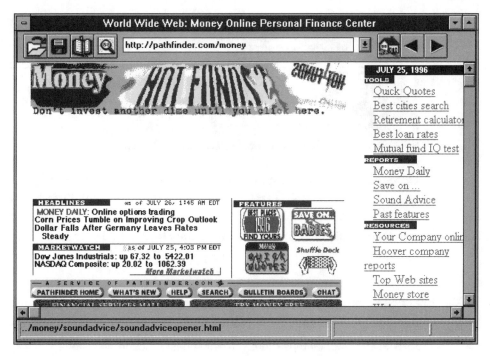

Figure 8.25 *Money* magazine's Website: loaded with hot-fund data.

the money with cyberspace investors. And the winner of this competition will not be Time Warner or Dow Jones; it'll be the individual investor.

Earlier we featured the *Money*/Vanguard fund investor's IQ quiz. This quiz is perhaps the essential first stop for every investor, both novice or expert. After the test, stick around and explore the wealth of investors' resources all here in one location on the Web: Fundwatch, headline news, market indexes, securities quotes, company research, current loan rates, and links to other key Websites for investors. *Money* also has a first-class search engine that lets you scan and retrieve important articles from their huge database. Also see *Money*'s buy/sell/hold ratings of the 25 largest mutual funds.

Pathfinder's aggressive cyberspace strategy is paying off. Not only with the broad consumer market, but with cyberspace investors generally and, most specifically, with the flood of mutual fund investors discovering this new world of do-it-yourself opportunities on the Web. This one's another winner. Bookmark it and return to it often.

Figure 8.26   *Money* magazine: screening best funds for investors.

MUTUAL FUNDS MAGAZINE: CYBERSPACE ROOKIE OF THE YEAR

Mutual Funds Online magazine is a rising star in the publishing arena. And they're rapidly moving to the pole position in the race for the cyberspace fund investor. Less than two years ago, the Institute for Econometric Research was just one of hundreds of financial newsletter publishers. The Institute published 10 excellent newsletters, and they were one of the early publishers featured on the NETworth Website.

All that rapidly changed two years ago with the publication of *Mutual Funds* magazine, and their new Website, Mutual Funds Online. The magazine is still the only one devoted solely to mutual funds, and they are winning awards for editorial coverage, among the best in the business. This Website is already a favorite among cyber-investors.

Mutual Funds Online provides an endless series of perspectives on star-performing mutual funds, top-gun managers and major families, sectors, globals and rookies, news, quotes, and trends in the mutual fund industry. Review their standard screening criteria in Chapter 7 to get a feel for the online power available to you in cyberspace. Better yet, get on the Web and see the action.

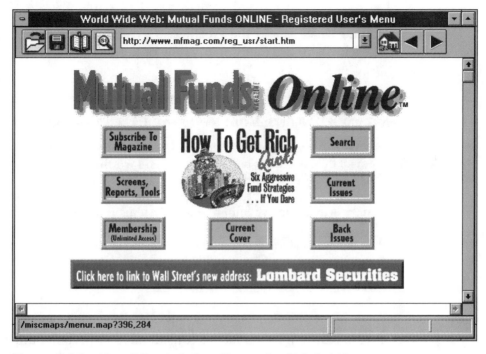

Figure 8.27   Mutual Funds Online: How to Get Rich Quick!

And here's another lesson: Compare Mutual Funds Online selection of the 24 top-gun fund managers with similar selections on Kiplinger Online or the Pathfinder Website. Once more you'll see what different criteria, formulas, databases, and editorial styles do to the process of selecting top guns and five-star winners; there's little overlap in the survey results. Discover why you cannot rely solely on the experts' best-funds lists. And why the ultimate, final investment decision—buy, sell, or hold—is *always* in your court.

The Mutual Funds Online Website is loaded with power tools that could make it not only your first, but possibly even the only resource you need in cyberspace. This is a must-see publication for fund investors, both online and in print.

SMARTMONEY: POWER HITTER IN DIGITAL DOW'S STARTING LINEUP

Dow Jones was a cyberspace pioneer for the institutional investor. The Dow Jones New/Retrieval was a mainstay and one of the few high-quality electronic tools open to investors until the early 1990s. The growing popularity of online services and the World Wide Web revolution changed all that. Today's investor has many, many new options available.

SMART MONEY WARNS: MOST NEW FUNDS AREN'T WORTH BUYING

The Wall Street Journal's SmartMoney magazine warns the serious investor that many of the new funds being offered aren't worth buying:

"With $25 billion a month flowing into mutual funds, new funds are sprouting like weeds. But of the 617 equity funds created last year, only seven are worth buying . . . all are led by managers with proven track records."

Only seven? That's scary. Another reason to do your homework.

SOURCE: Walecia Konrad, "The Best of the New Funds," *SmartMoney* (August 1996).

As a result, Dow Jones is facing considerable new competition from many news vendors, software developers, online magazine publishers, and others. And they have been slow in adjusting to the new competitive arena where they no longer have a near monopoly.

Fortunately, the new Digital Dow giant is now wide awake—growling and flexing its muscles. Barron's Online is a sure winner, as is the Interactive Journal. And now *SmartMoney* is entering the starting lineup of the Digital Dow team.

Hopefully, *SmartMoney* will carry its special editorial elitism into cyberspace. Other publications might focus on a list of the "Best 250 Funds," or even the "Top 50." One *SmartMoney* cover story read: "Super-Star Funds: There Are 2,034 Mutual Funds Out There. Only 7 passed Our Test." Another: "The Best New Funds . . . but of the 617 equity funds created last year, only seven are worth buying." And one of the magazine's articles gave us "Funds Fit for a Guru." Highly selective screening here for serious fund investors.

With so many other lists cloning each other today, *SmartMoney*'s special perspective is not only welcome, but cyberspace investors will clearly benefit by using *SmartMoney*'s selections as a benchmark, cross-check, or second opinion in narrowing their own picks to fit the asset allocations in their individual financial plans.

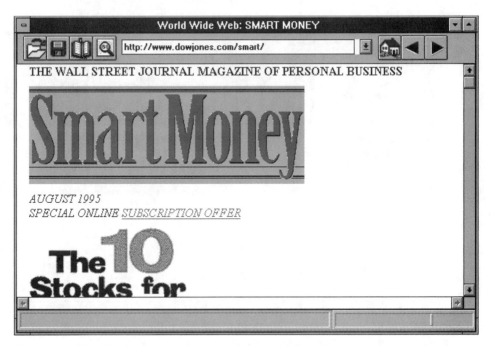

Figure 8.28 SmartMoney Online: tooling up for the Web

USA TODAY ONLINE: NATIONAL NEWS PLUS LIPPER DATABASE

Remember when skeptics said it couldn't be done? They said that about CNN and *USA Today*. Well, thanks to the visions of Turner and Newhouse, we have two super news vehicles. And now CNN and *USA Today* are again "going for the gold" in cyberspace.

USA Today is already doing surprisingly well, thank you, giving the online editions of the *monthly* magazines some solid competition. And a major part of its success with the do-it-yourself fund investor is due to the Lipper database. *USA Today* is proving to be the perfect retail delivery outlet for this highly respected fund database.

❐ Regular **editorial columns** of hot topics

❐ **Search engine** linked to archive of past issues

❐ **Quarterly reviews** of 3,500-plus equities and fixed-income funds

❐ Major mutual **fund categories rated** using Lipper's criteria

❐ Detailed performance of the **100 largest stock funds**

Figure 8.29   *USA Today's* Money Website: top financial news daily.

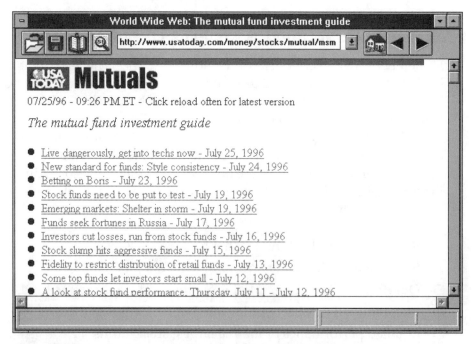

Figure 8.30   *USA Today's* mutual fund guide: researches top news stories.

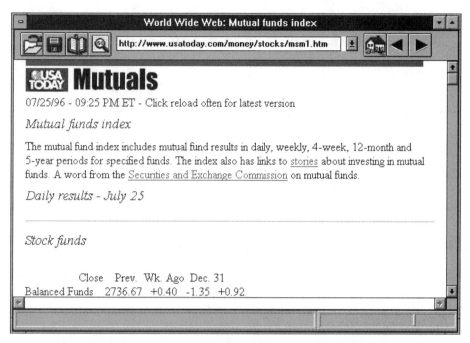

Figure 8.31 *USA Today:* mutual fund statistics, indexes, performance.

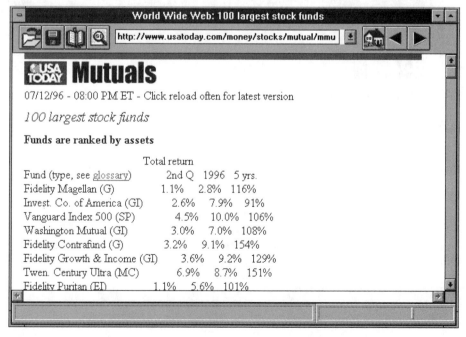

Figure 8.32 *USA Today:* performance of funds by size and objective.

❐ **Trend analyses:** shifts in stocks, bonds, and sectors
❐ Educational materials, glossary of terms, and Web links

USA Today's extensive fund coverage is quite remarkable, not because they do anything better or different than *Money, Kiplinger's,* or *Mutual Funds,* but because *USA Today* is a national *daily* newspaper. And because it is not a monthly *financial* periodical. Nevertheless, *USA Today* is out there in cyberspace, competing with the best of the electronic editions of the financial magazines.

The skeptics should be a bit more circumspect this time, because *USA Today* just might come out on top again—this time with the fund investors.

U.S. NEWS & WORLD REPORT: HONOR ROLL OF BEST FUNDS

U.S. News & World Report is another surprise in the delivery of mutual fund information in cyberspace. Their Website is a relative newcomer online. However, their print coverage of funds is quite solid, considering that they are a weekly magazine for a general audience. *U.S. News* also taps into the same Micropal database used by *Kiplinger's* magazine.

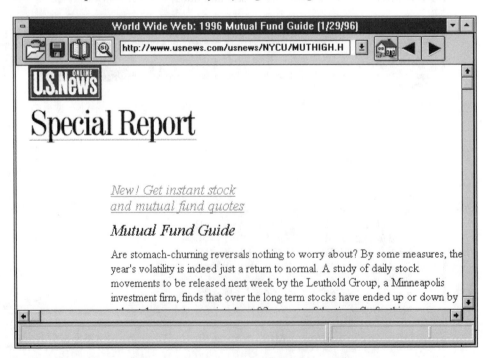

Figure 8.33 *U.S. News & World Report:* instant mutual fund quotes.

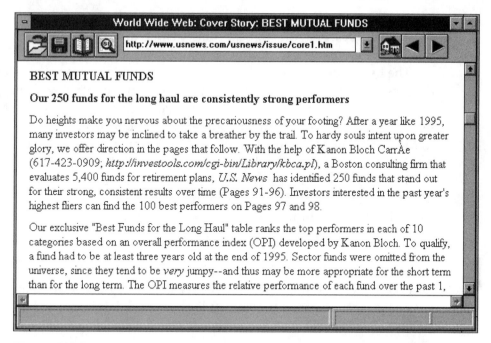

Figure 8.34 *U.S. News & World Report:* top-250 funds for the long haul.

In spite of the overlapping database, the "Top 50" highlighted by *Kiplinger's Mutual Funds '96* annual and the "U.S. News Honor Roll" of 45 funds shared only 8 funds in common. Once again, we see quite dramatically the need for each cyberspace investor to take full responsibility for the task of creating *your own* best-funds list with *your* favorite software system and *your own* criteria customized to fit *your* particular financial plan.

With *USA Today* as a role model for a nonfinancial publication in the cyberspace fund market, the new *U.S. News* Website could provide some solid competition, although perhaps not as intense as the coverage from the financial magazines. Early last year, the *U.S. News* print version included several best-funds schedules:

❏ **Honor Roll of the top-45** funds whose performance put them in the top 10 percent of their respective fund categories for three consecutive years

❏ **Top-250 "funds for the long haul . . . consistently strong performers"**

❏ Top-10 funds in each **of 10 primary fund categories**

❏ Ratings of the **50 largest** stock and bond funds

❏ Performance ratings of the **top-10 mutual fund families**

In fact, this *U.S. News* material is quite distinguished for a nonfinancial publication and deserves the highest praise. Hopefully, they will be repeating this feature regularly and posting it on their Website.

The list of fund families developed for *U.S. News* is from the Micropal database, and includes three fund families—Morgan Stanley, Pimco, and Strong—that are not included within the 20 largest families on the Morningstar database and the Worth Online list. Around this period, just prior to Morgan Stanley's acquisition of the Van Kampen family of funds, Morgan Stanley was 59th in total assets managed.

The reason for this variation is that *U.S. News* used a unique proprietary index, the Fund Family Performance Index (FFPI), which measures several criteria, including portfolio risk. *U.S. News'* reports also build on research from Morningstar and Kanon Bloch Carre, a Boston research firm specializing in mutual funds.

If *U.S. News & World Report* puts the same high-quality fund information on its Website regularly, cyber-investors will be fortunate in having yet another set of expert best-funds lists as second opinions for their own research.

THE WALL STREET JOURNAL: INTERACTIVE JOURNAL EDITION FROM THE NEW DIGITAL DOW

The new Interactive Wall Street Journal naturally leans more toward the securities markets in general rather than funds. This new electronic edition of the bible of the gray-pinstriped investor costs less than half the print version, and it's delivered around the clock. Technologically, it's state of the art. *Individual Investor* even concluded, "Given the awesome comprehensiveness of *The Wall Street Journal* interactive edition, there is remarkable little to quibble about." The content is a virtual copy of the print edition, with some noticeable bonuses and cyberspace conveniences. Their lineup looks like this:

❏ Three standard sections: **Front Section, Marketplace, Money & Investing.**

❏ **Personal Journal:** preselect favorite features, companies, news, etc.

❏ Programmed links to **company snapshots and briefs** on newsmakers

❏ A new **sports section** that is continually updated

❏ **Quick-jump links** from the main directory to sections of interest

❏ Search engine accessing to the **news archives** from the prior two weeks, which actually is too short a perspective for mutual fund investing

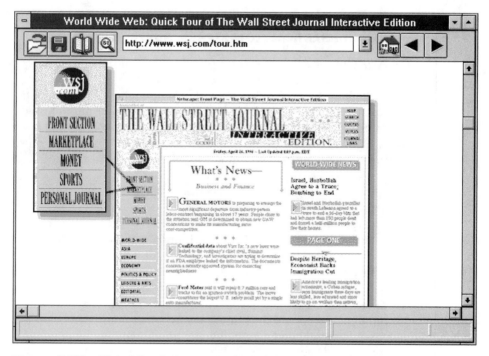

Figure 8.35   Digital Dow's Interactive Wall Street Journal.

From a strategic perspective, the Interactive Journal is an important element in the new Digital Dow, along with Barron's Online, SmartMoney Online, and Dow Jones News/Retrieval.

And while Barron's Online and SmartMoney Online appear to be more focused on in-depth mutual funds coverage, the Interactive Journal can be counted on to deliver its unique perspective with real-time urgency: features, news, and quotes, plus their extensive quarterly reviews of the mutual fund industry.

WORTH MAGAZINE: FINANCIAL INTELLIGENCE ON THE WEB

Worth magazine is a welcome maverick in cyberspace information industry circles. The lead banner of their Website reads: "Worth Online—Financial Intelligence," and that's their goal—*intelligence,* not just data. *Worth's* mission is beyond data delivery, beyond raw information: a commitment to financial intelligence. And *Worth* is emerging as an important cyberport for the new do-it-yourself fund investor operating in this high-tech, fast-paced world.

EIGHT PRACTICAL, LOW-STRESS, SUREFIRE STRATEGIES

The Wall Street Journal frequently offers some real down-home, keep-it-simple, sage advice to investors. Here's a few when all else fails:

"Take it easy. Other folks are working themselves into a lather trying to guess the market's direction, spot the next superstar mutual fund and find another hot initial public offering. And most, of course, will fail miserably. So why don't you do yourself a favor and focus instead on some surefire ways to improve your finances. Here are eight strategies:

Dump your savings account . . . consider switching to a certificate of deposit or money market fund . . .

Buy cheaper mutual funds. . . . Stick with money funds that charge less than 0.6% a year and no-load bond funds that levy less than 0.8%.

Use a discount broker. If you want advice, pay for it. But don't pay for advice you don't need . . . also check out the burgeoning number of no-load stocks, which can be bought directly from the company . . .

Get tax smart . . . make the maximum contribution to any tax-deductible retirement account [and] figure out whether you're better off in tax-free municipal bonds . . .

Nickels and dimes . . . consolidate individual retirement accounts. . . . Apply for no-fee credit card . . .

Save more. Socking away a few extra dollars every month . . . surer road to riches . . .

Contemplate your own death . . . a will . . . trust . . . gifts . . .

Avoid losses. "Get all your paperwork organized, just in case."

And when you stop and think about it a minute, there's a whole darn barnful of wisdom here filled with old saws that will add to your peace of mind without requiring you to beef up your hard drive or even go online.

SOURCE: Jonathan Clements, "For Investors Who Are Loath to Gamble, Here Are Eight Solid Money Strategies," *The Wall Street Journal* (July 9, 1995).

Worth's editors are doing an especially good job in the mutual fund arena. Their annual reporting on the top-20 fund families, for example, is financial intelligence at its best, and something every fund investor should bookmark for future reference as well as current research. Investors can also access *Worth*'s materials on America Online. On the Web, anyone in the world can access *Worth*.

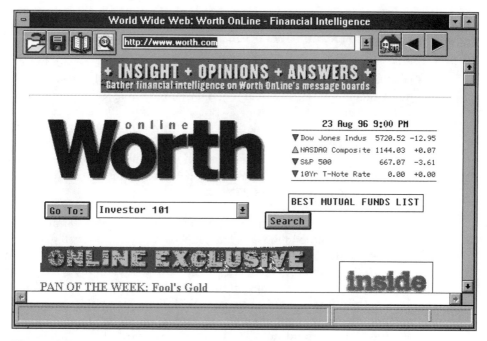

Figure 8.36 Worth Online—Financial Intelligence.

The Worth Online Website features virtually the same hot editorial content found in their print edition, including guru Peter Lynch, market indexes, and search provisions to past articles. *Worth* is a strong competitor, in print and in cyberspace, and will make giants like Dow Jones, Time Warner, and McGraw-Hill run a little harder.

Cyberspace fund investors with any reasonable degree of moxie (Worth calls it "financial intelligence") would be wise to bookmark Worth Online and return to it on a regular basis. Don't miss this one in your research.

YOUR MONEY MAGAZINE AND OTHER NEWCOMERS JOIN THE RACE

Your Money magazine is a relatively new bimonthly financial magazine, with editorial dynamics reflecting many of the basic features of the other consumer-oriented personal finance magazines, especially *Kiplinger's* and *Money* magazines, although *Your Money* may not be considered a major threat by the competition (yet).

RED FLAGS: HOW TO TELL IF YOUR MANAGER'S LOSING IT

"Pay attention to the key signs that may mean trouble ahead, but don't sell too quickly. Even the great managers hit dry spells. In most cases your best bet is to give them a year to get back on track . . .

"As Vanguard CEO John C. Bogle is so fond of saying, the performance of mutual funds, over time, tends toward mediocrity. Why? Within a fund's success often lie the seeds of failure. A half-dozen or so factors consistently conspire to undermine even talented managers—and their appearance should alert investors to pay close attention to what's happening at their funds. Among them:

Ballooning assets. A wizard makes his reputation with $30 million [then with] $1.1 billion ten years later, it became a different ball game . . .

Market creep. . . . Over time, markets change and your manager can't find the companies he or she prefers . . .

Fund pileup . . . adding new funds at a dizzying pace . . . asked to run another fund or, worse, charged with hiring lawyers, managers and administrative staff. Boom! . . .

Failing to keep good help. . . . When one or more [leaves], results may suffer."

SOURCE: Richard Teitelbaum, "Is Your Fund Manager Losing It," *Fortune* (December 25, 1995).

"A sampling of fund managers reveals that most fail to see their increased bulk as a significant problem. Nonetheless, management styles have been subtly adjusted, cash positions have increased and for the new, often highly segmented funds have accelerated. It's important for bettor on hot portfolio managers to watch for such signals."

SOURCE: Eric Savitz, "Warning Signs," *Barron's* (June 3, 1996).

However, *Your Money* already features mutual fund information in every print edition, and we fully expect to see the magazine featuring their best-funds lists on the Web, using Morningstar research data. Here are *Your Money*'s regular screens:

❐ **Top-15 stock funds,** based on one-, three-, and five-year returns
❐ Performance of the **10 largest stock funds**
❐ **Top-10 funds in 17 categories,** based on their objectives

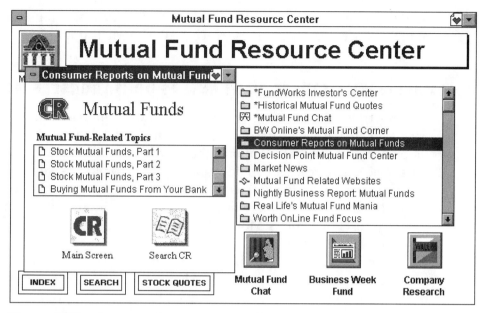

Figure 8.37 Consumer Reports' Mutual Fund Report on AOL.

In addition to *Your Money* magazine, the editors of several consumer magazines are featuring mutual fund articles more frequently. This trend is being fueled by the growing public interest in mutual funds, 401(k)s, social security, and retirement planning in general, creating new pressures to save and a huge influx of new money flowing into mutual funds. As a result, in the past year we began to see articles on mutual funds in diverse magazines; for example,

❏ *Consumers Digest:* "The Complete Guide to Mutual Funds."

❏ *Consumer Reports:* "Consumer Reports on Mutual Funds."

❏ *Playboy:* "Everything You've Heard about Mutual Funds Is Wrong."

❏ *Working Woman:* "The Ten Most Popular Mutual Funds."

And we expect to see more of this jump-on-the-bandwagon trend throughout the print media. However, with the exception of a *Consumer Reports'* survey on America Online, none of these magazines has emerged on the Web with any regular mutual fund coverage.

But don't write any of them off! Improbably as it may seem, recent cyberspace history is loaded with so many unpredictable and pleasant surprises, fund investors are strongly advised to have their search radar regularly scanning for new resources like these reaching the Internet stratosphere.

BLOOMBERG: WALL STREET GIANT ENTERS DO-IT-YOURSELF MARKET

Bloomberg is now focusing on the do-it-yourself market, another fortunate sign in the cyberspace revolution. In *Expert Investing on the Net*, Bloomberg was included among the *television* news organizations as a cyberspace resource. Our logic was simple. Bloomberg's supersophisticated, proprietary navigator is designed for *institutional* investors. It is priced out of the do-it-yourself investor market, at more than 50 times the monthly costs of Reuters Money Network, Quicken Investor Insight, or Dow Jones News/Retrieval.

On the other hand, the Bloomberg financial information team was helping the individual investor on Main Street with its television news reporting and newswire delivery systems, beamed to the print media, television, and the Internet. In short, Bloomberg was a broadcaster when it came to helping the do-it-yourself cyberspace investor.

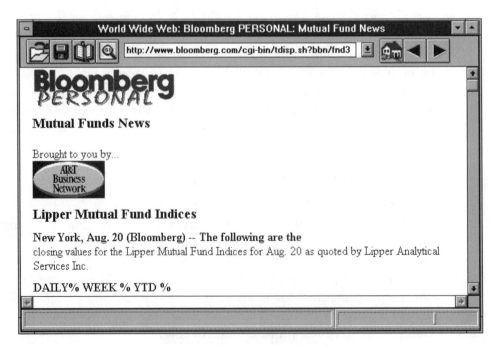

Figure 8.38   Bloomberg Personal: Lipper Mutual Fund Indices.

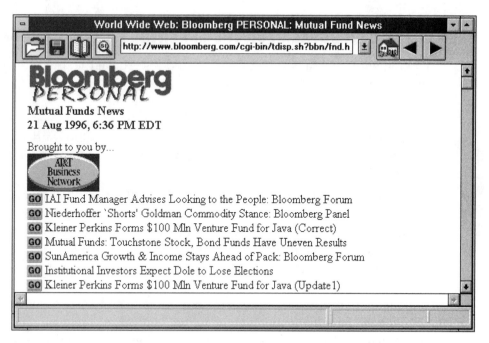

Figure 8.39   Bloomberg Personal: mutual fund news reports.

As a broadcaster, Bloomberg and the other two financial television broadcasters, CNBC and CNNfn, reported on hot stock news rather than the broader best-funds research investors need for a second opinion on mutual funds, and the magazines are now provided on the Web.

Now that's all changing. Last year Bloomberg began publishing *Bloomberg Personal,* a competitor of *SmartMoney, Worth,* and *Fortune.* More important for the cyberspace investor, *Bloomberg Personal* is now forced to compete with the other Web-based electronic editions of these consumer finance magazines, adding Bloomberg's special brand of reporting to the mutual fund industry . . . and leveling the playing field by giving the individual investor even more online resources.

As a result, we can see here another sign of the steady transfer of power from the Wall Street Establishment to the independent investor on Main Street—another element in the fulfillment of John Naisbitt's prediction in *The Global Paradox* that "all trends are in the direction of making the smallest player in the global economy more and more powerful." Welcome aboard Bloomberg . . . to the highly competitive new global *cyberspace* mass economy.

BOTTOM LINE: FIRST, BUILD YOUR OWN LIST OF WINNERS
THEN CHECK CYBERSPACE FOR THE EXPERTS' SECOND OPINIONS

Picking winners is a two-step process, and it's crucial that investors do not reverse the sequence of these two crucial steps:

☐ **First, you pick your own winning funds.**   Screen and select your own winners, using your own computer software system, online service, and your own criteria, after developing your personal financial plan, complete with asset allocations.

☐ **Then get second opinions from best-funds lists in cyberspace.**   After you use your online/software/computer mutual fund investing system to come up with some alternatives that fit your asset allocations, then double-check yourself. Get some second opinions by comparing your alternatives to those in some of the 16 key online magazines listed here.

There are numerous reasons for not relying solely on the second opinions you get from the experts at the various online magazines, *and definitely do not rely on them for your first opinion.* Otherwise, you'll give up your responsibility as an independent do-it-yourself investor.

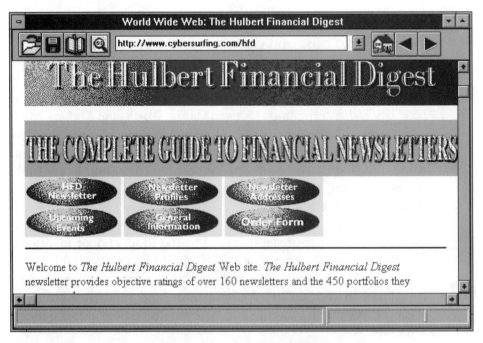

Figure 8.40   Hulbert Financial Digest: the complete guide.

TOP MUTUAL FUND NEWSLETTERS: MORE GREAT SECOND OPINIONS

Need more second opinions? Try a few financial newsletters, on a highly selected basis. Although most financial newsletters are of questionable value, here are nine top performers as rated by the *Hulbert Financial Digest*. Nine of the top-performing long-term newsletters for mutual funds (including other newsletters with mutual fund portfolios) include:

Timer Digest	(203) 629-3503
Fundline	(818) 346-5637
Fidelity Monitor	(800) 397-3094
Stockmarket Cycles	(707) 579-8444
Fidelity Insight	(617) 235-4422
Professional Timing Service	(406) 543-4131
Equity Fund Outlook	(617) 397-6844
No-Load Fund Investor	(914) 693-7420
Personal Finance	(703) 548-2400

SOURCE: "Long Term Performance Ratings," *Hulbert Financial Digest* (July 31, 1996). And for additional evaluations of financial newsletters, see the annual *Hulbert Guide to Financial Newsletters.* Hulbert's *Digest* is a valuable resource.

Complimentary sample copies are available from most of these publishers. The time period for Hulbert's various ratings were five and eight years. Performance records also included both Total Return and Risk-Adjusted Returns. Most of these mutual fund letters have print rather than electronic editions, but this is likely to change soon with the Web's expansion as the primary delivery system for financial information.

Five other excellent advisory letters for mutual fund investors:

The Asset Allocator	(800) 850-1522
Independent Advisor/Vanguard	(800) 211-7642
InvestTech Mutual Fund Advisor	(800) 955-8500
Moneyletter	(800) 433-1528
No-Load Fund Analyst	(800) 776-9555

SOURCE: Walter Updegrave, *The Right Way to Invest in Mutual Funds* (Warner Books, 1996), and other resources.

With the flood of best-funds lists now being published on a regular basis, it would be easy to surrender your decision-making power to these (presumed) experts. However, you can't afford to fall into the trap. If you do, it will only weaken your skill, judgment, and confidence as an independent investor. And then you'll be vulnerable to these cyberspace magazines in the same way you previously had to rely on all those brokers, advisors, newsletter writers, and other so-called professional gurus in the pre-cyberspace days.

Yes, definitely use these new Websites published online by these top-16 financial magazines. But whatever you do, be extremely skeptical of their limitations. For now, expect big gaps in their online data, see past the trend toward the sensational, and if you do use these Web resources, use at least two, always double-check one list against one or two others, and use them only as a second opinion to your own research.

Remember, these magazine experts use different databases and different criteria, criteria that aren't specifically your criteria. Moreover, they're human; they make mistakes, too. However, even with these limitations, this emerging network of cyberspace resources is a valuable resource for the do-it-yourself fund investor. Bookmark them and use them for *second opinions* in selecting *your* winners, *your* top-gun managers, and *your* superstar funds.

Choosing from the Top-20 Mutual Fund Families

The Powerhouses Controlling a Majority of Cyberspace Mutual Funds

Here in step 9 we'll identify the 20 largest families of funds. Together, these fund families control about half of all the mutual fund assets under management, in more than 3,000 mutual funds. We will help you find these fund families in cyberspace, tap into their databases, test their online and Internet services, and check out their management styles and track records.

THE BIGGEST MUTUAL FUND FAMILIES
WILL GET EVEN BIGGER AND MORE POWERFUL BY 2000

The cyberspace revolution is creating a major upheaval within the mutual fund industry and, indeed, the broader money management business. The retirement of the boomers, a national savings shortfall, massive corporate

---

CYBERSPACE REVOLUTION CREATES HIGH ANXIETY, SHAKING UP THE MUTUAL FUND INDUSTRY

"Many of today's mutual funds will be gone by the year 2000. That dire warning comes not from some quirky doomsday newsletter, but rather from the august firm of Goldman Sachs . . . widespread consolidation over the next few years . . .

"The battle will be made more intense . . . as investors get smarter about electronic investing and increasingly demand that fund companies offer better service, more information, and lower fees . . . that will mean an industry dominated by a handful of large companies. . . . For individual investors, these developments spell mostly good news . . .

"Even more damning for brokers is that only one quarter of the households surveyed plan to use a broker for their next mutual fund purchase. . . . Electronic fund supermarkets, like Charles Schwab's One-Source, will become even more dominant . . . more than half of the products sold by Schwab don't involve a salesperson at all.

"As power increasingly shifts to a smarter and better-equipped consumer, the big losers will be fund companies."

SOURCE: Carol Curtis, "Shake It Up," *Individual Investor* (April 1996).

"Goldman Sachs & Co . . . predicts that in five years the 2,900 companies that now actively run money will have winnowed down to between 20 and 25 giant institutions, each with more than $150 billion under management, and numerous niche players, each with less than $5 billion."

SOURCE: Julie Rohrer, "High Anxiety," *Institutional Investor* (February 1996).

downsizings, restructuring of the social security system, doubling of new moneys into mutual funds . . . all these factors make this revolution even more complex.

In a major report last year, Goldman Sachs, a leading, conservative, Wall Street investment banker, predicted a rapid global consolidation of the top money management firms. According to a summary in *Wall Street & Technology* magazine, "By the year 2000, the report continues, 'there will be 20 to 25 companies with at least $150 billion under management,' as compared to five such companies meeting that criteria today."

Goldman Sachs concludes that most American mutual fund, pension, and other money management firms "lack the capital, hardware and software to compete and reliably distribute information worldwide."

On the other hand, as more and more individual investors move into cyberspace, they do have the capital, hardware, and software to compete. Indeed, today's individual investors are now armed with so many new technologies, they have the power to easily pick the winning funds and reject the losers.

As a result, the mutual fund industry is in for a wild roller-coaster ride with this cyberspace revolution; look for major turmoil as it restructures.

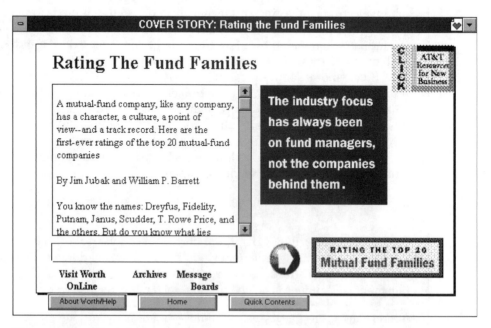

Figure 9.1 Worth Online: rating fund families on AOL and the Web.

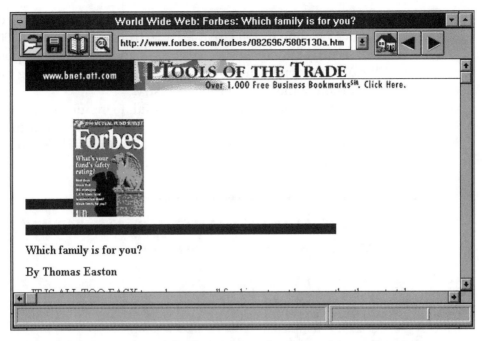

Figure 9.2   Forbes mutual funds survey: performance, data, and analysis.

Expect to see major consolidations, mergers and acquisitions, bigger families of funds . . . and the disappearance of many of the existing mutual funds.

Recently, Morgan Stanley bought the Van Kampen family, American Express acquired the IDS family, Zurich Insurance got Kemper, Mellon Bank now owns Dreyfus . . . and all are among the top-20 families of funds, which together manage and control over 50 percent of all mutual fund assets. And this consolidation game is still in the early innings, with more excitement to come.

THE TOP-20 MUTUAL FUND FAMILIES: POWER-PLAYERS CONTROLLING OVER HALF THE FUND WORLD

Perhaps one of the most striking facts is that a relatively small group of 20 companies controls more than 50 percent of the total assets invested in all mutual funds. In fact, just two of these families, Fidelity and Vanguard, together control about 20 percent. All are destined to grow bigger, much bigger, as investors pour more and more money into savings.

We know the experts are forecasting that mutual funds will double quickly, from $3 trillion in 1996 to at least $6 trillion in the year 2000. And if the social security system is privatized, as seems likely at some point, the total will double several times over in a decade or two, fueling an even greater expansion of the mutual fund industry.

As fund families grow in size and consolidate in numbers, one probable trend will be an increasing tendency as well as an opportunity for investors to satisfy their asset-allocation needs within a single large family with a well-rounded, diversified collection of funds.

WORLD WIDE WEB ADDRESSES: THE TOP-20 FUND FAMILIES

AIM Family of Funds	//pawws.com
Capital Research	*planned for 1997*
Dean Witter	*no information*
Dreyfus Group	//www.dreyfus.com
Fidelity Investments	//www.fid-inv.com
Franklin Templeton	//www.templeton.ca
IDS/American Express	//www.americanexpress.com
Janus Funds	//www.janusfunds.com
Kemper Funds	//www.kemper.com
Merrill Lynch	//www.ml.com
MFS Family of Funds	//www.mfs.com
Oppenheimer Funds	//www.oppenheimerfunds.com
Prudential Funds	//www.prusec.com
Putnam Investments	//www.putnaminv.com
Scudder Funds	//funds.scudder.com
Smith Barney	//www.smithbarney.com
T. Rowe Price	//www.troweprice.com
Twentieth Century	//www.twentieth-century.com
Vanguard Group	//www.vanguard.com
Van Kampen	//www.vkac.com

SOURCE: Stock and Bond Funds assets, Morningstar Research (2d quarter, 1996).

Convenience aside, however, this strategy could be very limiting, since there will inevitably be hundreds of other top performers outside any one family. And as we'll see in the final chapter, the new funds' networks like Schwab's OneSource and Fidelity's FundsNetwork make picking funds from any family easy to do from a single account, which may slow, but not stop, consolidations among the top-20 families.

Several popular fund advisory newsletters, including *Mutual Fund Forecaster, Moneyletter,* and *Fidelity Monitor,* have as regular features model portfolios for major families such as Fidelity and Vanguard. If the Goldman Sachs report proves to be an accurate forecast, by the year 2000 investors could regularly turn to many others for independent recommendations of model portfolios for every one of the top-20 families of funds.

The distinction between no-load and load families is neither arbitrary nor a mere convenience. As more fund investors move into cyberspace, there is a high probability the independent do-it-yourself investors will neither use nor pay for the advice of the load fund managers. Instead, they tend to pick high-performing no-load funds. This appears to be a universal trend noticed by independent experts.

BARRON'S: MOST INVESTORS LOYAL TO ONE FAMILY

"Almost every financial magazine in the country, this one included, provides reports on the best- and worst-performing mutual funds. This focus on individual funds certainly provides useful insights, but such rating rituals almost ignore the fact that *many investors don't have the interest or ability to cherry-pick funds of various types from lots of families. Many people,* including large numbers who are planning for retirement through corporate plans, *tend to stick to a single fund family.* Yet assessing the overall performance of any one fund family has never been a simple process. To fill the void, *Barron's* introduces its first performance survey of mutual fund families."

SOURCE: Eric Savitz, "It's All in the Families," *Barron's* (February 5, 1996).

The *Barron's*/Lipper study was quite comprehensive, covering the 62 largest fund families that collectively control $2.1 trillion, 78.7 percent of all mutual fund assets. Viewed another way, the top-20 families control over 50 percent, the next 42 families control another 30 percent of the assets.

So let's take a brief look at each of these 20 mutual fund powerhouses, identified from the Morningstar research database, and find out more about them as investment vehicles for today's new do-it-yourself investor in cyberspace. These include the following:

Primarily No-Load Funds Sold Direct by the Funds

Vanguard, Fidelity, American Express/IDS, Scudder, T. Rowe Price, Janus, and Twentieth Century. Interestingly, all of the major no-load families were on America Online early, while the load-fund families were noticeably absent, reflecting their rejection of do-it-yourself investing and their commitment to the continuation of sales commissions.

Primarily Load Funds Sold through Commissioned Brokers

AIM, American Capital, Dean Witter, Dreyfus, Franklin Templeton, Kemper, Merrill Lynch, MFS, Oppenheimer, Prudential, Putnam, Smith Barney, and Van Kampen. Several of these load-fund families, such as Smith Barney and Merrill Lynch, also offer no-load funds of other families. However, they load the no-load funds with high management fees, often equal to the total expenses of the no-load manager, thus eliminating the cost advantage of buying a no-load fund.

For monthly updates on the top 20, see *Mutual Funds* magazine. Quarterly and more frequent reviews appear throughout the financial press, including *BusinessWeek, Money, Kiplinger's,* and *SmartMoney. Worth* magazine publishes an excellent annual survey focused on the top 20. *Barron's* survey of the top 62 is great. And other periodicals have a wide range of coverage. The electronic versions of each can be found online and on various Websites.

EXPLORE THE WORLD WIDE WEB
WITH THE MAJOR NO-LOAD FUND FAMILIES

Of the top-20 families, seven are primarily no-load fund managers controlling over 25 percent of the total assets, slightly more than half of the assets controlled by this elite group of 20 families. Vanguard and Fidelity, of course, are the big guns. These two families together control approximately one-third of all assets under management by the top-20 families of funds.

The other 18 each manage between $25 and $150 billion in mutual fund assets, and are growing. And if the Goldman Sachs prediction is accurate, consolidations will result in many more of these families rising above the $150 billion mark soon.

These statistics from the Morningstar database exclude money market funds and assets other than mutual funds. Thus, for example, while Fidelity manages close to a total of half a trillion dollars of other people's money, only the $290 billion in the equity and bond funds are included in our statistics here.

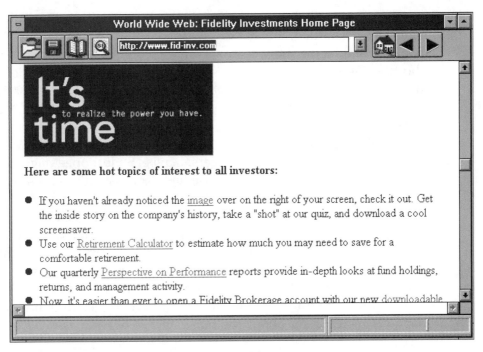

Figure 9.3   Fidelity: It's time to realize the power you have!

Obviously, all these figures are likely to increase as more money pours into mutual funds. Nevertheless, it's very likely that the actual membership of the top 20 will remain fairly constant.

With the exception of Vanguard and Fidelity, most of these Websites are little more than "digitized sales literature," as *Barron's* calls them: "slick graphics, daily fund pricing and a smattering of retirement-planning and portfolio-management counsel." Yet, while the information is thin and self-promotional on these Websites, the competition, and the pressure to invite repeat visitors, will force improvements.

FIDELITY INVESTMENTS: $290 BILLION IN 184 FUNDS

Last year *BusinessWeek* ran a cover story asking, "Has success spoiled Fidelity?" The $400 billion giant doubled assets in three years, but its "once-stellar performance is slipping." The problem: Aggressive-growth and growth funds lagged the S&P 500 for three straight years. *Smart-Money's* feature story asked rhetorically, "What's going on with Fidelity?"

By midyear, the management teams of 27 of Fidelity's 116 equity funds had been reshuffled. *Forbes* was worried about too many "bull market babies" running the show, many of whom were "in grammar school when the 1973–74 bear market began." *Kiplinger's* was looking to "Fidelity after the earthquake," and in *Money* magazine, Jason Zweig advised on "how to win with the new Fidelity lineup." Then the boss of Fidelity Magellan resigned.

What *was* going on? Answer: Go-go style, says *SmartMoney*. Maybe too aggressive. Will it change? Managers, maybe. Style, nope. Magellan's boss left, but "It's not likely to be because he took a risk. It's because he took a risk and failed. In that sense, nothing has changed. 'You perform, or else,' says Stansky [subsequently made the new head of Magellan]. 'That's what drove Fidelity when Peter [Lynch] was here. That's what drives it now.' "

Warning: Don't get caught up in the drama. By the time this "hot news" hit the street, it was old news. Virtually useless for short-term trading and exchanges. Besides, most mutual fund investors are long-term, buy-and-hold investors. But what you do have in this unfolding drama is a powerful reminder about the *importance of ongoing asset allocation and rebalancing.*

FIDELITY'S MODEL PORTFOLIOS WIN BY 5 POINTS

In spite of Fidelity's reorganization last year, Mark Hulbert, editor of *Hulbert Financial Digest*, the leading independent source evaluating financial advisory newsletters, concluded that "Over the last 12 months, investment portfolios that recommend only Fidelity funds made 5% more than the average non-Fidelity portfolio." So continue betting on Fidelity's winners.

SOURCE: Mark Hulbert, "Fidelity Hasn't Lost Its Touch," *Forbes* (July 29, 1996).

One more time we see that even the biggest heros will often let us down. The solution: Stick consistently to your own financial plan. Don't go chasing the latest portfolio of the month that the financial press bombards us with constantly.

As we've already seen, Fidelity still has a large share of five-star winners—and still offers a vast number of services to the do-it-yourself cyberspace investor. Even nonshareholders will profit considerably by checking with Fidelity regularly:

❐ **Internet World Wide Web site**
   Fidelity Online Investor Center for cyberspace investing.

❐ **Commercial online services**
   Fidelity Online Investor Center on Prodigy and America Online.

❐ **Offline analytic software**
   Thinkware, Fidelity's Retirement Planner software.

❐ **Electronic brokerage**
   Fidelity Online Xpress (FOX), discount brokerage service.

❐ **Network linked to nonproprietary mutual funds**
   Fidelity FundsNetwork, to over 2,200 mutual funds.

The headline of one of the Fidelity ads is aimed directly at the heart of the do-it-yourself cyberspace investor: "It's time . . . to realize the power you have." And that's especially true for the do-it-yourself cyberspace investor. Fidelity is spending over $350 million annually on high-tech information

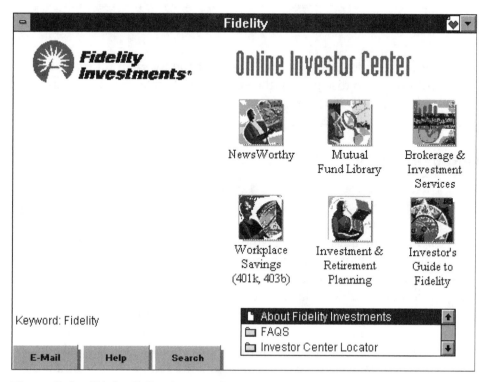

Figure 9.4 Fidelity Online Investor Center: Information and education.

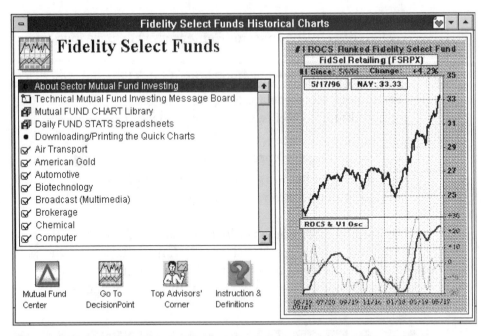

Figure 9.5   Decision Point's Fidelity Select Funds: on AOL and the Web.

systems, more than the total assets of the average mutual fund. They are committed to discovering the key that will make cyberspace investing profitable for individual investors as well as Fidelity.

VANGUARD GROUP OF FUNDS: $146 BILLION IN 73 FUNDS

Just before the Fidelity restructuring began unfolding last year, a *Forbes* cover story, "Which Way to a Happy Retirement?," compared Vanguard and Fidelity. The cover art succinctly illustrated the difference between the investment approaches of these two giants: The Fidelity salesman was shouting, "Hot Funds!"; Vanguard's, "Low Fees!" Low fees won the day.

Vanguard's low-expense index funds are a reflection of this conservative philosophy. In fact, index funds were invented by Vanguard's longtime CEO, John Bogle, in his Princeton thesis about 50 years ago. Today the Vanguard Index Trust 500 does effectively duplicate the S&P 500, while a large majority of all other mutual funds fall short of the indexes.

Vanguard's conservative investment style is also grounded in the fact that, as a result of a reorganization in the 1970s, Vanguard is actually owned by its shareholders, cutting corporate taxes while creating a natural incentive to minimize costs. Vanguard is a true family from this perspective.

In the past decade, the combined market share of Vanguard and Fidelity has risen from 10 percent to 20 percent, "and both of these giants are winning, at the expense of the rest of the fund industry," says *Forbes.* Fidelity is not only bigger, it has a higher profile pushing its "hot funds" image. According to *Forbes,* although Fidelity is not quite twice Vanguard's size, it spends over three times as much on advertising, $13.4 million versus $3.4 million. Still, *Barron's* awarded Vanguard its number one rating.

VANGUARD FAMILY: #1 ON *BARRON'S*/LIPPER CHARTS!

"In the year just ended, the top-performing funds tended to be those that bet on declining interest rates in their bond funds and large-company stocks in their stock funds. Conservatism ruled the day—an environment tailor-made for the Vanguard Group, which topped the *Barron's*/Lipper survey."

SOURCE: Eric Savitz, "It's All in The Families," *Barron's* (February 5, 1996).

Vanguard is clearly one of the pioneers of the emerging new Wall Street cyberspace. Like archrival Fidelity, Vanguard has been exploring several major cyberspace vehicles to support the new do-it-yourself investor. Vanguard's package includes:

❐ **World Wide Web.**   Vanguard University is especially notable.
❐ **Vanguard Group Online.**   Located at America Online.
❐ **Offline Financial Planner.**   Software for retirement planning.
❐ **Vanguard FundAccess.**   Online fund trading and exchanges.
❐ **Personal Financial Services.**   Unique, low-cost, over-the-phone advice on investments, retirement planning, estates, and trusts.

In the short history of the World Wide Web, Vanguard has clearly moved into a position of cyberspace leadership, which is adding to the strength and momentum of Vanguard's overall expansion in recent years, in accounts and total assets under management, as well as in superior performance.

Figure 9.6 Vanguard group of no-load funds at America Online.

Like Avis car rental of a generation ago, Vanguard may be number two behind Fidelity, but they try harder, and it's paying off. Cyberspace investors are encouraged to log on to the Vanguard Website on a regular basis. It is a true high-tech *graduate university* designed specifically for the new breed of do-it-yourself cyberspace fund investor. The Vanguard Website is guaranteed to be a profitable experience.

T. ROWE PRICE FUNDS: $50 BILLION IN 61 FUNDS

Actually, the T. Rowe Price family of funds is one good reason for *not* putting too much weight on past performance. And even more important, they are a testament to the rewards of staying loyal to a fund manager through the tough times. A *SmartMoney* cover story called the T. Rowe saga a "remarkable turnaround" and a "renaissance."

As recently as "five years ago only 29% percent of T. Rowe's long-standing equity funds had above-average five-year records compared with their peer groups, according to Lipper Analytical Services. Today, 80% of the company's stock funds meet that standard."

There is an important lesson here for the new cyberspace investor faced with the decision of how to pick a fund, a fund manager, and a fund fam-

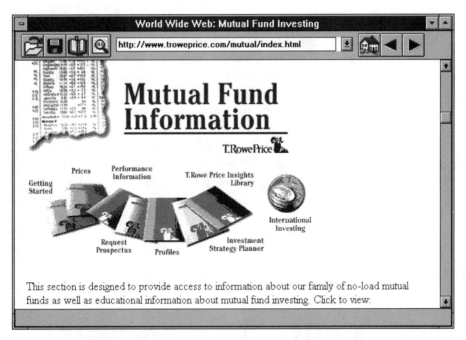

Figure 9.7   T. Rowe Price no-load funds: Mutual Fund Information.

Figure 9.8   T. Rowe Price: getting started investing in mutual funds.

ily as an anchor in your investment portfolio. T. Rowe didn't dump a bunch of managers and go "cherry-picking talent elsewhere. . . . Instead it's been a revolution from within—they have literally taught themselves to be better managers," according to *SmartMoney*. And we know that experience is the best kind of wisdom.

T. Rowe Price was one of the early pioneers of the no-load, low-cost funds. "It still offers its retirement-plan clientele some of the best bargains in the business [and] achieved the highest overall rankings of the 20 fund families," according to *Worth*'s 1996 survey of the top-20 families. With a no-load manager like T. Rowe setting the pace, why should a do-it-yourself investor ever consider a load fund, or pay a broker or adviser for second-hand advice?

TWENTIETH CENTURY FUNDS: $39 BILLION IN 47 FUNDS

The founder of Twentieth Century, James Stowers, titled his book, *Yes You Can . . . Achieve Financial Independence*. And that philosophy pretty much summarizes Twentieth's goal: Help investors do it themselves. For Twentieth, low cost begins in the lunchroom with the boss, who would regularly bring a peanut butter sandwich and apple to work rather than buy them in the company cafeteria, because he was saving $1,200 a year.

However, don't let that fool you. Stowers spent the money where it counted: on new technologies. According to *Worth*, "Stowers was an early user of computers in the mutual-fund business, and Twentieth Century

---

INVESTMENT SOFTWARE PROGRAMS FROM NO-LOAD FAMILIES

Janus Funds	Janus Asset Builder	(800) 525-1093
Fidelity Investments	Thinkware Planner	(800) 457-1768
Scudder Funds	Scudder Retirement Guide	(800) 520-7568
T. Rowe Price	Retirement Planning Kit	(800) 541-9478
Twentieth Century	The Investment Planner	(800) 690-3913
Vanguard Group	Retirement Planner	(800) 876-1840

Each of these software programs costs less than $20, and some are free. They provide basic educational materials, financial planning, portfolio asset allocation, investment strategies, fund selection, and, of course, promotional information. The load families offer no real do-it-yourself materials.

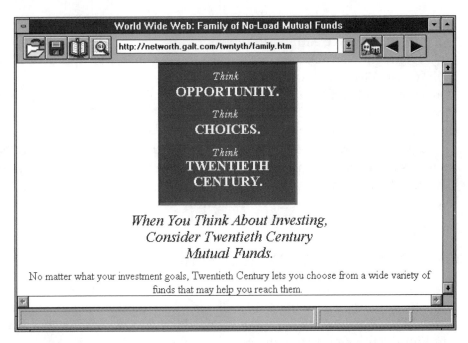

Figure 9.9 Twentieth Century mutual funds: NETworth Website.

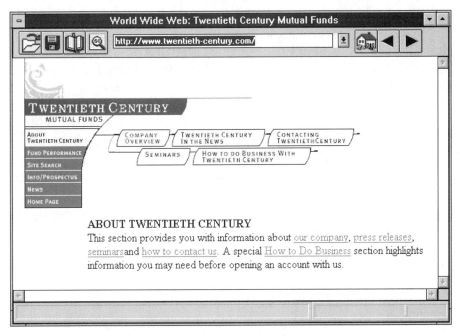

Figure 9.10 Twentieth Century Website: no-load mutual funds.

relies heavily on database searching and computer analysis to identify stocks with positive earnings outlooks."

Twentieth was also one of the early fund families to sign up with the NETworth Website, and recently created their own Website. You can get prospectuses and all the information you need about one of the leading no-load fund families out there.

Twentieth is smaller in size than Fidelity and Vanguard, but then, who isn't? In size, they're number 10 among all fund families, no-load and load, with a staff of more than 2,000. More important for the cyberspace investor, Twentieth has a solid roster of five-star, high-performing equity funds, as you'll quickly discover with your software power tools.

SCUDDER FUNDS: $30 BILLION IN 39 FUNDS

With over $100 million in assets under management globally, Scudder Stevens & Clark is also one of the oldest and largest money management firms. They are the sixth largest of the fund families using direct marketing, and fourteenth among the top 20.

The granddaddy of the no-loads, Scudder created the first one in 1928. They are a pioneer in several other areas: the first in-house research department in 1924; first American fund investing internationally in 1953; first small-company fund in 1970; and one of the first no-load variable annuities in 1988. Last year *Fortune* said the Scudder Global Fund and Scudder Global Small Company Fund were among "the best mutual funds for building wealth."

Scudder style of investment management is conservative, with a long-term perspective. Their management style is also unique in relying on collective decision making rather than star managers. By choice, the Scudder family maintains a low profile. Consequently, their top managers may also be less visible.

Scudder's conservatism is reflected in their tenure as manager of the AARP Investment Program. The American Association for Retired Persons is one of America's largest nonprofit membership organizations for individuals over 50 years of age. Scudder offers a portfolio of nine "pure no-load funds" for AARP.

Scudder also offers the Scudder Fund Access program, a "funds supermarket" like those discussed in Chapter 10, which helps their clients select funds from 20 other families of funds. Scudder's no-load, no-nonsense family is a wise choice for retiring boomers and Gen Xers alike.

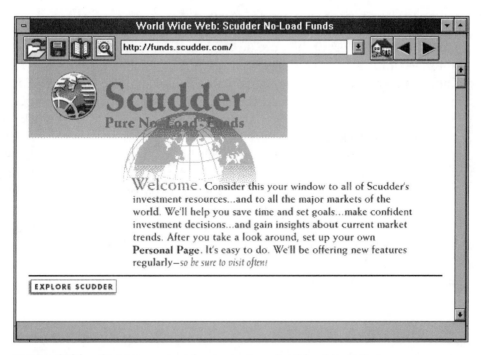

Figure 9.11   Scudder mutual funds: pure no-load fund investing.

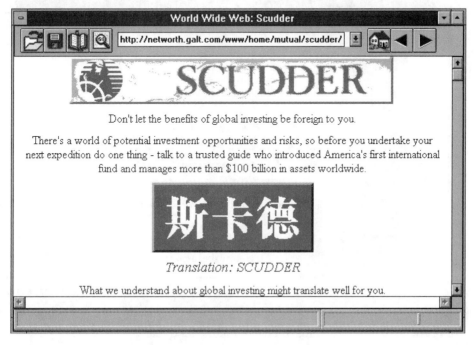

Figure 9.12   Scudder fund family: America's first global funds.

JANUS GROUP: $26 BILLION IN 15 FUNDS

Janus is the smallest of the pure no-load families and smallest of the top-20 families of funds. *Kiplinger's* says Janus Fund, which controls over half the Janus family assets under management, "is like a guiltless dessert. For the past five years it has matched the S&P 500's total return. But in rougher markets it suffers less than similar funds. If your investing framework is on the short side, this can be important."

The Janus family's management style builds on the collective talents of its small staff, with a heavy reliance on the new technologies. In fact, Janus even matches its bigger competitors with a reasonably priced software planner for the new breed of do-it-yourself investor.

Janus may lean a bit to an aggressive game plan, yet on performance it still fits solidly in the middle of the top-20 fund families. Janus focuses on helping investors who are "tired of chasing every 'hot' investment tip," and ready for a "consistent investment program" to meet a variety of lifestyle goals.

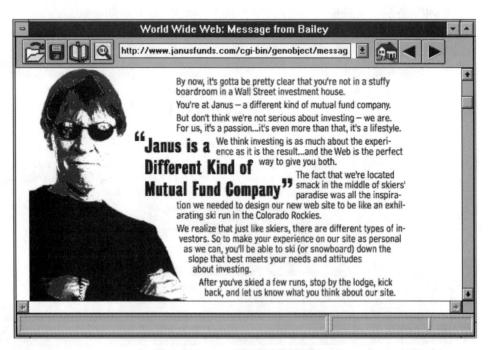

Figure 9.13   Janus Funds: a unique mutual fund team.

IDS/AMERICAN EXPRESS: $48 BILLION IN 61 FUNDS

The IDS Mutual Fund Group is an American Express subsidiary. IDS primarily sells a group of conservative, low-profile load funds through a huge staff of "financial planners." Moreover, mutual funds are only one of the many financial products IDS sells to customers, vying with variable annuities, insurance, and CDs for the attention of its commission brokers.

Recently, American Express added a new service, Financial Direct, which should be of special interest to the cyberspace investor. According to *The Wall Street Journal,* "American Express is eager to capture the legions of do-it-yourself investors who might otherwise bypass the company in favor of no-load fund companies or discount brokers such as Schwab, which runs a big no-load fund-trading network."

BusinessWeek's comment on the company's strategy revealed that the AmExpress/IDS team was able to quickly join the no-load crowd by using funds that already had track records. It accomplished this by *repackaging 13 existing IDS load funds* for direct marketing to investors, removing the sales charges. And it plans to add more no-loads and more nonproprietary funds later. IDS/American Express also offers discount brokerage accounts.

Figure 9.14 IDS/American Express: Financial Direct services.

American Express appears to be defecting from the Wall Street Establishment cartel that ignores the do-it-yourself investor while pushing its own loaded funds through brokers. Whether the IDS/American Express group will make a mass conversion to no-loads in the near future or not, their Financial Direct does represent a clear recognition of the growing power of the do-it-yourself investor by at least one Wall Street insider. The firm's 8,000 brokers who count on commissions may have something to say about the company's success in this new strategy, but the signs of change are certainly welcome.

THE MAJOR LOAD-FUND FAMILIES: SELLING FUNDS WITH ADDED FEES AND COMMISSIONS

The remaining 13 fund families manage load funds almost exclusively. They also rely heavily on the sales efforts of commissioned brokers and so-called independent advisors to sell their funds to the public. And, generally speaking, virtually all experts in the emerging new Wall Street cyberspace advise the do-it-yourself investor to avoid load funds and load fund families for two reasons:

❏ Do-it-yourself investors don't need to pay for investment advice if the investor is actually doing all the research and analysis.

❏ The fund's performance is reduced by the additional loads—expenses, sales commissions, fees, charges—which many fund managers rationalize, in part, as the way of their recovering research costs.

However, rather than blindly excluding all load funds, which is not recommended, use total return as your criteria. Let's face it, if a *load* fund's performance is superior to competing *no-load* funds, it has to be a serious alternative for your portfolio. The cream of the crop will rise regardless of the expenses.

Nevertheless, *even if you are comparing no-loads to load funds*, do-it-yourself investors are encouraged to use every possible cyberspace power tool available to do their own research, analysis, and decision making, and in the process, *avoid all advisory fees*. Otherwise, you're shortchanging your learning curve in the emerging new cyberspace investing, while paying for advice from someone who may be biased.

CAPITAL RESEARCH & MANAGEMENT: $145 BILLION IN 25 FUNDS

Capital Research is a low-key giant, number three in size among the top-20 families, close in total assets to Vanguard. Recently *Forbes* gave Capital the highest praise, extraordinary considering that *Forbes* has been promoting the virtues of no-load funds for a long time. In the case of Capital Research, *Forbes* made its one exception, recommending that do-it-yourself investors should favorably consider Capital's American Funds Group along with its no-load rivals.

EVEN *FORBES* MAGAZINE RECOMMENDS CAPITAL RESEARCH FAMILY OF LOAD FUNDS TO THE DO-IT-YOURSELF INVESTOR

"It rarely hits the top of the charts; its managers never make the cover of *Money* magazine. But in its quiet way, Capital Research does very well by investors. . . . There's something refreshingly old-fashioned about this outfit—reminiscent of prudent men and of responsibility . . .

"For years *Forbes* has lectured about the virtues of no-load funds . . . but we made an exception for the American Funds load family run by Capital Research . . . even if you buy funds entirely on your own, you may still find this family attractive; its sales loads are waived for very large purchases . . .

"Many broker-sold, load-bearing funds compete with the no-loads by disguising high sales charges with exit commission coupled with stiff annual 'distribution' fee. Not Capital. It puts its commissions in the front window . . .

"Capital's investment style is a splendid combination: low expenses, low risk, low portfolio turnover and low management turnover. All this, plus an old-fashioned sense of integrity."

SOURCE: Mary Beth Grover and Jason Zweig, "Capital Research: Steak, No Sizzle," *Forbes* (August 28, 1995).

Capital is slow getting a Website, and it won't mail you any low-cost software. But when you're screening for top-performers, Capital's funds consistently show up with the winners.

Cyberspace investors: When a Capital fund comes across your high-tech radar screen, stop. Take a close look, it's a friendly aircraft even for die-hard do-it-yourself investors. Take time to read their prospectus. And ask about Capital's unique Multiple Portfolio Counselor System, their team approach to investment advice.

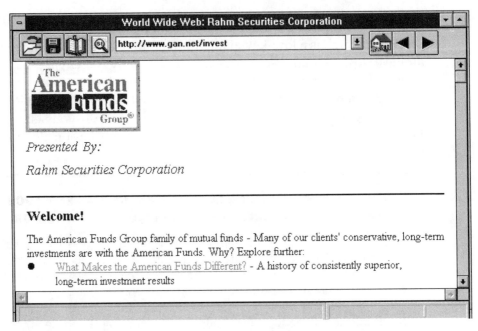

Figure 9.15   Capital Research & Management: The American Funds.

KEMPER FUNDS AND ZURICH INSURANCE GROUP: $27 BILLION IN 65 FUNDS

The Kemper family of funds is one of the top performers, number four among 62 included in *Barron's* survey last year and above average among *Worth's* largest 20 families. In fact, "thanks to the strength of its bond funds and its overseas stock funds," *Barron's* rated Kemper way up near the top of all families—ahead of Putnam, AIM, MFS, and even Capital Research, to name a few of the other top performers in this elite group of the 20 largest families of funds.

Kemper was acquired by the Zurich Insurance Group in 1995. *Worth* quoted Kemper's president describing his team as, "smart but not glitzy." However, that was before the recent addition of contrarian David Dremen's mutual funds, and before Kemper made changes at the top that included executive and policies. Translated, Kemper is a top-rated family of funds, and they intend to stay there.

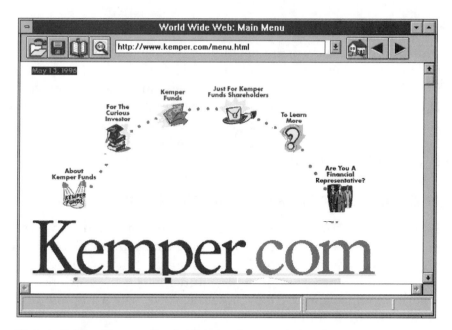

Figure 9.16   Kemper Funds Website: facts and planning.

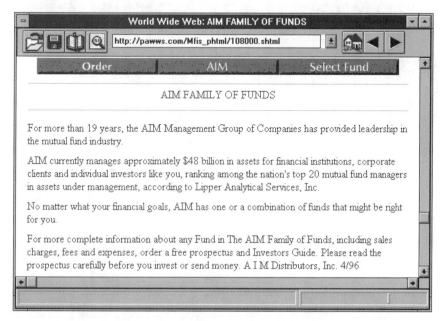

Figure 9.17   AIM Family of Funds at the PAWWS Website.

AIM FAMILY OF FUNDS: $33 BILLION IN 34 FUNDS

In its mid-1996 review of mutual funds, *Forbes* noted that "AIM is suddenly the hottest fund family around." Similarly, *Worth* rated AIM one of the top-four fund managers, along with three primarily no-load powerhouses, Fidelity, Vanguard, and T. Rowe Price, the number one family in the top 20. And *Barron's* rated AIM tops among the 20 largest families for its international as well as balanced funds, plus number seven among *all* fund families over a 10-year period.

PUTNAM MUTUAL FUNDS: $82 BILLION IN 142 FUNDS

Putnam is another top-performing family of load funds. Last year, *Barron's*, *Newsweek*, *Worth*, and others in the financial press all ranked Putnam high, not just among the top 20, but among all fund families. *Worth* went so far as to say Putnam's "group of equity funds is the only one on our list whose ranking approached those of AIM," focusing on their top-performing stock funds.

The Putnam tradition goes way back to 1830 Boston and Samuel Putnam, the judge who developed the "prudent-man rule" that is today's stan-

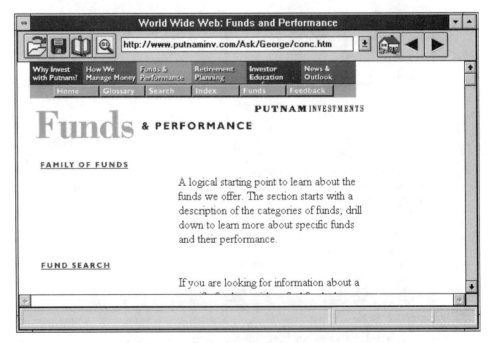

Figure 9.18   Putnam Investments: opportunities in cyberspace.

IS THE MANAGER OF YOUR MUTUAL FUND MISLEADING YOU?

"There are stricter labeling laws for a two dollar container of cottage cheese than a two billion dollar mutual fund. It's a little known fact. How a mutual fund is classified doesn't always indicate how it will be invested. Whether you're putting together your own portfolio or a 401(k) plan, this makes every decision more difficult. . . . We continually monitor each fund to ensure that year after year it still fits its classification."

SOURCE: Putnam Investments advertisement, *Fortune* (August 19, 1996).

dard for money managers. Today Putnam continues the tradition, with a conservative team-management approach rather than a team of superstars.

FRANKLIN TEMPLETON: $101 BILLION IN 147 FUNDS

The Franklin Group, one of the top bond fund managers for over 50 years, acquired the Templeton global stock fund five years ago and continues on

Figure 9.19 Franklin Templeton funds: Never follow the crowd.

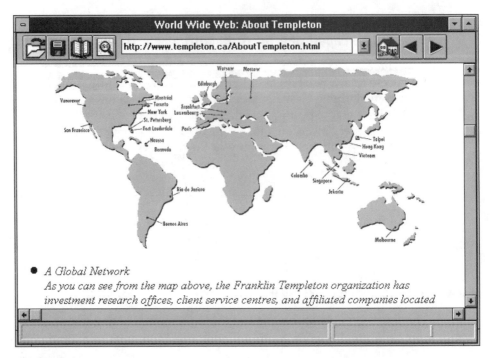

Figure 9.20   Franklin Templeton funds: global network of funds.

a rebuilding program while integrating the two families. Although Franklin is a load-fund family, its expense ratios are definitely some of the lowest in the business.

The Templeton global funds have grown considerably since the acquisition, reflecting the increasing interest in international investments as a major factor in building more and more portfolios. And the Franklin bond funds are known as extremely cautious and overly conservative to the point of being hampered in the recent bull market, a trait which, conversely, may be a major advantage in a bear market or even a lesser correction.

OPPENHEIMER FUNDS: $33 BILLION IN 101 FUNDS

The Wall Street world of investing has traditionally had a lot in common with stock-car racing, video games, and the military: "It's a guy thing." At least that was the conventional wisdom. Then along comes Oppenheimer Funds, the first fund family to go beyond myths and stereotypes: "Ignore Her at Your Own Risk" headlines one of their ads, "She earns more than a trillion a year. Owns almost 6.5 million businesses. And 4 times out of 5, she'll end up controlling a household's assets."

Oppenheimer is more than a family of funds. Oppenheimer considers its clients as members of the family, not just people investing money, and the company wants you to know of its open-door policy. A call will get directly to the boss if you want to talk to him or her. And fortunately, Oppenheimer's family style is matched by a conservative management team that regularly fits in the upper middle of most performance charts.

MFS FAMILY OF FUNDS: $27 BILLION IN 122 FUNDS

Massachusetts Financial Services (MFS) established the first mutual fund in 1924. Today, MFS is a wholly owned subsidiary of Sun Life Assurance of Canada, one of the world's largest insurers with over $300 billion underwritten. MFS is a solid above-average performer among the top-20 fund families; it combines excellent diversity among a stable of conservative, long-term funds with strong emphasis on team management.

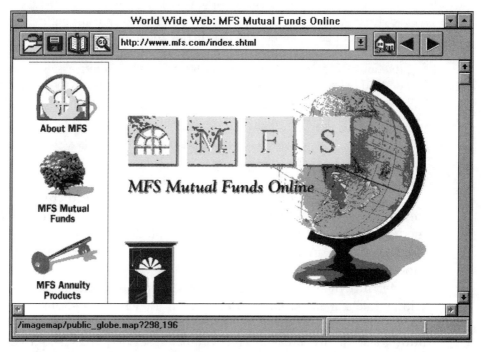

Figure 9.21 MFS Mutual Funds Online Website.

Definitely check out the MFS Website. For one thing, they have an excellent, easy-to-understand chart describing the relationship between investment strategies and style. Generally speaking, MFS is a congenial family of funds to work with, and independent rating-agency studies prove it, rating MFS high in quality of service and customer satisfaction.

MERRILL LYNCH GROUP: $62 BILLION IN 262 FUNDS

So far, Merrill Lynch has made it very clear that they are leaving the entire do-it-yourself market to the discount brokers and no-load funds. According to a *Fortune* cover story, "Merrill isn't courting the masses. Instead, it's aiming at a narrow segment, the wealthy and the near-wealthy." And "fortunate for Merrill, 36 million baby boomers lugging a trove of savings," will be their target "priority households" in the next decade or two.

MERRILL LYNCH'S TARGET: THE WEALTHY, NOT THE MASSES

Merrill Lynch "will never compete with a Schwab on price. . . . The advice and planning . . . will enable Merrill to keep charging rich prices for its products. . . . Merrill isn't courting the masses. Instead, it's aiming at a narrow segment, the wealthy and near-wealthy. The target is 'priority households' with $250,000 to $5 million in liquid assets: families headed by executives, doctors, lawyers, entrepreneurs, all too busy making money to manage it—or retirees who'd rather fish and travel than pick mutual funds."

SOURCE: Shawn Tully, "Merrill Lynch Bulls Ahead," *Fortune* (February 19, 1996).

Merrill does not offer any no-load funds, nor are there any no-load funds among their network selling almost 1,000 nonproprietary funds that include many load funds offered by the other Wall Street Establishment firms. And how do Merrill's own funds rank? Below average among major fund families.

Merrill Lynch plays the game conservatively, close to the chest. Risk taking takes a backseat to the Merrill Lynch reputation. Apparently, nothing is permitted to jeopardize the powerhouse reputation Merrill has built in so many areas of the financial services business over many decades.

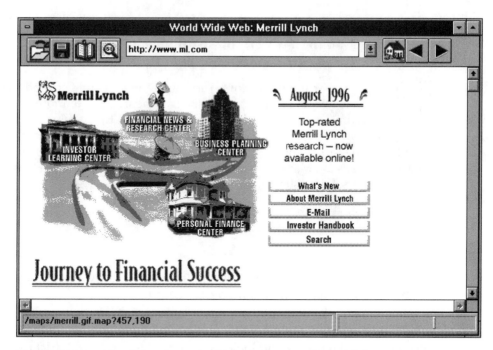

Figure 9.22 Merrill Lynch on the Web: Journey to Financial Success.

SMITH BARNEY FUNDS: $30 BILLION IN 81 FUNDS

Smith Barney took their time getting on the Web, and the results are impressive. Smith Barney has one of the Wall Street Establishment's snazziest Websites, and for that they deserve a pat on the back...even if they're one of the staunchest members of the Wall Street cartel dedicated to total customer dependency.

Last year one of Smith Barney's key executives bluntly asserted that "do-it-yourself investing is not a viable concept in the 1990s." That's an obvious put-down, not only of competitors like Schwab and other cyber-brokers, but of the new breed of high-tech, do-it-yourself investors. Today's independent investors are proving that Smith Barney not only "makes money the old-fashioned way," they even *think* in an old-fashioned way, like parents who don't trust their children.

Nevertheless, you should definitely check out Smith Barney's Website, they are packing it with a lot of high-tech bells and whistles, along with some solid content that must be the envy of archrival Merrill Lynch. Hopefully, we'll see more cyberspace competition between the two, as we have on the no-load side between numbers one and two, Fidelity and Vanguard.

SMITH BARNEY: "DO-IT-YOURSELF INVESTING IS *NOT* A VIABLE CONCEPT IN THE 1990"

"Smith Barney will offer a deluxe service that will include no-load fund transactions on mutual funds, stocks, and bonds; access to mutual fund and other investment research; and personal investment advice . . . betting that by acting as middlemen for the no-load funds they can please affluent investors who value—and are willing to pay for—personal service. . . . Says Jay Mandelbaum, executive vice president at Smith Barney: 'Do-it-yourself investing is not a viable concept in the 1990s.' "

SOURCE: Bethany McLean, "A Better Way to Buy No-Load Mutual Funds," *Fortune* (December 25, 1995).

Moreover, Smith Barney is part of the Intuit banking consortium, so you'll be able to use Quicken with a modest account.

And if one of your fund searches turns up a Smith Barney five-star fund (and they definitely have a number of them) based on total return, you'd better give it a second look, even if it's a loaded fund. Just remember

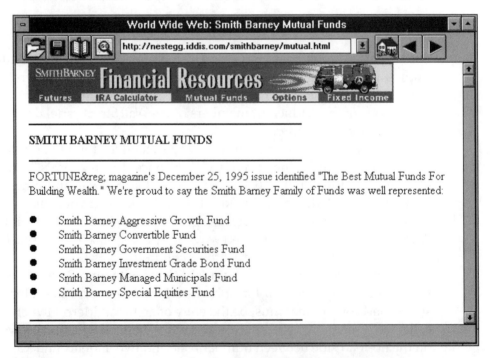

Figure 9.23   Smith Barney Mutual Funds at IDD/Tradeline Website.

this when the smoke clears: If you're serious about do-it-yourself invest-ing, you will be an outsider to the Smith Barney family, like the proverbial black sheep.

DREYFUS GROUP AND MELLON BANK: $32 BILLION IN 203 FUNDS

Mellon Bank acquired the Dreyfus Corporation, one of the oldest and largest mutual fund companies, in 1994 and has been slowly rebuilding. The *Worth* magazine 1996 survey called Dreyfus the family in the top 20 with the "worst overall performance rating," noting that "revitalizing Dreyfus may take some time."

Watch out though, the turnaround may be happening faster than expected. In an article titled, "Dreyfus: The Lion Awakens," *Mutual Funds* magazine says, "After years of sleepy performance, Dreyfus' equity port-folios are posting eye-opening numbers. Year-to-date the firm's stock funds are up 16%, nearly double the performance of the venerable S&P 500. That's surprising, given that *no* Dreyfus stock fund has bested the benchmark over the latest ten-year period."

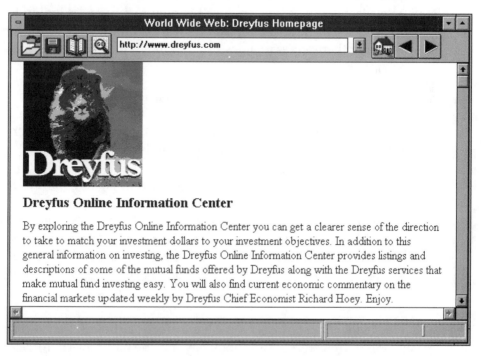

Figure 9.24   Dreyfus Online Information Center on the Web.

Looks like Dreyfus' partnership with Mellon Bank is turning into a winning combination, giving the lion the heart transplant it needed to turn Dreyfus back into a roaring king of the jungle of funds.

DEAN WITTER FUNDS: $41 BILLION IN 52 FUNDS

Dean Witter has a secret, and it's not high performance. *Worth* rates Dean Witter as "mediocre," while *Barron's* stacked it in the middle of all families, ahead of Merrill Lynch and other load and no-load families. Our research came to the same dead end with Dean Witter as did *Worth's*: Dean Witter was the only family of funds that didn't cooperate.

With an army of 8,500 in-house brokers to support and a "mediocre" performance, *Worth's* warning may be well deserved: "Investors might consider taking their money elsewhere—at least until Dean Witter demonstrates it is as serious about performance as it is about sales."

Like the rest of the Wall Street Establishment, Dean Witter is fearful of the impact of the cyberspace revolution. They are holding on ever more tenaciously as power continues shifting away from the traditional Wall Street firms to the discount brokers, to no-load funds, and to the new do-it-yourself technologies. In denying this new reality and clinging to the old concept of client dependency, many in the Wall Street Establishment are committing themselves to a destiny that may ultimately prove fatal.

PRUDENTIAL MUTUAL FUNDS: $27 BILLION IN 130 FUNDS

Prudential has been restructuring its mutual funds operation for a while. Last year *Individual Investor* magazine noted:

> . . . *in the aggregate, the percentile performance rankings for Prudential funds can be summed up in one word: rocky.*
>
> *On the average, Prudential funds over the past ten years have ranked in the 67th percentile. That means two-thirds of other companies' funds outperformed Prudential's offerings. . . . Morningstar's database shows that over the past five years, only five out of 57 Prudential funds that have been around that long finished in the top quartile within their investment objective.*

Individual Investor was a very harsh critic, although they did see a "Silver Lining: Investors should look beyond the bad news before saying 'no

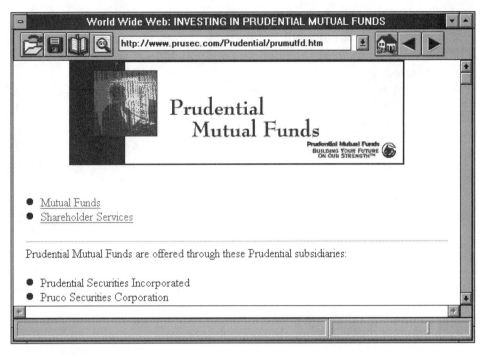

Figure 9.25   Prudential Mutual Funds: helping build your future.

thanks' to Prudential. The company does offer some funds worth considering."

And remember T. Rowe Price: In five short years this company went from 29 percent of its funds below average to 80 percent. Miracles often happen fast in this volatile revolution that's upending the mutual fund business. And Prudential is likely to be another one in the near future.

VAN KAMPEN FUNDS AND MORGAN STANLEY: $26 BILLION IN 115 FUNDS

When Morgan Stanley acquired Van Kampen last year, *BusinessWeek* (and many others) asked, "What's a top-drawer investment bank doing buying a decidedly second-tier mutual-fund firm." True, Van Kampen has a 70-year history of investment management experience, but it is clearly an "undistinguished record."

The answer: Morgan Stanley is combining the best of both firms—Morgan's own first-class money management stars with Van Kampen's distribution network of 2,500 organizations. The result remains to be seen; performance is what counts. However, if anyone can pull off such a gamble, Morgan can. Their acquisitions are usually solidly grounded in long-term strategies.

However, without some major changes, the do-it-yourself cyberinvestor won't get much here. Van Kampen's Website makes their philosophy quite clear: "Some may feel that investing . . . is a simple, do-it-yourself affair. We disagree . . . we believe so strongly in the value provided by professional, full-service investment representatives. And that's why all our funds are available only through them."

Unfortunately, Van Kampen's performance contradicts their strategy, which reflects the dominant mind-set of the Wall Street Establishment cartel. Hopefully, Morgan's vision will evolve.

The do-it-yourself revolution is not only a reality, it is an overwhelming reality. Morgan knows it. Morgan underwrote Netscape. They wrote the book, *The Internet Report.* They should see beyond Van Kampen's self-restricting denial of the do-it-yourself investor.

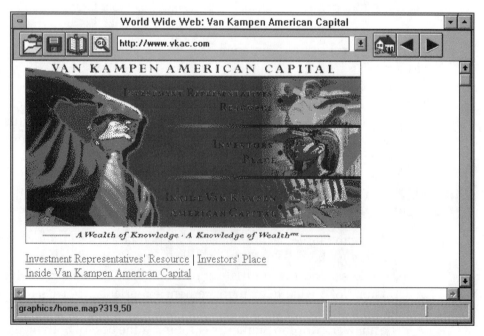

Figure 9.26　Van Kampen American Capital: Morgan Stanley subsidiary.

The Morgan style may be just what's necessary to break up the Establishment cartel. The cartel has had its head in the sand for far too long. And if not, well, then Schwab and the other online discount brokers will continue reaping the enormous rewards of the cyberspace revolution.

CYBER-WAR: WALL STREET'S CARTEL BATTLES NO-LOAD FUNDS, DISCOUNT BROKERS, NEW DO-IT-YOURSELF TECHNOLOGIES

It's important to realize that at $25 billion even the "smaller" of the top-20 largest families have enough individual funds to help investors satisfy all their diversification needs within a single family. Moreover, the big ones—Fidelity, Vanguard, and Capital Research, for example—are loaded with top performers.

And soon they'll be facing more competition as other fund families grow larger, faster. If the Goldman Sachs prediction materializes as predicted by the year 2000 (rapid, massive consolidation into fewer and larger money managers), then investing with a single fund *family* may produce the following benefits:

- ❐ Psychologically satisfying
- ❐ Financially compelling
- ❐ Requiring much less of your time

Warning: Don't fall into this trap. At least not until you first do your homework. Cyberspace investors now have the power tools to do the work themselves. Use them. Do it yourself first, every step of the process, *even if you eventually decide to work with one family,* because, in spite of the advantages, there are some significant shortcomings:

- ❐ **Biased source of information**
  Remember, you can't count on getting an *independent* evaluation of the current condition of any one of these funds or the whole family *from the family itself.* They simply can't be objective, and never will be.

- ❐ **Limited data at fund Websites**
  Not only is their printed material biased, each family's Website is a very limited corner of a huge galaxy. Visiting one site would be only one small element in your overall research.

❏ **Limited selection of total funds**

Besides, no family is going to give you any reliable information about the *other* 8,000 funds and the *other* 62 key fund families. If you limit yourself, you will have automatically screened out about 90 percent of this huge universe of opportunities.

In other words, don't limit yourself, because even if you ultimately choose to work with one family you'll at least need the power tools to compare your favorite family to its peers among the 8,000 other funds out there.

And that's where the new software packages come in—Reuters Money Network, StreetSmart, Steele's Mutual Fund Expert, Value Line's Fund Analyzer, Morningstar's Ascent, Quicken's Investor Insight, and other mutual fund investment packages. Any one of these powerful new cyberspace systems can help you make your own investment decisions independently.

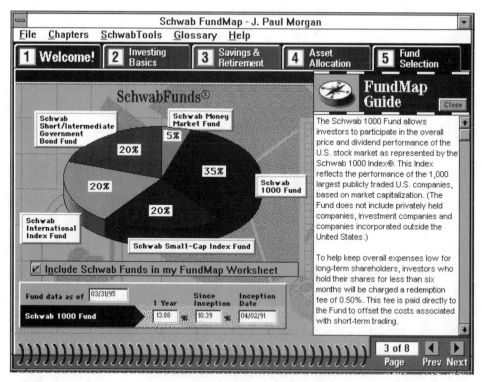

Figure 9.27   Yes, you can diversify within a single family.

BOTTOM LINE: EVEN IF YOU INVEST WITH ONLY ONE FAMILY, MAKE EVERY DECISION ON YOUR OWN

There's nothing inherently wrong with investing in a single family; in fact, it can be a perfect strategy. If the performance and diversification are there, it's a workable strategy. Remember *Hulbert Financial Digest*'s research, for example, which concluded that model portfolios investing only in Fidelity funds had outperformed non-Fidelity portfolios by five points. However, *you must still do your own independent research:*

❒ Monitor, evaluate, and manage your portfolio.

❒ Regularly update your financial plan.

❒ Check and rebalance your asset allocations.

❒ Independently confirm how well your funds and your fund family are performing against their peers.

After all, it's your money and your future; stay on top of it. *Use your own independent judgment,* even *after* selecting a single family, if that's your choice. Even if you like the racing stables, you still have to pick a specific jockey and horse to bet on.

In the final analysis, when you're faced with the choice of this or that specific fund, the battle is not between load and no-load funds. Although *Forbes* and most major financial publications consistently recommend no-load funds, there are exceptions to the rule. Whether you're in cyberspace or in a branch office, the real test is the bottom line. If the performance ratings signal a "total return" winner on your radar, then it's a winner . . . whether the fund is a load or a no-load.

New Mutual Funds Networks
One-Stop Shopping on the Net

How Cyberspace Works as the New
Marketplace for Mutual Fund Investors

One-stop cyberspace shopping for funds is our focus here in step 10. These new networks of funds give investors instant, one-stop access to thousands of no-load and load funds from a single source. Investors enjoy many benefits, including centralization of all their accounting, management, and trading.

CYBERSPACE MUTUAL FUND NETWORKS: ONE-STOP SHOPPING IS REVOLUTIONIZING THE MUTUAL FUND WORLD

The growing number of mutual fund networks is another trend that's shifting power to the individual do-it-yourself investor. These new networks, like Schwab's OneSource, link hundreds of unrelated funds and fund families into single systems in cyberspace, making it easy for independent investors to "go direct" to almost any fund from a single source.

These "fund supermarkets," as they're often called, are replacing traditional financial marketplaces and exchanges. The primary forces behind the spectacular growth of this worldwide network are the millions of computer-savvy investors going online to tap into the power of these rapidly expanding networks.

NEW FUND "SUPERMARKETS" ARE MORE POPULAR THAN MUTUAL FUND FAMILIES

"Are mutual fund investors bypassing fund supermarkets? A recent report by Cerulli Associates and Lipper Analytical reveals financial advisors' loyalty to fund families is waning. Can individual investors be far behind?

"The percentage of financial-advisor-managed assets placed directly with fund families dropped from 57% in 1992 to 29% in 1995. The report concludes, 'The emphasis on fund families is fading fast.' Meanwhile, supermarkets are raking in assets."

The reasons are obvious. Fund supermarkets offer wider selection, no-fee switching, and convenient consolidated statements.

SOURCE: "Supermarkets Outdrawing Fund Families," *Mutual Funds* magazine (May 1996).

The World Wide Web is the ultimate "network of networks." The Web is a new force in the financial and business communities, introduced just a few short years ago. Already, however, the Web has become the supernetwork of networks that has the potential of linking all 43 million mutual fund shareholders and 52 million stockholders to the same financial information resources previously available only to the Wall Street Establishment. The Web is indeed a major force in revolutionizing the mutual fund industry.

Consider, for example, these emerging alternatives that have been announced recently. Each is designed to eliminate the necessity for investors to work with many separate funds and fund families, while expanding the fund investors' opportunities using these new cyberspace connections:

Internet Mutual Fund Network

The World Wide Web is rapidly becoming the electronic "access of choice" to all mutual funds, the new "800 number" service giving investors direct access to prospectuses, quotes, news, educational materials, portfolio management, research reports, analytical tools, transactions, and account information.

ONLINE SERVICES ARE ALSO BECOMING FUND "MARKETPLACES"

"Mutual fund trading will soon be available on the nation's biggest computer online services. America Online Inc., the nation's biggest service, and CompuServe, which ranks second, plan to offer shareholders of participating fund companies an electronic avenue to open new accounts, check balances, redeem shares and transfer money within a fund family."

SOURCE: "Leading Online Services to Offer Mutual Fund Trading," AP newswire, *Los Angeles Times* (April 1, 1996).

Mutual Fund Supermarkets

Single-source accounts where investors can access many unrelated funds and fund families to buy, sell, exchange, and manage their portfolios, often through an Internet discount-trading account. Schwab's OneSource and Fidelity's FundsNetwork are examples.

Trading through an Online Service

America Online now permits account transactions using its online connection, which some investors prefer as a potentially more secure electronic link than the Internet.

Funds of Funds

Many new funds are now being offered that don't even pick stocks; they only invest in *other* mutual funds as a new way of solving an investor's diversification and asset-allocation goals.

Self-Managed No-Load Mutual Fund

Using the option of buying stocks directly from corporations and maintaining a dividend reinvestment program—no-load stocks as they're called. In effect, you are building your own mutual fund of established companies, and minimizing all brokerage loads.

Keep an open mind, because more opportunities will surface that break from the conventions and norms of the past, outdating much of what you know about investing.

In each of these instances, the center of financial power continues its rapid shift away from the Wall Street Establishment. Networks are decentralizing power into the hands and minds of millions of individual investors loosely connected all over this new worldwide financial network.

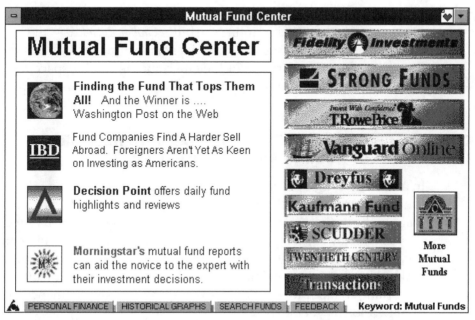

Figure 10.1 Mutual Fund Center at America Online: opening menu.

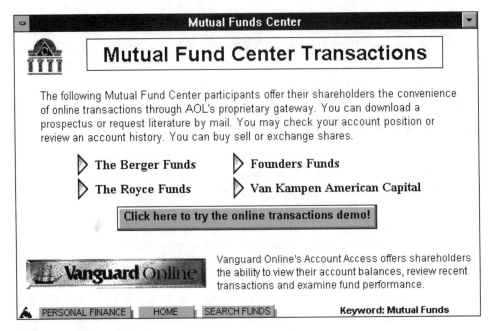

Figure 10.2   Mutual Fund Center Transactions: buy, sell, manage.

In the larger context, the financial world is witnessing the incredible phenomenon identified in John Naisbitt's *Global Paradox*—"the bigger the world economy, the more powerful its smallest player." This is the battle cry and the guiding formula of the emerging new cyberspace network of individual investors. And the power is shifting to them quite rapidly.

CYBERSPACE: THIS GIGANTIC FINANCIAL DATA NETWORK IS NOW PART OF YOUR PERSONAL COMPUTER

In many ways, the specifics of these new opportunities being offered by the fund industry are much less important than the underlying trend that is making the individual investor a self-sufficient technological powerhouse.

All the new cyberspace technologies (new software, online and Web services) are making it possible for the individual investor not only to make decisions independent of the Wall Street Establishment, but more important, to tap into what is now emerging as a single financial network of networks in cyberspace.

Moreover, the new breed of high-tech investor can capitalize on powers far beyond his or her own computer's hard drive, tapping into and

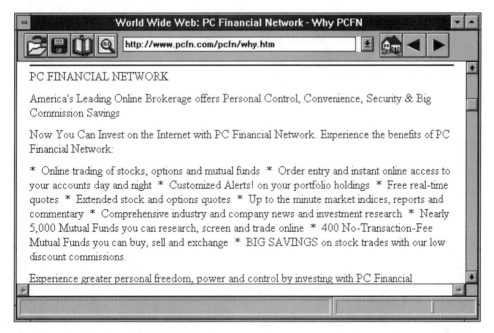

Figure 10.3   PCFN: research, screen, and trade 5,000 funds.

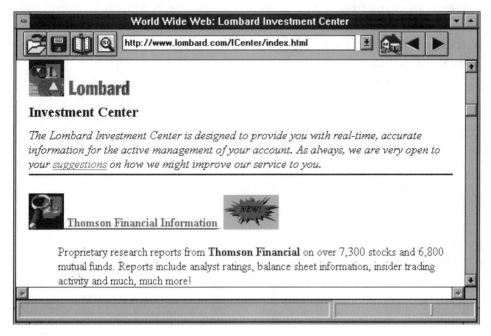

Figure 10.4   Lombard on the Web: fund analysis and trading.

leveraging this vast new resource called cyberspace—*out there in cyberspace*, in that network of networks, the World Wide Web, the whole network in your computer, including every other computer linked to this gigantic financial and information supermarket.

MUTUAL FUND SUPERMARKETS ARE GROWING IN POPULARITY AS INVESTORS BYPASS FUND FAMILIES

"Are mutual fund investors bypassing fund families for fund supermarkets?" asked *Mutual Funds* magazine in introducing a research study conducted by Lipper Analytical Services and Cerulli Associates in 1995.

The Lipper/Cerulli report focused on a major shift in the loyalties of professional financial advisors to fund families. Specifically, they concluded that "the emphasis on fund families is fading fast." How fast? Fast! In a short three years, the percentage of funds placed with fund families by financial advisors dropped precipitously, from 57 percent to 29 percent. "Can individual investors be far behind?" asked *Mutual Funds* magazine.

The question went beyond rhetoric. "Meanwhile," the report added, "supermarkets are raking in assets. Those of Schwab, Fidelity, and Jack White control nearly $80 billion." The answer is obvious. Individual investors prefer the enormous financial benefits of this new vehicle, primarily a wider selection of top-performing no-load funds from one convenient, centralized account.

Of course, some of these supermarket fund networks, such as Schwab and Fidelity, also manage their own large families of funds. As a result, these funds networks are also increasing the power of already powerful financial-services companies.

Since 1990, for example, the Fidelity and Vanguard families have each grown almost 300 percent, while the mutual fund assets of Merrill Lynch and Smith Barney have grown less than 100 percent. Consequently, this networking trend has become a wake-up call for all the fund families, forcing improvements in their services, all of which is beneficial to the do-it-yourself investor.

In fact, the real battle for the attention of the mutual fund investor is not just between the Wall Street Establishment and the no-load fund managers. The no-loads advocates are also fighting among themselves for a piece of the action.

MAJOR NO-LOAD FUND NETWORKS ("FUND SUPERMARKETS")

The trend to mutual fund networks—buying and managing all your funds through one discount brokerage firm—is accelerating and will soon be the industry norm. Fortunately, investors can also buy load funds from these same brokers. PCFN, for example, "gives you instant access to nearly 3,500 funds—all at the click of your mouse." Also keep in mind that in *Barron's* annual survey of mutual fund families, only 62 families were reviewed. Here are some of the current leaders:

No-Load Network of Funds	Funds	Families
AccuTrade //www.accutrade.com	576	113
Fidelity Investments //www.fid-inv.com	443	48
Lombard Internet //www.lombard.com	400	120
National Discount Brokers //www.pawws.com	95	15
Charles Schwab & Co. //www.schwab.com	600	70
Muriel Siebert & Co. //www.msiebert.com	470	47
PC Financial Network //www.pcfn.com	472	52
Waterhouse //www.waterhouse.com	250	45
Jack White & Co. //pawws.com/jwc	747	126

Interviews and other sources include: "Buying Mutual Funds a la Carte," Manuel Schiffres, *Kiplinger's* (November 1996); "A Better Way to Buy No-Load Mutual Funds," Bethany McLean, *Fortune* (December 25, 1995).

A word of caution: Recently the traditional Wall Street Establishment firms have also started selling no-loads. Unfortunately, Wall Street often adds on some high annual management fees that can effectively more than double the management fees of a no-load fund, and they offer no discount trading.

Figure 10.5   Charles Schwab Website: Mutual Fund OneSource Service.

Figure 10.6   Schwab Mutual Fund OneSource: hundreds of no-load funds.

Figure 10.7 SchwabFunds Family: one-stop no-load asset allocations.

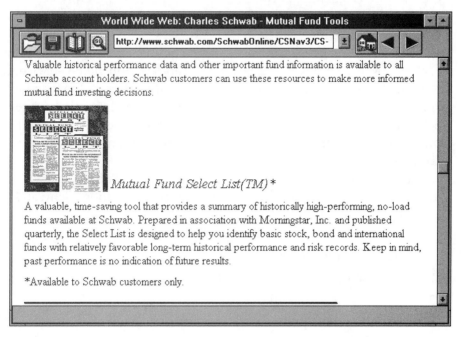

Figure 10.8 Mutual Fund Select List: best no-loads for the long haul.

The Wall Street Journal put this revolution in perspective in blunt terms: "Schwab and Fidelity are locked in a bitter battle to control the various lucrative mutual funds business. Fidelity runs more mutual-fund assets than any other fund company. Schwab's mutual-fund marketplace is one of the more popular trading systems for the nation's small investors."

And this squabbling leaves the entire no-load industry open to a counterattack from the Establishment, which is, in fact, what's happening, because the prize—trillions of mutual fund dollars—is such a massive lure.

SCHWAB'S ONESOURCE: THE WAL-MART OF CYBERSPACE FUNDS

Every investor is by now familiar with the Charles R. Schwab organization. It is the largest discount broker in America and the fifth-largest brokerage firm behind old-line Wall Street institutions like Merrill Lynch, Smith Barney, Dean Witter, and PaineWebber. Although a relative newcomer, Schwab manages over $200 billion in assets.

More important, the Schwab OneSource supermarket network of funds has nearly a thousand no-load and load mutual funds. Moreover, its growth rate is sizzling, between 50 and 75 percent annually according to recent reports on OneSource in *Forbes, Fortune, Mutual Funds,* and *Individual Investor* magazines.

The revolutionary significance of OneSource certainly was obvious to *Fortune:* "Master innovator Charles Schwab has launched a service that is revolutionizing the funds market just as his invention of the discount brokerage rocked the world of stocks 20 years ago. . . . Called OneSource, Schwab's service offers investors a virtual Wal-Mart of funds. With one phone call, you can choose from a menu of more than 350 funds in 50 fund families."

And so the revolution shifts into high gear. And here's what fund investors can look for from this cyberspace innovation, Schwab's One-Source:

1. Better selection: bigger choice of mutual funds
2. Consolidated account and tax statements
3. Frequent switching without transaction fees
4. Distributions swept into single money management account
5. Online and software tools for planning, research, and analysis

6. Convenient securities trading on the Internet at a discount

7. No additional management fees (for non–Wall Street supermarkets)

8. Select List: a quarterly summary of top performers by fund type

9. Family of proprietary funds, including a fund of funds

10. Financial planning advice: in-house and independent consultants

Actually, Schwab has had a similar network of funds for over 10 years. However, the Mutual Fund Marketplace, a larger universe of well over a thousand funds, is made up primarily of load funds, plus other Schwab services.

DISTINCTIONS BETWEEN WALL STREET'S RETAIL FIRMS AND THE DISCOUNT FIRMS ARE VANISHING INTO CYBERSPACE

"Charles Schwab has ridden the bull market to a splendid present, but its future is in boomer retirements. . . . Schwab's San Francisco–based company, though only 22 years old, is well ensconced now among America's top five brokerages. . . . Schwab says you haven't seen anything yet . . . talks of quintupling Schwab Corp.'s customer base over the next decade, from 2 million households [Merrill has 4 million] to 10 million . . .

"Schwab's heavily advertised OneSource mutual fund service . . . is the fastest-growing element of a company that, in client asset terms, has swelled at a 43% compound annual rate since 1990 . . .

"With their higher cost structure, their commissioned brokers and in-house mutual funds, the full-service brokers can scarcely afford to trade mutual funds without imposing direct charges on the consumer. Industry leader Merrill Lynch, though it provides access to 1,000 mutual funds, still lacks a no-load . . .

"The differences between Schwab and Fidelity and the full-fee brokerages have blurred . . . for many smaller firms with good performance but no sales clout, OneSource and Fidelity's FundsNetwork are godsends."

SOURCE: Tim Ferguson, "Do It Yourself," *Forbes* (April 22, 1996).

The revolutionary aspect about OneSource is that OneSource includes *only* no-load funds: no sales fees, no management fees, and no commissions. In other words, this new approach is aimed directly at the do-it-yourself investor, and it is forcing a whole new level of competition among

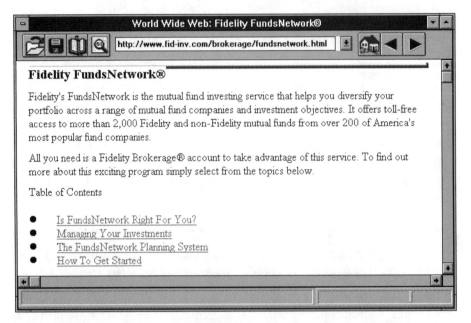

Figure 10.9   Fidelity FundsNetwork Website: one stop supermarket.

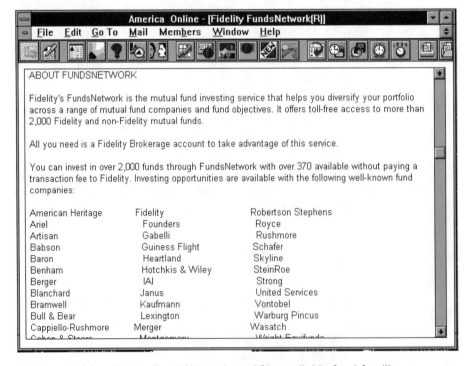

Figure 10.10   Fidelity FundsNetwork on AOL: available fund families.

no-load as well as loaded mutual fund managers, and especially for loaded funds controlled by the Wall Street Establishment.

What's next with the expanding Schwab network of financial services? *Mutual Funds* magazine characterized Schwab's enormous influence, "Now, in moves that are sending tremors throughout the financial community, Schwab is building its own proprietary family of mutual funds, and preparing for the first time to dispense advice that would ultimately lead clients into one of a handful of pre-designed 'fund of funds.' " Fasten your seat belts; the mutual fund revolution's just beginning.

FIDELITY'S FUNDSNETWORK:
CYBERSPACE SUPERMARKET OFFERS CHOICE OF 2,200 FUNDS

The success of Schwab's OneSource immediately spawned many "copycat" supermarkets, as *Fortune* called them. In quick-fashion Schwab's biggest competitor became the giant of all fund families: Fidelity Investments.

FIDELITY'S FUNDSNETWORK HAS 2,200 FUNDS:
ONE BIG HAPPY EXTENDED FAMILY OF FUNDS IN CYBERSPACE

"With more top-rated funds than anyone else, we're not afraid of competition. . . . We sell it. . . . We didn't get to be the leading mutual fund company overnight. We built it fund by fund. And today we manage over $350 million in assets. Based on the sheer strength of our talent and expertise.

"But we didn't stop there. We went on to build FundsNetwork. It lets you buy hundreds of funds from over 200 other well-known companies. . . . At Fidelity, we refuse to settle for being anything less than the one and only source for mutual funds you'll ever need. After all, the more successful an investor you become, the more successful an investment company we become."

SOURCE: Fidelity Investments ad in *L.A. Times* (January 14, 1996).

Fidelity quickly matched and possibly even one-upped Schwab with FundsNetwork, a mixture of the best of OneSource and the Mutual Funds Marketplace. Today, Fidelity's FundsNetwork offers over 2,200 funds, a group that includes about 360 no-load funds with no transaction fees whatsoever.

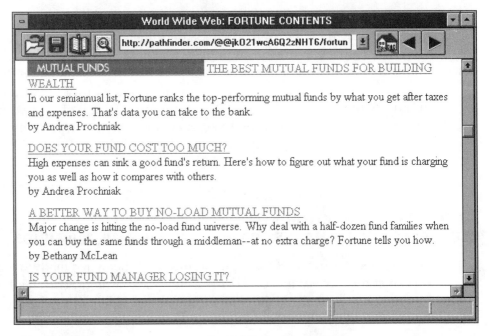

Figure 10.11   *Fortune:* new trends driving funds networks.

Fidelity also offers its investors the many other basic features investors have now come to expect from these fund supermarkets, including a wide selection of funds, consolidated statements, low cost, ease of management, and other privileges common to discount brokerage accounts.

Fidelity also provides investors with their own printed list of top-performing mutual funds, similar to Schwab's Select List. This competitive best-funds list is also based on data from Morningstar ratings, and Fidelity's list includes the Lipper Quintile Rating of each fund. In addition, Fidelity's FundsNetwork makes available a pencil-and-paper investment planner to help any remaining computerphobic investors develop their own asset allocations.

Because Fidelity's FundsNetwork is so extensive, Fidelity's printed research material is a valuable backup resource to their computer database. However, the investor should be aware that this approach still requires a lot of time-consuming paperwork on an incomplete database. In contrast, Value Line's Fund Analyzer, Steele's Mutual Fund Expert, and Morningstar's Principia, for example, would not only cover a more complete database, they will save a lot of time.

FUNDSNETWORK AND ONESOURCE CLONES ARE NOW EVERYWHERE: OFFERING INVESTORS ONE-STOP ACCESS TO MUTUAL FUNDS

Schwab introduced its OneSource supermarket in 1992, before the Web became popular. OneSource "set off a copycat scramble, and not just among rival discount brokers," according to a *Fortune* year-end report on investing. Fidelity quickly followed suit with FundsNetwork. Commercial banks have also joined the battle to become no-load funds middlemen, as many are also offering customers Quicken and Microsoft's Money. Why? These institutions see major revenues being generated by this powerful new trend toward do-it-yourself investing.

WALL STREET'S FUND FAMILIES: BELOW-AVERAGE PERFORMERS

"Acknowledging a brokerage house for having the best fund family on Wall Street is like handing out first prize at the 'tallest dwarf' contest: Any way you look at it, the winner comes up short. Prudential's domestic diversified stock funds have the best five-year combined average . . . 77%, *just short of the average gain that all fund families registered.*"

SOURCE: "Wall Street Comes Up Short," *Mutual Funds* magazine (September 1995).

And "even bigger news is around the corner. The rise of OneSource has helped break the resistance of Wall Street's full-service brokers to selling no-load funds." Smith Barney and other big brokerage firms are setting up their own one-stop mutual fund shops, with their own spin. And in marked contrast to the discounters' approach, the Wall Street Establishment is adding on a management fee, *loading the no-loads!*

In the final analysis, of course, Wall Street firms can pile on all the loads they want; ultimately, it's the bottom-line performance of a fund that will determine whether they fall by the wayside.

Certainly, if the central conclusion of the Goldman Sachs report we discussed in Chapter 8 materializes (that by the year 2000, most of today's fund companies will either disappear or be consolidated into 20 to 25 megamanagers, each controlling $150 billion), then both the megamanagers and the emerging supermarkets are reflecting the same basic trend toward do-it-yourself investing.

In other words, underlying this trend toward consolidation of funds into bigger and bigger management companies, the individual investor is

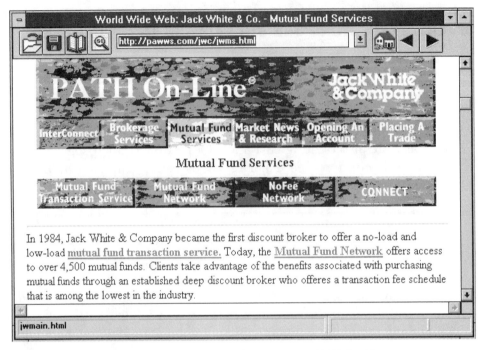

Figure 10.12   Mutual Fund Network at Jack White's PATH On-Line.

paradoxically calling the shots, armed with high-tech information and focused on bottom-line fund performance. Ultimately, the individual investor "votes" on the direction of the trend by cherry-picking the best funds through fund supermarkets or through fund families. So let's see what some of the best supermarkets are offering the individual investor.

CYBERSPACE DISCOUNTERS: JACK WHITE & COMPANY OFFERS THE LARGEST SUPERMARKET OF NO-LOAD MUTUAL FUNDS

Schwab and Fidelity may be the heavyweights when it comes to total no-load fund assets. However, solid organizations like Jack White & Company, a regional broker physically based in San Diego, California, are also pushing rapidly into this new frontier. White, for example, is simultaneously building a powerful network of no-loads and also winning a loyal following of independent investors as a discount broker. The White organization has distinguished itself in several key areas:

❑ Cyberspace pioneer: Jack White's PATH On-Line Website was one of the first of its kind on the Internet when the company joined the

PAWWS World Wide Web site a few years ago. White was also one of the first brokers offering client trading online and on the Internet.

❏ Mutual fund supermarket: Jack White & Company has created the largest of the fund supermarkets, with access to over 800 funds from 120 families through their NoFee Network.

❏ *SmartMoney* magazine has ranked Jack White & Company the number one discount broker for overall service for the last three years, even ahead of Charles Schwab.

While Jack White & Company does offer the largest number of free no-load funds, Schwab, with fewer funds, is the most selective of all fund supermarkets, including White. Schwab's funds network has a high percentage in the top 25 percent of its respective fund categories. Nevertheless, the Jack White team has a remarkable track record.

SUPERMARKET FOR INDEPENDENT-THINKING INVESTORS

"We were attracting an unusually enlightened client. A client who had confidence, an independent mind, and the ability to make an important decision without the advice of a salesperson. . . . They want: quality customer service, professional executions plus large commission savings. . . . They don't want: high cost services or sales pressure."

SOURCE: Jack K. White, "Letter to an Independent Thinker" (1996).

According to *Forbes,* White's retort to Schwab was, "We don't agree with their approach." White makes no "judgmental overlay." You get to choose from 1,600 funds at White versus 800 at Schwab. And if you're a true do-it-yourself investor, you'll appreciate more alternatives for your screening and selection.

White's NoFee Network does have an excellent selection of top-performing funds. And savvy independent investors who know how to screen and cherry-pick the winners from any database love it.

Also check out Jack White's other services in cyberspace discount brokerage. Among the early pioneers, White continues pushing the envelope today. Their latest innovation is the new InterConnect trading service, the first crossing network for individual investors, which directly matches Nasdaq buyers and sellers without going through a market maker, saving

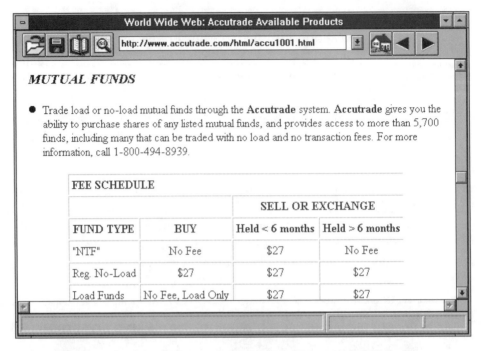

Figure 10.13   AccuTrade: discount broker with network of 5,700 funds.

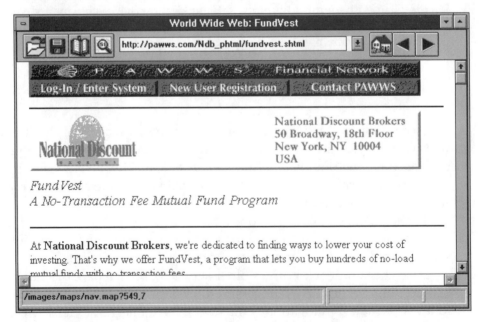

Figure 10.14   National Discount Brokers FundVest: mutual funds network.

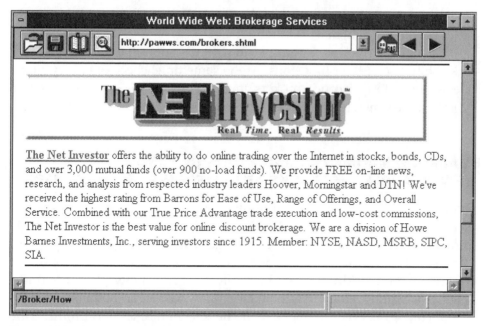

Figure 10.15 NET Investor: 900 no-loads and over 3,000 mutual funds.

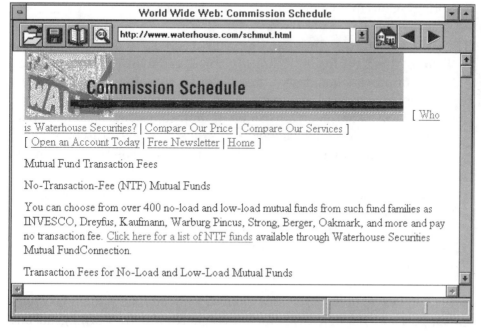

Figure 10.16 Waterhouse Website: 400 no-load and low-load funds.

on the spread. White champions the individual investor, in both cyber-space and traditional markets.

Cyberspace investors interested in a funds supermarket should make Jack White one of their first stops. At the same time, check out every single one of these top discount brokers in the *SmartMoney* surveys; this is a cybertrend destined to *replace* the Wall Street Establishment's closed network.

SUPERMARKETS, MINIMARTS, AND FUNDS OF FUNDS: MANY NEW FINANCIAL NETWORKS ARE EMERGING IN CYBERSPACE

Cyberspace technology is pushing the frontiers of Wall Street into a new dimension of reality. Schwab, Fidelity, and Jack White have been quickly joined by many other discount brokerage firms offering fund supermar-kets. And some of the best include top discount brokers already set up for trading on the World Wide Web, and offering funds networks: AccuTrade, Lombard, Muriel Seibert, National Discount Brokers, and others.

Of course, as often happens while new technologies and products are developing, the hype and promise from insiders often far exceeds the end result. For example, the intense competition for the investor's money is also bringing out many new products and services:

❏ **Fund MiniMarts.**   *The Wall Street Journal* says, "Most investors know them by their confusing technical name—variable annuities. Yet vari-able annuities, though baffling to most investors, are essentially smaller versions of fund supermarkets . . . they enable investors to buy and sell shares of funds from different fund companies . . . but . . . with a smaller selection—and higher process costs . . . fewer discount 'prod-ucts.' . . . Unfortunately for investors, this trend has been leading to even higher prices."

❏ **Funds of Funds.**   In a separate article, the *Journal* quotes John Bogle, founder of Vanguard Funds and "the fund industry's apostle of low-cost index investing." The *Journal* noted that Bogle is "naturally opposed to funds of funds with an extra layer of management fees. Over time, he figures, most such funds won't beat a fixed portfolio of comparable index funds."

   On the other hand, *Mutual Funds* magazine found much favorable support for this new investment vehicle from both Morningstar and Value Line, even though the added layer of management increases operating expenses and eats into the investor returns.

WINNING FUNDS OF FUNDS: VANGUARD AND T. ROWE PRICE

"The funds offer professional management, and because they invest in several other funds, more diversification than can be achieved by a single fund; hence less risk. . . . Diversity and expertise doesn't come cheap. The average fund of funds has an expense ratio of 1.56% versus 1.34% for the average stock fund . . ."

One solution: "Vanguard and T. Rowe Price have an enormous cost advantage over the competition. Since both Vanguard Star and Price Spectrum invest wholly within their respective families, running them is essentially free."

SOURCE: Jonathan Burton, "Let a Pro Pick Your Funds," *Mutual Funds* magazine (February 1996).

Cyberspace financial networks are increasing exponentially: supermarkets, minimarts, and funds of funds; Internet trading, discount brokerage, and online research; Schwab, Fidelity, and Smith Barney. Information technology is changing the financial landscape, substantially increasing the options available to the independent investor in cyberspace. Do-it-yourself

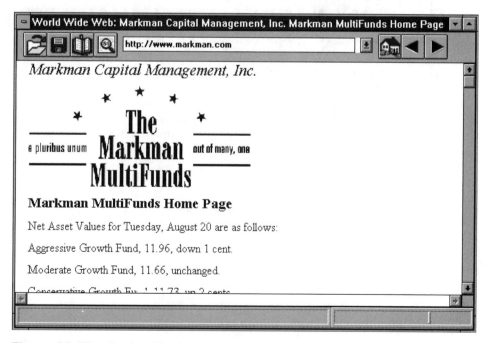

Figure 10.17 Funds of funds: alternative to funds networks.

investing—*not* the institutions—is the moving force underlying all these networks. This is no mere fad.

WALL STREET'S COUNTERATTACK ADDS NEW COSTS TO NO-LOADS: TRANSFORMING THEM INTO "LOADED NO-LOAD" FUNDS!

The Wall Street Establishment is finally reading the handwriting on the wall. Some are breaking ranks. While Merrill Lynch's network of 800 funds still lacks a no-load, last year Smith Barney announced that it would start offering no-load funds in its network. So the brokers are still motivated, and little changes for the customers of this Wall Street Establishment, other than the marketing spin.

According to *The Wall Street Journal,* "Broker-sold funds have been losing ground to no-loads, and Smith Barney feels driven to go with the tide. Moreover, brokers who steer clients into no-loads won't go hungry. They'll get annual fees." In most cases, these new services will add on another load of at least 1.5 percent to the cost of a previously no-load fund.

> ### *KIPLINGER'S:* LOADING NO-LOAD FUNDS CAN DOUBLE EXPENSES AND TOTALLY DEFEAT THE PURPOSE OF A NO-LOAD FUND
>
> "Brokers are seeing their dominance of the fund business steadily eroding in favor of direct-marketed funds . . . these funds will hold a majority of fund assets within about a decade. By selling shares in no-load funds in addition to their traditional commissioned-based funds, brokerages hope to broaden their clientele and keep present customers from bolting . . .
>
> "Loaded No-Load Funds. It's a sound strategy, but investors will pay a price . . . 1.5% of the assets of those funds a year, in addition to the expenses incurred by the funds. If you add 1.5% to the 1.27% average expense ratio of a U.S. diversified stock fund . . . it totally defeats the purpose of no-load funds—namely, low cost."
>
> SOURCE: Tracy Longo, "Guess Who Wants to Sell You No-Load Funds?," *Kiplinger's Personal Finance Magazine* (September 1996).

Call it whatever you like—annual fees, brokers' commissions, or kickback—the Wall Street Establishment has added some clever marketing spin here. We've seen similar tactics earlier, as firms renamed brokers "independent advisors," another subtle misnomer. Now Wall Street is loading no-load funds with management fees and commissions, converting no-load funds into loaded funds.

In other words, Wall Street has invented a new hybrid fund type: the "loaded no-load fund." And unfortunately, since the fund families of Wall Street brokerage firms are historically below-average performers, this trick of loading no-load funds will obviously (on a total return basis) tend to drag down many solid no-load funds to the lower performance levels of the Wall Street brokerage funds.

In all fairness to the Establishment, we should emphasize again that these programs offered by the Wall Street Establishment are not aimed at the average investor. Wall Street has little interest in independent investors. In fact, *Fortune* specifically reported that Merrill Lynch is targeting only the well-to-do and not the do-it-yourself investor. The wealthy investors Wall Street wants as customers are too busy making lots of money, so they don't have the time necessary for do-it-yourself investing; this class of investor *does* have the money to pay for Wall Street's advice. Targeting these investors seems a reasonable business strategy . . . until the majority of the next generation become do-it-yourself investors.

GROUND ZERO IN THE WAR ZONE: WALL STREET BATTLES NO-LOAD FAMILIES, DISCOUNTERS, AND THE RUSH TO DO IT YOURSELF

And in another article, *Fortune* quotes a Smith Barney executive vice president as saying, "Do-it-yourself investing is not a viable concept in the 1990s." Another major money manager is equally blunt, again emphasizing the huge gap between Wall Street and the independent-thinking investor.

Wall Street aggressively pursues customers who are the rich, people who are either too busy *making money* or too busy *spending money* (on vacations or in retirement), to waste their time managing their money as do-it-yourself investors. In fact, Wall Street is a major purchaser of telephone lists of prime candidates that fit their demographic profiles; these lists are made available to their cold-call salespeople.

The battle lines are drawn: on one side of the field, the Wall Street Establishment and the well-to-do; on the opposite side, no-load funds and the do-it-yourself investor. The central challenge boils down to this:

❑ *If an investor can achieve optimum diversification by picking 10 funds in the right categories, and*

WALL STREET'S OUTDATED, OLD-FASHIONED PATERNALISM: INVESTORS ARE CHILDREN WHO NEED ALLOWANCES

In addition to Wall Street's denial of the do-it-yourself investing trend, the advertisements of other major investment institutions are even more revealing of Wall Street's paternalistic ideas about investors. Consider the message of these headlines for two recent ads:

One Day You'll Get to **Act Like a Kid** Again. But for Now, Let's Discuss Your Allowance.

Forget Retirement—We're Talking About a **Second Childhood.** This Time Make Sure You Get a Big Allowance.

SOURCE: Aetna Retirement Services and ITT Hartford, *Money* magazine (June 1996).

❏ *today's new cyberspace technology and research are making it so darn easy to pick the right categories,*

❏ *how much longer will the Wall Street Establishment be able to keep selling so little for so much?*

BUSINESSWEEK: "NEWFANGLED THINKING" AT SMITH BARNEY? OR IS LOADING NO-LOAD FUNDS AN "OLD-FASHIONED" TRICK?

In August 1996 "Smith Barney began selling 2,700 no-load funds alongside its own proprietary funds, marking the first time a major Wall Street broker has sold no-loads. Smith Barney could see a big drop in both revenues and assets if too many customers buy no-load funds, which carry a 1.5% annual 'wrap' fee instead of the 5% up-front sales load charged by Smith Barney's in-house funds."

Smith Barney is "gearing up to exploit one of Smith Barney's biggest untapped assets: a network of 37,000 insurance agents and brokers in the Travelers organization [Smith Barney's parent] licensed to sell mutual funds. That's more than industry leader Merrill Lynch & Co.'s 13,800 brokers." They have also improved the performance of Smith Barney's in-house funds.... Smith Barney's 70 funds have advanced from being below average in 1993 to 'about average' through June."

SOURCE: Geoffrey Smith, "It's Nice to Have This Stuff in Your Blood," *BusinessWeek* (August 12, 1996).

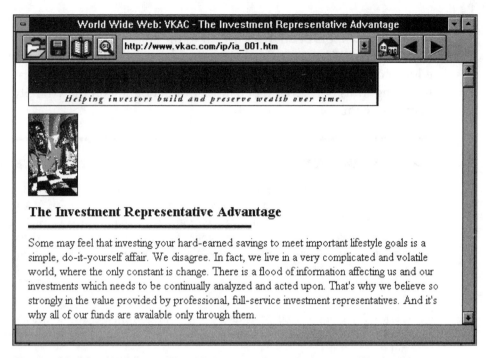

Helping investors build and preserve wealth over time.

The Investment Representative Advantage

Some may feel that investing your hard-earned savings to meet important lifestyle goals is a simple, do-it-yourself affair. We disagree. In fact, we live in a very complicated and volatile world, where the only constant is change. There is a flood of information affecting us and our investments which needs to be continually analyzed and acted upon. That's why we believe so strongly in the value provided by professional, full-service investment representatives. And it's why all of our funds are available only through them.

Figure 10.18   Wall Street Establishment rejects do-it-yourself investing.

The simple answer is The Wall Street Establishment will be able to continue this aggressive game as long as the performance of their funds warrants it. Then the illusion will be replaced by the harsh realities. The bottom line will decide the outcome, and the bottom line is brutally neutral when viewed from the databases and computer technologies that expose it.

WALL STREET'S ESTABLISHMENT IS STUCK IN AN OLD PARADIGM: "OLD-FASHIONED" INSTITUTIONAL PATERNALISM AND DEPENDENCY

The Wall Street Establishment firms are stuck in the old paradigm; as Smith Barney is fond of saying we're "old-fashioned." More accurately, they are paternalistic fundamentalists who dogmatically adhere to a belief system that says investors are either incapable of making or unwilling to make intelligent investment decisions by themselves. Consequently, Wall Street lives in fear that do-it-yourself investing is a serious threat to the very survival of an existing system that pays the bills of the Establishment.

As a consequence, the Wall Street Establishment spends large sums of money on research and advertisements to counteract this perceived inability of the investing public. Meanwhile, the funds, the accounting, and all the electronic tools of analysis are all in the sole control of the all-knowing "old-fashioned" brokers. Furthermore, the Establishment neither acknowledges nor makes any effort to educate customers regarding do-it-yourself investing, thus perpetuating customer dependency on the Wall Street brokerage system.

THE WALL STREET ESTABLISHMENT. . . . ON THE DEFENSIVE

Last October, the headline in a *Money* magazine ad read, "Smith Barney just broke down the wall between load and no-load funds." And in smaller type they note that they charge "an annual advisory fee." Independent investors familiar with cyberspace are unlikely to be misled by any such extravagant claims by the Wall Street Establishment. Rather, do-it-yourself investors know the facts:

1. **Wall Street is way behind the discounter brokers:** Charles Schwab's OneSource, Fidelity's FundsNetwork and Jack White's No-Fee Funds Network actually "broke down those walls" many years before Smith Barney, *and without the added fees*. Wall Street is on the defensive here.

2. **Wall Street may double your fund's expenses:** The Wall Street Establishment is now loading the no-load funds with new fees which may in some cases effectively double the fund's expenses (the overall expenses of many funds are actually *less* than Smith Barney's add-on 1.5 percent fee). This, of course, substantially reduces the total return to the investor.

3. **Wall Street's fund families are so-so performers:** Generally speaking, mutual fund families managed by the Wall Street Establishment are not top performers, in spite of their ads. Research in *Mutual Funds* magazine concluded that even the best Wall Street families are merely average among all mutual fund families.

In the long run, the relentless competition from the discounters will force the Wall Street Establishment to surrender to the realities of the do-it-yourself cyberspace revolution.

Wall Street's conservative leadership would be wise to listen closely to the underlying message of last year's historic welfare reform legislation, which reversed a generation-old mind-set. Economic dependency—whether dependency on the government or on Wall Street—is an outdated concept, a fading paradigm in an era of individualism and independent thinking. Listen to the voices of investors defecting to Schwab, Fidelity, and Jack White.

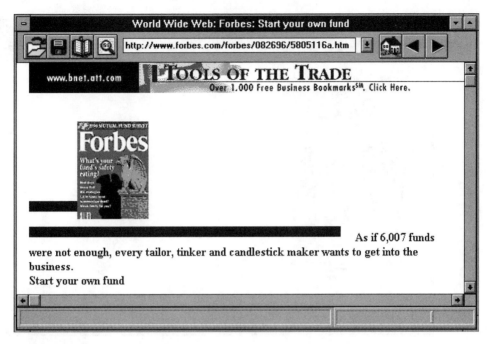

Figure 10.19 *Forbes:* another new trend, start your own fund.

NEW CYBERSPACE NETWORKS ARE UNDERMINING WALL STREET'S POWER AND LEVELING THE PLAYING FIELD

The new breed, firms such as Charles Schwab and Fidelity, are offering a new kind of full-service electronic advice to the computer-savvy investor who doesn't need or want to talk to a broker about no-load funds, and who refuses to pay Wall Street's high fees and commissions for advice that's often late and usually no more valuable than what's widely available (and often free) from your home computer. But what do we name these new entities? What do you call these powerful new multitalented organizations? In fact, nothing quite fits yet.

No matter what Merrill Lynch says, Jack White, Lombard, Aufhauser, and Schwab are evolving into more than mere discount brokers. They all offer rather sophisticated *electronic full services* using do-it-yourself power tools, as well as those new no-load-fund marketplaces that are pushing the Wall Street Establishment firms to the wall and driving them crazy. Moreover, there are now many more discount cyber-brokers entering the competition, forcing Schwab and the better online discounters to run an even stronger race into the uncharted territories of cyberspace.

Figure 10.20   *BusinessWeek:* technology + globalization = high anxiety.

All of which is driving the Wall Street Establishment firms even crazier, into a state of confusion, if not panic. The real panic, however, is of their own making, for *the enemy is within.* As the paradigm continues shifting, Wall Street's "old-fashioned" ways no longer work. And as long as Wall Street clings to its paternalism, denying the do-it-yourself trend, the tension is guaranteed to increase.

BOTTOM LINE: DO-IT-YOURSELF INVESTORS ARE THE DRIVING FORCE BEHIND THE NEW MUTUAL FUND NETWORKS

In this chapter networks have been the focus: all the emerging networks of funds, the supermarkets, and the World Wide Web that are all making possible an emerging new global financial community that links everything electronically in cyberspace. These include fund networks with high-concept name tags such as OneSource, NoFee Network, and FundsNetwork, as well as fund supermarkets, fund minimarts, and funds of funds. Professional money managers often consider these networks as their personal property, managed and controlled by their professional expertise.

HIGH ANXIETY AND THE PSYCHOLOGY OF MONEY MANAGEMENT

"High anxiety. it's money managers' new malaise. The symptoms are red eyes, jet lag, nervous tics—and doubts about their firms' future . . .

"Money management professionals would make good poster children for the Age of Stress. Yet it's not their harried travel schedules alone that induce anxiety. Clients have become more demanding, of performance and service both; investment instruments have become more complex; markets have become more volatile—and treacherous; schedules have become more stretched as globalization ushers in the true 24-hour workday; and worst of all, competition has become far more ferocious as the whole money management business undergoes a serious shakeout . . .

"Another of money management's modern plagues: information overkill. The sheer quantity of data that investment professionals feel obligated to track boggles the mind . . . the belief is growing that psychology is a key factor in investment decisions."

SOURCE: Julie Rohrer, "High Anxiety," *Institutional Investor* (February 1996).

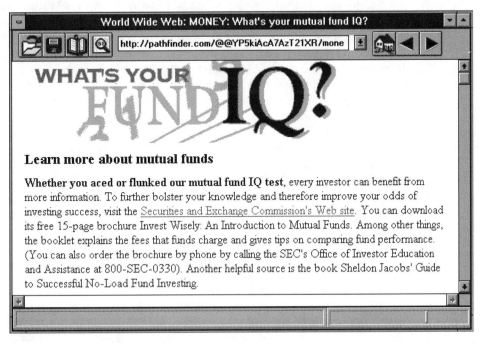

Figure 10.21 Bottom line: Be a winner, perfect your game!

In fact, *the money managers have little control here. The underlying power here is in an emerging network of individual investors.* The emerging new cyberspace technologies are helping these investors bypass these institutions by creating this vast amorphous network of networks:

❏ Intranets and the Internet

❏ Online services loaded with real-time news and quotes

❏ Powerful offline software

❏ Direct access to the best financial databases

ANALYSTS NOW FOCUSING ON MUTUAL FUNDS NETWORKS

The Mutual Fund Investors Association publishes a number of newsletters. Last year MFIA came out with the first one devoted solely to the emerging new mutual funds networks, *FundsNet Insight,* which is another valuable "second opinion" for cyberspace investors. MFIA's President, Eric Kobren, had this to say about the new service:

"These services provide a tremendous opportunity for mutual fund investors like you. With Fidelity's FundsNetwork, Schwab's Mutual Fund Marketplace and Jack White's Mutual Fund Network you can buy and sell hundreds of top mutual funds from dozens of fund families with the same ease and convenience as trading from within one fund family. And in many cases, the cost of this added convenience is—zero . . .

"Out of the thousands of available fund *FundsNet Insight* will simplify your decisions by selecting a diversified portfolio consisting of 5–6 of our highest-ranked funds tailored to your investment goals.

"If you're seeking long-term capital growth, are comfortable taking market risks and have no income needs for at least 5 years, follow our FundsNet **Growth Portfolio.**

"Our FundsNet **Growth & Income Portfolio** is targeted for investors who want solid growth, but with less volatility than the market. A good choice for those retiring in less than 5 years, as well as many younger retirees.

"If you need current income and want to protect your portfolio and stay ahead of inflation, follow our FundsNet **Income & Preservation Portfolio.**"

EDITED FROM: How to Avoid a Mutual Fund Disaster, Eric Kobren, President, Mutual Fund Investors Association (800) 537-2280. MFIA's Website is coming.

❐ Electronic tools for everything from financial planning and online banking to trading and portfolio management

The power is in the Net. Call it what you will, a network of networks, the Internet, the World Wide Web, or cyberspace. The power of the network comes from the individual do-it-yourself investor. Each is leveraging themselves by being connected to this network of networks, cyberspace, that is linking each to an infinite number of resources and *to every other individual investor on this network, creating a universal intelligence.* Each has the power of the whole.

Sun Microsystems has been telling us for well over a decade that "the network is the computer." Now that we know the Net is the computer, we also know it is no longer the exclusive property of the Wall Street professional; today the power also belongs to the independent Main Street investor. And those investors are the underlying force of all these networks.

The Future Is Already Here. You've Got the Power; Do It Yourself

That's right. You already have everything you'll ever need to successfully buy mutual funds and manage your own portfolio of funds, thanks to today's new cyberspace technology. You don't need the Wall Street Establishment. Wall Street's "old boys' club" is locked in an old paradigm and an old way of thinking built on two related principles that are no longer valid:

❏ Wall Street had a *monopoly* on market and financial information, and controlled financial cyberspace as their private domain.

❏ Customer *dependency* was essential; investors had to rely on the presumed superior intelligence of the Wall Street's brokers.

The cyberspace revolution changed everything a few years ago. Now Wall Street is in the blast zone, at ground zero. As more and more individual investors discover the infinite supply of financial information and power tools in cyberspace, more and more power shifts away from Wall Street to Main Street.

Charles Schwab and Jack White, Vanguard and Fidelity, and many other discount brokers and no-load funds have been chipping away at the power of the Wall Street cartel for two decades, undercutting Wall Street's outmoded commission structure. More important, today these same pioneers are also offering *full-service* brokerage and research using the latest cyberspace technology, new *electronic* services that are superior to Wall Street's antiquated broker-controlled "full service."

POWER SHIFT: FROM WALL STREET TO DO-IT-YOURSELF INVESTORS

Are the discount brokers and no-load funds winning the war with Wall Street? Yes, and Wall Street's worried. But the real winner is the Main Street do-it-yourself investor: Market Wizards and Motley Fools, Gen Xers and Beardstown Ladies. Street smart, they are independent souls who love the freedom cyberspace investing offers.

Today the cyberspace investor can manage a portfolio far better and far cheaper than the Wall Street Establishment. As a cyberspace investor, you never have to deal with a Wall Street broker again—not for mutual funds, securities, research, or portfolio management. You can be totally independent, in charge of your own destiny.

The reason is simple. Today's mutual fund investor can get better information online and on the Net. In fact, many cyberspace financial data providers now use this headline, "Get the same information as the pros." It's all there waiting for you, faster, cheaper, and with more options and more objectivity than you'll get paying unnecessary commissions to a Wall Street broker.

WALL STREET'S COUNTERATTACK AND THE SPIN DOCTORS

But watch out. The Wall Street Establishment recently marshaled a massive counterattack, a sustained marketing blitz. Fortunately, some of the major financial publications are questioning this new image-making. And this battle to control the individual investor's mind promises to heat up. Here's a few late-breaking news items that investors should keep in mind concerning Wall Street's defensive stance and their new advertising face:

Behind Those New Name Tags, a Broker Is Still a Broker

Don't be fooled by the new name tags the Wall Street brokers are wearing. Wall Street's spin doctors have obviously read several studies that show the public distrust of "brokers." Their solution: Give brokers some new names. So the Wall Street Establishment invented new name tags for brokers, labels such as "advisors," "consultants," and even "your partner."

This charade is part of a subtle attempt to hypnotize the public. Main Street investors are supposed to believe that Wall Street's brokers are now offering *independent, objective* advice, with more integrity than existed the day before these new name tags were pinned on. It's an illusion.

The Wall Street Establishment may have convinced the SEC, NASD, NYSE, and FTC that this is not false advertising, but don't you be fooled. More than ever, you'll have to protect yourself as Wall Street floods the press with this clever new spin. In the end, however, a wolf in sheep's clothing is still a wolf, and a broker is still a broker.

Do-it-yourself. Manage your own mutual fund portfolio in cyberspace.

Buying No-Load Funds from Wall Street Doesn't Pay

Their advertisements tell us the Wall Street Establishment has finally come around after many years of refusing to sell no-load funds. In fact, soon, all of the Wall Street Establishment firms will be offering no-load mutual funds.

But there's a catch—and it's a very costly one for their customers—one the street-smart investor will see through immediately. Wall Street is now adding huge annual management fees, often as much as 100 to 200 percent, *on top of* the low management fees typically charged by the better-managed no-load funds, for relatively little services.

As a result, the main advantage of buying a no-load mutual fund—low management fees—has been wiped out by the Wall Street Establishment. Moreover, Wall Street is using this ploy as a marketing tool to sell customers a host of other "advisory" services, for even more fees.

Put another way, Wall Street has invented a costly new hybrid mutual fund; call it the "loaded no-load fund." They had to. In recent years, Wall Street's share of the mutual fund market has dropped dramatically. Wall Street's brokers need product to push, and "loaded no-load" funds are a clever way of beefing up commissions and fees again.

However, street-smart investors can go directly to the no-load funds, avoid Wall Street, and substantially increase their returns. So do it yourself. Any investor can manage their own mutual fund portfolio in cyberspace.

Discount Brokers Still Outscore Wall Street by a Wide Margin

Another key reason Wall Street's monopoly is disappearing is the relent-less competition from the discount brokerage firms. Today, these firms are offering not only huge discounts, but also *full service* to the *computerized* investor, at a very reasonable price. New cyberspace investors are finding more and more discount brokers offering trades in the $10 to $30 range, while the Wall Street Establishment often charges commissions that are more than 25 times higher for the same trade.

Wall Street's argument is that they have high in-house research costs, while the discounters provide no research. Today that's pure nonsense. Wall Street no longer has a monopoly on financial information. It has dis-appeared into cyberspace. Today, cyberspace is one gigantic "research cen-ter" readily accessible to any do-it-yourself investor in the world, thanks to computer technology. In other words, not only is there no advantage in dealing with the Wall Street Establishment, it's an expensive luxury.

THE FUTURE IS NOW: YOU CAN DO IT YOURSELF IN CYBERSPACE

All this cyberspace competition is welcomed and encouraged. *Competition will drive down costs on all sides*—for discount brokers, no-load funds, and data vendors, as well as the Wall Street Establishment. No matter what happens, the individual investor will benefit from this highly competitive battle.

In *Megatrends,* John Naisbitt calls this era "the Age of the Individual." Translated into the cyberspace investing arena, this is the "Age of the Do-It-Yourself Investor." Forecasts suggest that by the year 2000 virtually every mutual fund investor and every stockholder will be online and on the Net, over 100 million of them. Get on the cutting edge.

Bottom line: The future is now. And cyberspace is where the action is. You've got all the power tools you need to do it yourself today. You can successfully manage your own mutual fund portfolio in cyberspace.

Directory: World's Top-100 Mutual Fund Websites

Mutual Fund Educational Websites

American Association of Individual Investors	//www.aaii.org
Fidelity Investments	//www.fid-inv.com
Mutual Fund Education Alliance	//www.mfea.com
Mutual Funds Online	//www.mfmag.com
PAWWS Financial Network	//www.pawws.com
U.S. Securities and Exchange Commission	//www.sec.gov
Vanguard Group of Funds	//www.vanguard.com
100% No-Load Mutual Fund Council	//networth.galt.com

Fund Databases and Analytical Power Tools

AAII Quarterly Mutual Fund Update	//www.aaii.org
The Advisors	//www.advisorsw.com
Barron's Online	//www.barrons.com
CDA/Wiesenberger Mutual Funds Update	//www.cda.com
Disclosure Incorporated	//www.disclosure.com
Institute for Econometric Research	//www.mfmag.com
Lipper Analytical Service	//www.lipperweb.com
Manhattan Analytics	//www.manhattanlink.com
Micropal	//www.micropal-us.com
Morningstar Research	//www.morningstar.net
Mutual Funds Magazine Online	//www.mfmag.com
Reuter Money Network	//www.moneynet.com
Steele Systems	//www.steelesystems.com
StreetSmart and eSchwab	//www.schwab.com
TeleChart 2000: Mutual Fund Database	//www.worden.com
Telescan	//www.telescan.com
Tradeline/IDD Information	//nestegg.iddis.com
Value Line Mutual Fund Survey	//www.valueline.com

Financial Publications: Best-Funds Lists

Barron's	//www.barrons.com
Bloomberg Personal	//www.bloomberg.com
BusinessWeek	//www.businessweek.com
Financial World	//www.financialworld.com
Forbes	//www.forbes.com
Fortune	//www.pathfinder.com/fortune

Individual Investor	//www.individualinvestor.com
Kiplinger's	//www.kiplinger.com
Money	//www.pathfinder.com/money
Mutual Funds	//www.mfmag.com
SmartMoney	//www.smartmoney.com
USA Today	//www.usatoday.com/money
U.S. News & World Report	//www.usnews.com
Wall Street Journal	//www.wsj.com
Worth	//www.worth.com
Your Money	//www.consumersdigest.com

Top-20 Mutual Fund Families

AIM Family of Funds	//www.pawws.com
Capital Research	planned for 1997
Dean Witter	no information
Dreyfus Group	//www.dreyfus.com
Fidelity Investments	//www.fid-inv.com
Franklin Templeton	//www.templeton.ca
IDS/American Express	//www.americanexpress.com
Janus Funds	//www.janusfunds.com
Kemper Funds	//www.kemper.com
Merrill Lynch	//www.ml.com
MFS Family of Funds	//www.mfs.com
Oppenheimer Funds	//www.oppenheimerfunds.com
Prudential Funds	//www.prusec.com
Putnam Investments	//www.putnaminv.com
Scudder Funds	//funds.scudder.com
Smith Barney	//www.smithbarney.com
T. Rowe Price	//www.troweprice.com
Twentieth Century	//www.twentieth-century.com
Vanguard Group	//www.vanguard.com
Van Kampen	//www.vkac.com

No-Load Mutual Fund Networks

AccuTrade	//www.accutrade.com
Fidelity: FundsNetwork	//www.fid-inv.com
Howe Barnes: NetInvestor	//www.pawws.com
Lombard Securities	//www.lombard.com
National Discount Brokers	//www.pawws.com
PC Financial Network	//www.pcfn.com
Charles Schwab: OneSource	//www.schwab.com
Muriel Siebert & Co.	//www.msiebert.com
Waterhouse	//www.waterhouse.com
Jack White: NoFee Network	//www.pawws.com/jwc

Major Mutual Fund Website Resources

America Online: Mutual Fund Center	//www.aol.com
CompuServe: Money Investor Center	//www.compuserve.com
Data Broadcasting Corp.	//www.dbc.com
Edgar Online	//www.edgar-online.com
FundsInteractive	//www.fundsinteractive.com
Hoover's Company Reports	//www.pathfinder.com/hoovers
Hulbert Financial Digest	//www.cybersurfing.com/hfd
IBC Financial Data	//www.ibcdata.com
Internet Closed-End Fund Investor	//www.icefi.com
InvestSIG PC User Group	//cpcug.org/user/invest/funds.html
Investment Company Institute	//www.ici.com
InvesTools	//www.investools.com
Investorama-Mutual Funds	//www.investorama.com/funds.html
Mutual Fund Company Directory	//www.sc.cmu.edu/~jdg/funds.html

Mutual Funds Home Page	//www.brill.com
Mutual Fund Investors Research Center	//www.fundmaster.com
Mutual Fund Research	//www.webcom.com/~fundlink
Netmoney	//www.ypn.com
Prodigy: Business & Finance	//www.prodigy.com
Stockmaster	//www.stockmaster.com
TrustNet	//www.trustnet.com.uk
Zacks Earnings Reports	//aw.zacks.com

Discount Brokers: Internet, Web, and Online

AccuTrade	//www.accutrade.com
All American Brokers	//www.ebroker.com
Aufhauser	//www.aufhauser.com
Bull & Bear	//networth.galt.com
Datek	//www.datek.com
E*Trade	//www.etrade.com
Fidelity Online Xpress	//www.fid-inv.com
R. J. Forbes Group	//www.rjforbes.com
Howe Barnes	//www.pawws.com
Investex	//www.pawws.com
Lind-Waldock	//www.ino.com
Lombard	//www.lombard.com
National Discount Brokers	//www.pawws.com
PC Financial Network	//www.pcfn.com
Quick & Reilly	//www.quick-reilly.com
Charles R. Schwab & Co.	//www.schwab.com
Muriel Siebert & Co.	//www.msiebert.com
Max Ule's Tickerscreen	//www.maxule.com
Waterhouse	//www.waterhouse.com
Jack White & Company	//www.pawws.com/jwc

Personal Financial Planners: Online and Software

Fidelity Retirement Planner	//www.fid-inv.com
FundMap (Schwab)	//www.schwab.com
Kiplinger's Simply Money	//www.cai.com
Managing Your Money	//www.mymnet.com
MS-Money (Microsoft)	//www.microsoft.com
Plan Ahead (Dow Jones)	//www.dowjones.com
Portfolio Manager (Telescan)	//www.telescan.com
Prosper (Ernst & Young)	//www.ey.com
Quicken Financial Planner	//www.intuit.com/quicken
Retirement Planner (Vanguard)	//www.vanguard.com
Retirement Planning Kit (T. Rowe Price)	//www.troweprice.com
WealthBuilder (Reuters)	//www.moneynet.com

Internet Search Engines: Discover New Resources

Altavista	//www.altavista.com
Excite	//www.excite.com
InfoSeek	//www.infoseek.com
Lycos	//www.lycos.com
Magellan	//www.mckinley.com
Metacrawler	//www.metacrawler.com
Netscape	//www.netscape.com
Webcrawler	//www.webcrawler.com
Yahoo!	//www.yahoo.com

Index

Page numbers for illustrations (computer screen representations) are in italics. Page numbers for references to boxed text or quotations from magazines, newspapers, newsletters, and books are in boldface type.